T0365142

I PLAYED FOR SCOTUS
VOLUME 1

The Shamrock Athletic Legacy as told by the people who built it

Edited by
John Kopetzky and Mark Kurtenbach
Scotus Class of 1980

I PLAYED FOR SCOTUS VOLUME 1
THE SHAMROCK ATHLETIC LEGACY
AS TOLD BY THE PEOPLE WHO BUILT IT

iUniverse books may be ordered through booksellers or by contacting:

iUniverse
1663 Liberty Drive
Bloomington, IN 47403
www.iuniverse.com
1-800-Authors (1-800-288-4677)

ISBN: 978-1-5320-1315-7 (sc)
ISBN: 978-1-5320-1316-4 (e)

Library of Congress Control Number: 2016920611

Print information available on the last page.

iUniverse rev. date: 12/30/2016

Contents

Preface

It's a conversation that has taken place countless times in college dorms, at rec league gyms, or over a cold beverage at the local watering hole.

The question is posed: "Did you play in high school?"

"I did," the response begins, followed by a short pause. Then, accompanied with a hint of well-deserved pride, four all-important words:

"I played for Scotus."

If the person asking the question knows anything at all about Nebraska high school sports, they have an immediate set of images - tough, hard-working, disciplined, determined – characteristics of that blue-collar city in Platte County and the people who are proud who call it home.

"I played for Scotus."

For the person privileged to say *I played for Scotus*, other images immediately come to mind: rugged practices, exacting coaches, expectations of excellence every moment of every day. Those words also mean representing not only yourself and your teammates, but thousands of people over the years who, as players, coaches, fans, and friends of the school, were proud to call themselves Shamrocks.

Other images also come to mind. Forty-four times in the past eighty-five years, the Shamrocks of St. Bonaventure and Scotus Central Catholic have captured state championships in both boys and girls sports. There have been innumerable district and conference titles, monumental victories on the biggest stages in Nebraska high school sports. There have been All-State players, Shamrocks who went on to collegiate glory and careers in professional sports, hall of famers, and coaches who are among the legendary names in the annals of Nebraska prep sports.

"I played for Scotus."

But it's not just about the star players or the coaching legends. It's also the story of the young men and women whose athletic careers ended the last time they took off a Shamrock jersey. Those players, too, added to the magnificent tradition of the green and white and gold. These were the players, who as grade-schoolers attended games at Pawnee Park or Memorial Hall or the Dowd Activity Center and dreamed about someday playing for St. Bonaventure or Scotus. The years went by and their dreams were realized, and they took their place in the long line of Shamrocks. They embraced the tradition that was handed on to them, added their own contribution, and then proudly handed it on the generations that followed.

"I played for Scotus."

It's also about the students who never were listed on any team roster, but nonetheless made their own unique contributions to the Shamrock legacy as fans. It's about the faculty and staff who dedicated year after year of their lives to the school and its students. It's about the parents who made deep sacrifices to ensure their children had a chance to attend St. Bonaventure or Scotus. It's about the countless friends and supporters of the school who did their part to make sure that remarkable school on 18th Avenue was there for generation after generation of young people.

"I played for Scotus."

When those athletes wearing the green and white and gold stepped into the arena, they weren't just playing for themselves or the members of their current team. They were playing for the entire Green Nation; thousands of people spread over the years who were part of the Shamrock legacy as players, coaches, students, parents, and fans.

And when those athletes wearing the green and white and gold stepped into the arena, they weren't playing *by* themselves. They had the entire storied history of Shamrock athletics backing them up – a intimidating legacy of excellence that few schools anywhere can hope to attain.

This book is the story of the men and women who helped build and sustain the Shamrock legacy. In their own words, this is how the players, coaches, and fans from the 1940s until today made their mark in the long and storied history of athletics at St. Bonaventure and Scotus. In the pages that follow, you'll hear about the championships, the outstanding individual performances and performers…and the behind-the-scenes events that had such a profound impact on the lives of our authors.

Quite simply, this is the story of the Shamrocks … *by* the Shamrocks.

Acknowledgements

This development of this book goes back several years. About a decade ago, Mark Kurtenbach (Scotus Class of 1980) suggested to classmate John Kopetzky that they collaborate on a book about the history of Scotus athletics. The untimely death of Gregg Grubaugh (Scotus class of 1975) in February 2015 provided the impetus for them to get the project off the ground. Gregg was a senior when Mark and John were seventh graders at Scotus. That season, he led the Shamrocks to a 19-5 record and Scotus came within an eyelash of qualifying for the state tournament for the first time in nearly 40 years. In their minds, Gregg Grubaugh was - and still is - one of the best basketball players in Scotus history. Losing a legend like him made them realize that this book was something needed to be done now in order to preserve for future generations the stories of the Shamrocks.

This book would not be possible without the assistance of many people: Gary Puetz and the Shamrock Club for their assistance in getting the project off the ground; Scotus Alumni Director John Schueth and Shamrock Hall of Famer Annette Hash who provided invaluable assistance in helping us invite submissions; and Angie (Naughtin) Rusher '95 and her Scotus Journalism students for locating photos of our authors, and for design work on the cover. To all of them, the editors are most thankful.

Most of all, a special thank-you to the people who submitted their thoughts. We hope their insights of what it means to be a Shamrock bring as much enjoyment to you and it has to us in compiling this book.

Go Big Green!

THE ATHLETES

Jack Miller

St. Bonaventure High School 1944 - 1948

- Football letterman, 1945 – 1948
- Basketball letterman, 1945 – 1948
- Honorable Mention All-State basketball 1948
- State track qualifier, Broad Jump, Pole Vault

My name is Jack Miller. I was a student at St. Bonaventure High School from 1944 to 1948. At that time, it was a small school classified as Class C. If memory serves me correctly, there were 26 people in our class; 13 girls and 13 boys.

The varsity sports that I participated in were basketball, football, and track. At that time, those were the only ones available to all students. One of my vivid memories is that we always had classy green and white athletic uniforms. I believe that in addition to normal school funding there were probably private people who helped fund the athletic programs. Generally speaking, players were small compared to today's standards. Those over six feet tall and/or 170 pounds were few.

Reflecting back on those times I will always remember Coach Paul "Dutch" Ernst. He did it all: basketball, football, and track with no assistant coaches. In addition, he worked for the *Columbus Daily Telegram* newspaper. You would often see him walking from his work along 15th Street to the practice sessions. Basketball was in the very little gym on 16th Street, and football was in the front yard of the high school. I never saw him lose his cool or temper with any of his players.

Scheduled home basketball games were played at the Columbus Kramer High School gym and football at the field at Pawnee Park. As a side note, several of us worked one summer for the construction company that was building the new stadium on the west side of the field. An interesting note is that most of the concrete was poured using wheelbarrows. Our jobs were usually working with the mixers or handling the wheelbarrows.

There was a good group of athletes at that time - no hot shots, etc. We played hard to have fun and win. There were none of the amenities many players enjoy today. No training room, special coaching, etc. Most of your development was up to the individual player.

Your memory can have a little difficulty remembering events that happened over 65 years ago, but I do recall several incidents. One was we were playing Silver Creek in basketball; a team that was pretty highly rated. Our team had a great start and was being fouled a lot. The coach of the Silver Creek team pulled his team off the court because he felt the refereeing was not fair. We won on a forfeit.

Playing football at St. Joseph in Omaha at Creighton University was a game that was hard to describe. Creighton had given up football and the field was used by ROTC for drill and training. It was completely devoid of grass. Heavy rains prior to the game turned the field into a quagmire. Your shoes had so much mud on them you could hardly move, let alone run. I doubt if the game was played using more than twenty yards of the field. Sad to say, we lost the game by a touchdown when a St. Joseph runner got through the line and plodded over the goal line with several of us trying to catch him.

I ran the hurdles in track and remember hitting a hurdle near the start of the race. I managed to roll to my feet and gave it all that I had to finish third. Madison had a good football team when we played them in Madison. I remember punting near our goal line and the ball went over the safety's head and ended up around their twenty-yard line. We won the game 14-0. A girl named Norice Ketelsen played in the Madison High School band. I met her a few years later in college and we got married. That was over sixty years ago and we're still going strong.

A pleasant surprise in 1948 was receiving a letter from Floyd Olds, the Sports Editor for the *Omaha World-Herald* for my selection of Honorable Mention on the annual All-State basketball team.

After graduation, my friend Maurice Melcher (also a St. Bonaventure graduate), myself, and eight other fellows from Columbus joined the U.S. Marine Corps. Morrie and I served four years from 1948 – 1952, including time in Korea. Morrie went on to get an engineering degree from Nebraska, and I earned on from Oklahoma State. Sadly, Morrie died in 2006.

Dick Tooley

St. Bonaventure High School 1948 - 1952

- Football, basketball and track athlete
- Babe Ruth Award winner, 1952
- Longtime member and past President of the Shamrock Club
- Shamrock Athletic Hall of Fame inductee, 2001

Being a Shamrock has been a way of life for me for the past 70 years. It was instilled by my parents and five brothers.

The greatest influences on me were two coaches – Cletus Fischer and Paul Ernst.

My most memorable game-day experience was beating Seward our senior year in football. They were very good and won the Central Eight championship that year.

The best Shamrock athlete I saw was John Blahak. He scored 168 points in eight football game as a senior. The best I competed against was Jimmy Decker of Omaha Holy Name, who started three years at quarterback for UCLA.

I am most proud of winning the Babe Ruth Award my senior year.

One story that has to be told was when LaVerne Torczon was kicked out of the end zone during a football game at Loup City.

One other story: The original St. Bon's basketball uniforms in 1940 had Tooley Drug on their shirts (we sponsored the team).

Ken Cielocha

St. Bonaventure High School 1951 - 1954

- Class B All-State in football as a Halfback, 1953
- Member of the undefeated 1953 football team
- Honorable Mention High School All-American
- Shamrock Athletic Hall of Fame inductee, 1999

It was an honor to wear the green for St. Bonaventure High School for four years, from 1951 to 1954.

The greatest influence on me as a student and as an athlete were the priests, the sisters, and my coach Cletus Fischer. Clete came to St. Bon's in 1950 and turned the football program around. We went from playing eight-man football to eleven-man. We were taught the fundamentals for four years, plus other fundamentals that you use in everyday life from Coach Fischer.

My fondest memory was being named All-State in football in Class B as a halfback my senior year.

As far as remembering a particular game day experience, no game in particular was my favorite game. In 1953 we were undefeated and finished #2 in the state.

When I came to St. Bonaventure as a freshman, the upperclassmen taught us how to play. They were great; plus, all my classmates were great also: Bob Wemhoff, Jim Hoshor, John Tooley, Dean Soulliere, etc. Dean Soulliere became the head football coach at St. Bon's after graduating from college.

As I mentioned, I played for Cletus Fischer; he was a great guy to play for. He was the best. We worked hard. His philosophy was to know your

A-B-C's of football and also in life. Clete went on to be a great coach at the University of Nebraska.

In my time at St. Bonaventure, I am most proud of learning how to be a good sport. Whether you win or lose, you have to work hard and be honest in everything you do in life. A life lesson I learned while in school was to always bring the Catholic faith that was taught by the priests and sisters of St. Francis.

It was always great how people remember those years of success at St. Bon's. When we talk about those years and the turnaround of the football program in the 1950's, it gives me a great sense of pride. I always remember Bon Shadle; he was a great fan who always had words of encouragement.

In high school, my nickname was "Chili". I also wore one of the first helmets with facemasks ever used at St. Bon's.

One of my most memorable moments was being inducted into the Shamrock Hall of Fame along with my son, Mike.

I have also enjoyed seeing our children and grandchildren follow in our footsteps by attending Scotus and participating in the programs they have in athletics, academics, etc. It has been a joy to follow them and watch them grow.

It has been a great ride.

Clinton Gates

St. Bonaventure High School 1951 - 1955

- Four-Year letterman in football
- Member of the undefeated 1953 football Team
- Class B All-State and All-State All-Class in football, 1955
- Member of the St. Bonaventure/Scotus football chain gang for more than 30 years and active member of the Shamrock Club and 250 Club
- Shamrock Athletic Hall of Fame inductee, 1999

I went to a country school (District 9) from first grade through fourth grade.

Being a Shamrock athlete and playing football for St. Bonaventure meant a great deal to me. Also the whole team and my teammates were very important to me.

The most significant influence on me as an athlete was Coach Cletus Fischer. Clete was a great coach and a great person. He coached me through all four years in high school. Being coached by Coach Fischer is something I will never forget. He treated everyone the same.

One great memory I had was beating Sidney my junior year 33-13. It was really fun beating them (because they thought they were so good!). It was difficult getting beat by Omaha Holy Name my senior year 30-0 (ouch).

We played Sidney again my senior year in Columbus. We had them backed up to their goal line and they ran a play and fumbled the ball in the end zone. I recovered it for a touchdown, beating them 18-12.

The best athletes I played with were Jim Hoshor and Joe Bonk. The best athletes I played against was Dick Haggerty from Omaha Holy Name.

Being able to go to St. Bon's and being with my classmates for eight years was very important to me. They all taught me lessons I will never forget. We really had some good times at good ol' St. Bon's.

Bill Backes

St. Bonaventure High School 1957 - 1961

- Member of the 1959 state runner-up baseball team
- Athlete of the Year, 1961
- Shamrock Athletic Hall of Fame inductee, 1999
- All-Nebraska Conference running back 1963 and 1964 at Kearney State College
- 22 career rushing touchdowns at Kearney State College

What was it like to be a Shamrock athlete after graduating from 8th grade at St. Anthony's in 1957, then taking the next big step of walking the halls of St. Bon's? You might say it was a process of joining other graduates of St. Anthony's and venturing up to the Big House on 15th Street and 18th Avenue. Beginning the freshman year, all students had to prove to other students that they belonged in the system. In my case, I had to stand up for my rights in the locker room with a 98-pound body which was all I had. My encounter with a St. Bon's classmate was not pretty, but got the respect from other athletes that I would mix it up! I learned the skill of survival. Initiation from upper classmen was always around the corner, so I learned early on to be seen but not heard, otherwise there were consequences. Today, they would call it "bullying".

My freshman year I played football and baseball, and also tried out for the basketball team but did not make the team, which was a great disappointment. On the baseball team, I was fortunate to be on a Shamrock team that played in the Class B finals at State and that finished runner-up to Imperial, getting beat 6-5. It was special because I had the opportunity to play with my brother Ken, who was a senior.

On to my sophomore year, a year in which I put on 20 more pounds, weighing in at 118, and played defensive end. I played and started against the likes of John Kirby and his brother Dennis from David City St. Mary's. They had a powerful team going as they were undefeated for three years. John later played at the University of Nebraska and then for the Minnesota Vikings. I played on the reserve basketball team in 1958 when the new gym was dedicated. My claim to fame was that I made the first basket in the new facility.

Starting my junior year, I tipped the scales at a whopping 138 pounds - a great weight if you wrestle in the 138-pound division, but in football playing at this weight you are at a great disadvantage. That fall of 1959, St. Bon's had a very competitive football team. The record was 6-2-1. The team had a good group of seniors and was rated in the Top Ten in Class B, tying a very good Lincoln Pius X team 19-19. However, the winter basketball season was a character-builder; our team only won two games. We always felt our team made the other teams feel good about their basketball program. Our track season was fairly successful, winning the Fremont Invitational and placing in the top half of most meets.

The Shamrock football team my senior year, which was the fall of 1960, made us all hope to survive until the season's final game – we finished 1-8-1. That season there was a ten-game schedule. Why there were ten games was a mystery. The coach the previous year resigned and handed the reins over to Coach Dean Soulliere, his first year as a head coach. During the 1-8-1 season, I definitely believed in the power of prayer. Before each game I would journey across the street to the church to ask God to spare my life for another week. Our line averaged 150 pounds from end to end. And playing fullback at 145 pounds, you needed a Higher Power to survive. Probably the lesson in life our team was most proud of was never to complain or give up during a game when we were overmatched. Our motto was: "Don't steal, don't lie, don't alibi"; but that's all we did.

Coach Soulliere did not throw in the towel after our 1-8-1 record, but kept his eye on the future and went on to win many games in the following years. The 1963 season was a good year for the Shamrocks, winning seven games in the fall, going on to win the state championship in track that spring. Coach Soulliere had two players from the football team play in the

Shrine Bowl: Dave Kretz and my brother Dave Backes. Couch Soulliere was named the *Lincoln Journal Star* Coach of the Year. What a turnaround!

As I look back fifty-five years later, I see my senior year as a launch pad for success in the future. Our coach was persistent with a never-give-up attitude that rubbed off on the athletes. Our win-loss record was sub-par, but the coaches and Booster Club respected and recognized the effort of the athletes with a great year-end banquet getting none other than the greatest quarterback in professional football, Johnny Unitas of the Baltimore Colts, to give us an inspiring speech.

Moving forward to today, this past year Scotus proudly received the trophy for the State Championship Class C All-Sports award that the Nebraska School Activities Association gives out each year. I had the opportunity to attend the state championship football game at Memorial Stadium versus Norfolk Catholic. The Sea of Green was at its best, cheering the Shamrocks on to victory. All the Scotus alumni should be proud of the academic standard testing results reported by President Wayne Morfeld, showing that 96% of the Scotus Class of 2015 had a composite score on the ACT test of 25.9, compared with the Nebraska state average of 21.5 and the national average of 21.0. This was the highest ever achieved in the school's history. Congratulations!

In conclusion, these are a few events and activities that I had a privilege to be a part of with students and staff at St. Bon's from 1957-1961. The lessons that were learned during this period of time enabled me to attend Kearney State College after graduation and be a part of a football team that compiled a 30-6 record from 1961-1965. So, thanks for the memories and valuable time spent at St. Bon's High School. Go Big Green!

John Torczon

St. Bonaventure High School 1959 - 1963

- Four-year letterman in football, basketball, and track & field
- Class B All-State football player, 1962
- Shrine Bowl participant, 1963

Editors Note: Although St. Bonaventure didn't field a wrestling team and John didn't wrestle during his high school days, he was inducted into the Nebraska Scholastic Wrestling Coaches Association Hall of Fame as a wrestling official in 1995.

Being a Shamrock athlete means more to me now than when I played. There's a sense of great pride following the success of not only athletics but also the other accomplishments in the classroom as well. The greatest influence on me was my fellow teammates.

One of my favorite memories is upsetting Omaha Holy Name, playing the game at the Omaha Benson field. One particular memory I would like to forget is playing as a freshman defensive end and not being able to find the ball against the Seward-Concordia option game (or against David City Aquinas any time).

The best Shamrock athlete I ever played with is Bill Backes. The best opposing players I played against were Steve Balkavic from Omaha Holy Name and Dan McGinn from Omaha Cathedral. Also the Kirby brothers from Aquinas.

I am most proud of being disciplined both on and off the field, and that I was able to hang on to my faith.

Chuck Hagel

St. Bonaventure High School 1960 - 1964

- Three-year letterman in football, basketball, track & field

I was very proud to be on the teams I played on because I was part of something important with friends.

Coach Dean Soulliere had the greatest influence on me as a Shamrock athlete.

One of my funniest memories was stealing the basketball and running the wrong way on the court to score a lay-up for the other side.

My most memorable game day experience was during my sophomore year (1961) against Fremont Bergan. I was starting my first game, and intercepted a pass and ran it back for a touchdown.

The best Shamrock athlete I played with was Dave Kudron (1964). The best athlete I played against was Don Grubaugh (from David City Aquinas).

I remember Coach Soulliere's expressions when waiting for us to get to him during practice: "Come on, *HUSTLE!* We've got a dollar waiting on a dime."

During my time at St. Bonaventure, I am most proud of being part of a wonderful group of people and having an opportunity to make a contribution.

The life lessons I learned during my time as a student and an athlete were to: Play by the rules, work hard, believe in yourself and others, and have fun with good people and people you like.

Another story I remember is putting on Zorro masks in the 4th quarter of the 1963 football game against Omaha Cathedral on Halloween night. Coach Soulliere was not happy and we lost. My three years playing on Shamrock teams were three of the best years of my life. I've said enough!

Editor's note: In April 2014, United States Secretary of Defense Chuck Hagel made an official visit to Mongolia. While there, Mongolian Defense Minister Bat-Erdene Dashdemberel presented Secretary Hagel with the traditional gift given to foreign dignitaries visiting the mountainous Asian country - a horse. Secretary Hagel announced that the horse was to be named "Shamrock", explaining to his hosts and the American news media traveling with him that "Shamrock" was the mascot of his high school. Unfortunately, there was no room aboard the plane to bring Shamrock back to the United States, and he remains in Mongolia, where he reportedly follows the exploits of the Scotus Shamrocks via the World Wide Web.

Dave Kudron

St. Bonaventure High School 1960 - 1964

- Four-year letterman in football, basketball, and track & field
- First gold medal winner at state track meet in school history (High Hurdles, 1964)
- All- State Honorable Mention in football, 1963 and basketball, 1964
- St. Bonaventure Athlete of the Year, 1964
- Shamrock Athletic Hall of Fame inductee, 1999

To me, being a Shamrock athlete meant being able to contribute to the athletic tradition of the school. The greatest influence on me as an athlete would have been the group of teammates you played with year after year. The older guys were always a great influence on the younger guys, following their example to achieve what was possible.

One of my fondest memories is during my senior year of football, being selected the Homecoming King. Joe Pensick led off the second half of our Homecoming game by missing the ball on the tee (even though we weren't trying for an on-side kick!). Another memory would be scoring 29 points in back-to-back basketball games my senior year. One memory I'd like to forget is placing second at the state track meet my junior year.

The best athlete I played with was Tom Kretz; Tom was always a hard-driving force. Ed Peters was a "take control" type of leader. My Head Coach, Dean Soulliere, was a great coach on the field and a great teacher in the classroom. Coach Soulliere helped St. Bonaventure earn recognition as a small Class B school.

One time during a basketball game, I blew out a sole in my sneaker. I got a pair from Assistant Coach Rich Grennan and had one of my best games ever. Coach Grennan let me keep the shoes(!).

I will never forget getting to suit up for a varsity football game as a freshman, traveling to Omaha in one of those old Greyhound buses. On the way home they put me in the overhead luggage rack, but I think that made me feel like a part of the Shamrock team.

Bill Mimick

St. Bonaventure / Scotus High School 1962 - 1966

- All-State football player, 1965
- Member state track championship team, 1964
- Scotus Athlete of the Year, 1966
- Shrine Bowl participant, 1966
- Shamrock Athletic Hall of Fame inductee, 2000

It was an honor and privilege to be a Shamrock athlete and wear the green, white, and gold.

My parents taught me a good work ethic and commitment. The coaches taught me values and team work. The Shamrock Club, teachers, fellow students, and community taught me caring and concern. Paul Ernst comes to mind as the coach who got athletics going at St. Bonaventure and then he wrote for the *Columbus Daily Telegram.* He was a great example.

I always got so excited for games and going to practice. One day I got dressed so fast for track practice I forgot my gym trunks. Needless to say, I left my sweatpants on for practice. I never told anyone that story.

On game days, we'd all go to church and light a vigil candle both before and after the games. I learned this from my first game as a freshman against West Point. My guardian angel was already praying for me and still does today.

Everyone has a passion or a period in their life that they enjoy. I hope everyone has that opportunity. Mine was high school athletics at St. Bonaventure. I was fortunate to be able to play college football, teach, coach, and officiate sports. Fast pitch softball was a great experience, but high school sports at St. Bon's is at the top of the list.

Each time renew an acquaintance or meet a new person that went to St. Bonaventure before me or Scotus after me, a sense of loyalty goes through me. I was very fortunate to have the opportunities I did at St. Bon's. Almost everyone is proud of the schools they went to, and St. Bon's / Scotus alumni sure have that pride. This will continue with all the efforts of people to keep Scotus running and the pride and efforts of the students who attend. St. Bon's / Scotus has a proud history in both boys and girls athletics and will continue with community, alumni, coaches, parents, school, and the athletes' support and efforts.

I was born in 1947 and the first sports I remember was watching an uncle (Ted Mimick) playing football for St. Bonaventure in the early 1950's at Newman Grove. I got to go to a St. Bonaventure vs. Fremont St. Patrick basketball game played at Kramer High School when a cousin (Rich Mimick) played for St. Pat's. St. Bon's played home basketball games at Kramer High School until Memorial Hall was built in the late 1950's. The Shamrocks practiced at an old barn until then.

After seeing some athletic events, I had a passion for sports. When there was time at home I practiced kicking and passing a football, shooting baskets, high jumping with bamboo poles, hurdling over saw horses, throwing weights like shot puts, throwing baseballs and hitting with a bat or bitching against a brick wall. We lived in the country so I was usually by myself doing this.

I just couldn't wait to get to junior high and high school to get to play. During the playing days and summers, I spent a lot of free time thinking of sports and trying to figure out who was returning for schools we were going to play in the future. I was fortunate in sports in high school. I never missed a practice in any sport. My parents taught me commitment and a work ethic by example. I had younger sisters and brothers and we lived on a small farm and did carpentry work on my father's construction crew. We did chores in the mornings and evenings before and after school and on weekends. My parents and siblings helped so I could be at practice. This was very much appreciated.

Some good memories include playing in my first game as a freshman against West Point in football. I kicked four extra points and we won 40-12. I lettered as a freshman. I kicked the first field goal in school history in 1965 against David City St. Mary in a 3-13 loss. I had three school records at one time in track (the high jump, shot put, and discus), but all those have been broken. In 1966 I played in the Shrine Bowl game. Another great memory was being inducted into the Shamrock Athletic Hall of Fame in 2000. This was special to all four of my children; they were able to come to Columbus for the event at the Athletic Banquet.

Coach Paul "Dutch" Ernst helped start football at St. Bonaventure in the late 1940's. He deserved a lot of credit. After coaching he wrote a newspaper column called "Sport Shorts" for the *Columbus Daily Telegram*. It was an honor to be mentioned in his column.

I played under Dean Soulliere in football and track, Lowell Roumph in basketball, and Pat Keitges in football and track. The assistants were Larry Timmerman and Rich Grennan. Coach Soulliere always wanted to beat Omaha Holy Name (probably going back to his playing days in the early 1950's). Coach Roumph went to Wayne State. We played Wayne my junior and senior years; we lost to them in the City Auditorium in 1965, but defeated them in overtime in 1966. I believe this was Coach Roumph's highlight when he was at St. Bon's. Coach Roumph used to say when we'd play Omaha schools to "Be careful; the officials might be some men of the parish."

These opposing coaches stood out to me when we played because of their coaching ability, sportsmanship, and long tenure: Gene Torczon (Schuyler), Roger Higgins (Omaha Cathedral), Lou Wewel (Fremont Bergan), Jerry Sherman (Hastings St. Cecilia), Fred Northup (Grand Island CC), Lyle Nannen (West Point CC), Jim Micek (North Bend), Gene Pillen (David City St. Mary).

Athletes that played at St. Bon's before me stood out. Before Memorial Hall was built, the junior high and high school kids at lunch at the social hall at the grade school. As a grade-schooler, I looked up to all those athletes and if they acknowledged us it was a thrill. I hoped I would be a good example to younger people by saying "hello" or learning their names like the older athletes did.

I vividly remember this night: We were warming up at Memorial Stadium when Omaha Cathedral showed up in three big chartered buses drove into Pawnee Park together by the train engine and old swimming pool. Quite a sight. One bus for the players, one for the pep-club cheerleaders, and the last for their fans. This was a good hard fought game, a 20-13 win. After the game where all four buses (the three chartered buses and our school team bus) were parked at the north end of the playing field, the chartered bus with the Cathedral pep-club cheerleaders got stuck in loose sand. Some of us team players went to help push as the Cathedral girls got off the bus. They encouraged us with "Push them back, push them way back." It was a good sign of sportsmanship and respect both ways.

Starting lineups were mostly seniors. Cathedral juniors were Kro, Voorvart and McGinn, St. Bonaventure juniors Shank and Mimick. Both teams were final ratings placed in Class B in 1964 and again rated the next year 1965.

In 1964 both St. Bonaventure and Columbus High football teams were undefeated. In the middle of season Columbus High hosted Fremont Friday night and St. Bonaventure hosted Aquinas. Both Fremont High and Aquinas were also undefeated at the time. It was a great weekend for football in Columbus. Both sides of the stadium were filled plus standing room. Both crowds were estimated at about 4,000 people each night. Columbus High defeated Fremont 13-6 and St. Bonaventure defeated Aquinas 6-0. At the end of the season there was a big banquet at Memorial Hall for both teams. There were a couple of other events for both teams also.

My top team memories in high school (not in any particular order) were the state track & field championship in 1964, the 1964 undefeated football season, defeating Aquinas in football 1964 and in basketball 1965, defeating Omaha Holy Name in basketball when they were state rated in 1965 and 1966, defeating Wayne (79-78 in overtime) when they were state rated.

The first Centennial Conference track & field meet was in Fremont. Our track & field team won the meet. I was fortunate enough to win the high jump and place in shot put and discus. At that time track & field meets only scored five places. At that time there was also a conference playoff championship in football until the state football playoffs in the 1970s.

My biggest disappointments were in losing 0-6 to Aquinas in football in 1963, not being able to repeat our 1964 undefeated football season in 1965, losing to Schuyler in overtime in district basketball in 1966, despite defeating Schuyler in regular season. Schuyler went to state behind 6'10" sophomore Chuck Jura who went on later to play for Nebraska, then professionally in Europe.

Coach Paul Ernst in the late '40s and early '50s would have the athletes over to his home for sandwiches and go over the sports season with them. Then Cletus Fischer (later a Nebraska football coach for years) took over. The Shamrock Club organized the Athletic Banquet as we know it now and started "Athlete of the Year". Some of the first guest speakers were pro athletes in their prime and later were inducted in the Hall of Fame in their sports: Johnny Unitas, Bill George, Mick Tingelhoff in football and Bob Cousy in basketball. Other guest speakers included Joe Foss, former governor of South Dakota and Commissioner of the American Football League when it merged with the National Football League and started the Super Bowl, Olympic Decathlon winner Bill Toomey, and Jocko Conlon, the major league baseball umpire.

During high school the Shamrock Club took the basketball team to a college basketball game. One year it was a Nebraska game and the next year a Creighton game. I got to see Paul Silas play for Creighton who became one of the top rebounders in college and the pros. He was also a head pro basketball coach.

Fifty or sixty years ago "social media" was not anywhere like today. There were phone services, usually "party lines" until each home or business got their own private line and number. Local radio station KJSK did not broadcast sports. When KTTT started in the 1960's, they had a sunrise to sunset license. They would tape-record an out of town football or basketball game on Friday night and re-broadcast the game the next morning. Their first sports announcers included Ron Bogus, Joe Stavas, and Ed "Scoop" Ridenour. I remember listening to games rebroadcasted while cleaning chicken coops, hog and cattle sheds on Saturdays. The *Columbus Daily Telegram* had a really good sports page. Ray Gattermeyer, Rich Gaver, and Paul Ernst wrote sports for the paper. They did a great writing job with pre-season, pre-gram, post-game, after the season write-ups and pictures.

Steve Shadle

St. Bonaventure / Scotus High School 1963 - 1967

- Football letterman
- Basketball letterman
- All-Class gold medal & state record in 440-yard dash
- Scotus Co-Athlete of the Year, 1967

Being a Shamrock athlete was fun - it was important to me, to Shamrock supporters and to my family. People in the community knew who you were.

The person who had the greatest influence on me was Coach Dean Soulliere (probably also my role model). The athletes who influenced me were Bill Backes (arguably the best athlete ever) and Aaron Kudron (my neighbor). My parents Bon and Helen Shadle both loved sports. At age 92 Mom attended a football game in the fall of 2015.

One funny memory I have is eating a burger, Coke, and fries at the Black Angus before a football game and then throwing it all up after a long run. The pre-game meal was not a concept!

One memory I'd like to forget is not being able to anchor our 880 relay at the state track meet and letting three guys down. No one believed me that I had a broken leg. I think I had a stress fracture the week before at the district meet. It got much worse at the state meet. The next day the doctor looked at the x-ray and said "I bet competing on that really hurt". This was back when athletes were told to "walk it off"; it didn't matter what the injury was. I never claimed to be too bright.

A memorable game-day experience was my senior year. We were playing Omaha Cathedral the last game of the season. We had a good team and finally had all our players back from injury. Late in the game we were driving the ball to 'ice' the game. George Kretz probably weighed 140 pounds and was playing across from a 230-pound All-Stater from Cathedral. We ran an off tackle play and coming back to the huddle, George is standing over this kid saying "Get up because I'm going to knock you down again". We won the game and I think ended up ranked 8th or 9th. Desire seemed to be why we excelled.

Probably the two best athletes I played with were Jim Legenza and Tim Korgie. Jim could do all sports very well, especially shoot the basketball from the corner. We might have won a few more games with the three-point line. Jim could shoot. Tim was the biggest kid on our football team so that made him a lineman. Watching film one day, we busted a long run and Tim ran down our tailback to escort him into the end-zone. At any other school he would have been an All-State tailback! Other great athletes include Bill Mimick, Joe Blahak, and Bill Kosch; they were in the classes above and below me. John Shank was the first Scotus kid that transformed his body weightlifting. Nobody lifted weights back then. John did and started three years.

The best athlete I played against in football was Reggie Smith from West Point Central Catholic. They played a 7-1-2 defense; Reggie was 1! Also Fremont Bergan quarterback Chris Roumph. In basketball it was Chuck Jura from Schuyler. All twelve players on his team could dunk the ball during warm-ups. Also Chuck Wallersted from Omaha Cathedral. In track it was Joe Orduna in the hurdles and Henry Hunter from Omaha Central in the jumps.

I spent 39 years coaching at the high school level so I must have learned a lot. Dean Soulliere would talk to every kid so they felt like they mattered. Pat Keitges wasn't afraid to physically and mentally challenge his team. Lowell Roumph preached that sometimes patience was the best choice. I was fortunate to have played for great coaches.

My best memory was Coach Soulliere challenging the running backs to hit the holes hard. He was standing in front by a chalkboard saying, "Hell, if

I held an egg up against the board I doubt you could hit it hard enough to break the damn shell!" Thirty years later I was listening to John Torczon talk to his team and I swear it was Coach Soulliere.

I am most proud of the relationships I still have with my former classmates; both athletes and non-athletes. We enjoy seeing each other whenever our paths cross. In fact, returning from our 45th class reunion I told my wife, "Old people shouldn't have that much fun."

I have learned that life is fun. Life is a long time. We have the ability to change. Working at something makes a difference. Many of my most successful classmates were not considered the best and brightest by school standards. They were good hard-working people that developed along life's journey and successfully met life's challenges.

We would have had a great wrestling team, so it's good to see that Scotus added wrestling. I always felt bad for basketball Coach Roumph since our best jumper and center was 5'8" Kevin Wibbels.

During fall football it was unacceptable to have any water during practice. Coach had a pump up weed-sprayer that he would fill with water. We'd get in line and get a little spray in your face. I think the better players got a little more but you seldom got any sprayed at your mouth. I just hope he had rinsed the sprayer after killing the weeds on the practice field!

In 1967 there were no girl athletic teams though there were plenty of athletes. We have to wonder how many people have been limited by the words, "That's the way it is" without ever asking "Why?". My classmate Gene Konwinski started a girls' softball team that summer that had some very good players. My cousin Gayle Steiner was an outstanding 800-meter runner at the AAU level. Thank you Title IX for asking "Why?"

One story I shouldn't tell: Mary Dvorak was a classmate and always had people over to hang-out at her house. Her dad made wine. I don't remember many drinkers in our class. If you were caught you were done for the year. One day we were at Mary's house and a couple of guys found

Mary's dad's 'bottom of the barrel' under the stairs in unfiltered mix fruit-mash-chunks…whatever. But it must have been good and at least 80 proof. About two pulls of that, chunks and all, and heads were spinning. I don't know if it was from the alcohol or the mix in the bottom!

Looking back over the past fifty years I'm very grateful for the influence of a Scotus education and the families that made the sacrifice to send their kids to Scotus. It was an honor to attend school and play for Scotus. I have enjoyed the continued success of Scotus graduates and current students professionally, athletically and academically.

Bill Kosch

St. Bonaventure / Scotus High School 1964 – 1968

- All-State running back, 1967
- Scotus Athlete of the Year, 1968
- Shrine Bowl participant, 1968
- Shamrock Athletic Hall of Fame inductee, 1999
- Nebraska Football Hall of Fame inductee, 1997
- Starting defensive back and All-Big Eight selection on Nebraska National Championship teams, 1970–1971

Like the three leaves of a shamrock, being a Shamrock can be summed up in three words: faith, family and friends. I am very proud to say I grew up in Columbus and that I was a Scotus Shamrock. My wife, Linda, and our five children (Jesse, Laura, Jill, Rebecca and Jeff) all graduated from Scotus. They have great memories and long-lasting friendships from their years as Shamrocks. I was glad to be there during the transition from St. Bonaventure to Scotus Central Catholic High School. Junior high memories of the old brick school house with old desks on metal runners bolted to the floor, Sister Hermalonda's detention closet under the creaky wooden stairs, steam heat and leaky windows are priceless. My education from St. Bonaventure/Scotus provided a moral compass that guides me through life.

The greatest influence came from those who played before my time at Scotus. The classes of 1964 and 1965 won a state track championship and had an undefeated football season. Why would you not want to be like them? I remember when I was a freshman and we were running 100-yard sprints at track practice. I was in the middle of the pack. One senior track star and school sprint record holder picked me out of that crowd and pulled me aside. He said, "Lean forward, use your arms and relax, you can beat them all." I knew him but he had no reason to know me; what a kind gesture. Larry Liss was his name and in later life we became very good friends. Lesson learned: You never know how an act of kindness may positively influence someone's life.

Despite all of the talent St. Bonaventure/Scotus had in football and track (when I was in school), this talent did not translate well to basketball. If a team won half of its games it was an outstanding year. After the regular season of my senior year, we had three wins and sixteen losses. We played an all-Class B schedule but we were a Class C team and we were sent to Albion for district play. I remember warming up for the first game when the Scotus pep club came marching into the gym all decked out in their uniforms and shouting the school cheers. The opposing team pep club and fans just sat there in disbelief with their jaws precariously close to their popcorn. That episode set the stage for a bizarre ending.

Teams from Genoa, Fullerton, Newman Grove, Madison and others were in this district. We won the game by 40 points. The following night more of our fans showed up and the margin of victory was around 30 points. You could feel the anti-sentiment growing towards the Shamrocks from the Big City. What were they doing here?

We were paired up to play Humphrey St. Francis for the championship. The gym filled early and was contentious. We took an early lead in the first half but fouls were piling up on us. Some Scotus fans were letting the refs know it, too. After three quarters, we held a ten-point lead, however, we had three starters on the bench that had *mysteriously* fouled out. Once the fourth quarter started, the whistles continued to blow. Coach Younger argued and he got the big "Heave-Ho". On another call against a teammate, I politely asked the official what the infraction was and he said to me," One more word out of you and you are out of here"! St. Francis lived on the free throw line the whole fourth quarter and we lost by ten points. But, it was the first time in my basketball career that we won two games in a row. I guess the people of rural Nebraska misinterpreted our exuberance as invasionary.

It was a Friday, the day of the very first Scotus varsity football game ever; the year was 1965. This was the first time ever I put on the Scotus game day uniform. I was a sophomore and was a starter in the backfield with juniors Steve Shadle, Jim Legenza and Keith Feilmeier. The new locker rooms were pristine. The tradition was to make your way over to St. Bon's church for a personal prayer. This was part of "game" preparation. I remember the click, click, click of the football shoes on the parking lot – it seemed kind of militaristic. These few moments allowed you to put it all into perspective – if we performed at our best as a team, no one could ask more of us.

I need to mention Steve Shadle as he was a superb trackster and our starting quarterback and also was on the basketball team. However, I would have to say Joe Blahak was the best athlete I played with. His combination of speed, natural strength, sports I.Q. and desire to win made him an invaluable teammate. On the flip side, I would say John Riggins from Kansas University. He was the Kansas sprint champion in high school. At Kansas, he was a 6'2", 235-pound running back. He went on to be an All-Pro player for the Washington Redskins.

It was the summer of 1967 and my senior year was about to start. We knew that we were going to have all new coaches at Scotus that year. I remember seeing an article in the *Columbus Daily Telegram* about Claire Stramel, Jim Puetz and Vern Younger. It included photographs of Claire and Jim. The seniors would lead some preseason workouts and we thought Claire sounded like a reasonable person. What caught our attention was the picture of Jim Puetz – it was rather dark and we couldn't tell his ethnicity. It turned out he had a really good tan! Regarding Vern, when we first saw him, we thought he was the new kid in the senior class. He still looks like his last name! It didn't take much time to appreciate this group of coaches and their contributions to Scotus.

My father, Howard, strongly believed in a Catholic education. When a fund drive for the new gymnasium was held in the late 1950s, he was a major donor. A huge display was hung on the wall in the entry way to the gym along with all of the other donors. His name tag was in the very top row. Within a few days, I noticed his name tag was no longer displayed. I asked him about it and he said he had personally removed it explaining that recognition was not important, only the deed. He set a good example for me, and hopefully I have done so for my children.

The most important lessons are: be honest with yourself, practice hard and play harder, give credit and respect to your opponents. Also, how do you act when no one is around? So, study as hard as you can and gain knowledge until you come to the realization that you know very little.

I have to tell this story: It was a beautiful spring day for a track meet at Pawnee Park. We had a dual meet with David City Aquinas. After what seemed to be an endless warm up, Coach Puetz told us all to sit down in the stadium bleachers because the Aquinas bus broke down and would be half an hour late. We all sat down except my brother Bob (an unbridled sophomore). He had a pole vault pole and was doing a run through. He yelled at us and said, "Watch this." He proceeded to jam the pole in the box and break it in two! BOOM. We were in shock. He got up and walked back, grabbed another pole and did it again! BOOM. It sounded like a shotgun going off. We all roared and before we could wipe our eyes dry – again a BOOM!!! Coach Puetz came running out and asked who was shooting a gun off. We all pointed at Bob laying on the pole vault padding. We had no pole vault poles left. Jim kicked his rear all the way up the steps. Well, that was only the start of the day and what followed is shamefully remembered by the 1968 track team.

Aquinas eventually showed up and we wanted to shut them out for being late and we were doing a pretty good job of it. The next-to-last event was the 880-yard relay. We approached Coach Puetz and asked if we had to run all-out. He said, "Run to win." Lead off runner Al Bruner provided a good lead for sophomore Dave Swierczek. Dave extended the lead and then things started to happen. The crowd noticed I did not remove my sweats and had sun glasses on as I got into the exchange zone. I got the baton and broke into a casual trot. I let the Aquinas runner catch me on the curve so I ran with him for a while. Then I saw Joe Blahak on the back stretch so I picked up the pace. As I neared him, I saw he was in full sweats, too. He had one pant leg rolled up so as to pose like a cheap date trying to hitch a ride. I started to do a windmill action with the baton for the hand off. I blew by Joe as he just stood on the track. He grabbed the baton and didn't move. The crowd was now really curious and loud. Aquinas again took the lead. After a sizable lead, Joe did a little dance then turned on the jets. The crowd was in a delirious stupor as Joe crossed the finish line first. We all ended up in the middle of the football field sharing a high-five. I saw Coach Puetz nearing us with a grin on his face until he was intercepted by the Aquinas coaching staff. After a few heated words, he turned to us without the smile. It was at that moment that we realized we were *Stupidicus Maximus.*

Later we wrote a letter of apology to Aquinas. I hope they accepted our confession as I have fond memories of our competitions and have been friends with many of the Aquinas Monarchs over the years. God later punished us as this very same relay team was disqualified at the district meet and ended up losing the state meet by two points. I guess we did not deserve it after that stunt.

This final message is for those who have not yet graduated from high school. Challenge yourself to participate in all that you can. You are only young once. I have never heard anyone say they tried to do too much. However, I have heard many former classmates regret they didn't stick it out, or even worse, they did not even try. Don't be one to look back at your senior class year book and say to yourself, "I could have done this or that or I could have been on that team or I could have ...". No excuses - just do it!

I have always liked this poem by Robert. H. Smith:

> *The clock of life is wound but once, And no man has the power*
> *To tell just when the hands will stop At late or early hour.*
> *The present only is our own, So live, love, toil with a will.*
> *Place no faith in tomorrow, For the clock may then be still.*

Joe Blahak

St. Bonaventure / Scotus High School 1965 - 1969

- All-State running back, 1968
- Track gold medal winner in 100-yard Dash, Two-time gold medal winner in Long Jump, 180-yard Low Hurdles
- Still holds Scotus Long Jump record (23'0") set in 1969
- Scotus Athlete of the Year, 1969
- Shrine Bowl participant, 1969
- Shamrock Athletic Hall of Fame inductee, 1999
- Nebraska Football Hall of Fame inductee, 1990
- Nebraska High School Sports Hall of Fame inductee, 2011
- Starting defensive back and All-Big Eight selection on Nebraska National Championship teams, 1970-1971
- Played six seasons in the NFL, including the 1975 Minnesota Vikings Super Bowl team

---

OPENING STATEMENT

The committee that is responsible for the publication of this book asked me to assist in writing memories of one of greatest, if not *the* greatest, athlete ever to attend Scotus Central Catholic High School; I am humbled and honored. Joe Blahak touched many lives and I am sure many of you who grew up around his time have your own tales of his shenanigans in your memory bank. I would encourage you to share those stories with friends as time passes by. This will be the best testament to honor Joe. In the last years of his life he struggled with the effects of a stroke. He did his best to keep the laughter up and spirits high. He would tell me stories of his sons, Chad and Ryan, and how proud he was of them; of his daughter, JaNae, he would say she was the most talented athlete in the family and the most challenging. I would kind of chuckle under my breath when he would say this because she was Joe Junior! However, over the years they found common ground and he would finish each story with "I love my boys" and "I truly love JaNae". I would have to say that Diane was the "perfect" wife for Joe. She was the glue of the family, the element that made the family chemistry work. I humbly present the prose presented below.

Sincerely,
Bill Kosch

SUMMER OF 1969

It was a hot dry summer in Columbus. My brother Bob, Joe and I all had jobs at Behlen Manufacturing that summer along with many other Columbus kids. It was customary for the three of us to take turns driving to work each week for the 7:00 a.m.to 3:30 p.m. shift. This particular week had Bobby driving. He was known to collect cars in the $20 to $60 range. His choice this week was the 1960 black 465 cubic inch Cadillac. The riders would sit in the back seat to catch a few more z's before work. Joe and I worked together with crew leader Mark Kobus (a St. Bonaventure grad from the 50's) this particular day. We had just finished loading a flatbed trailer with various building materials that would find a new home somewhere in the USA. We lowered the trailer supports so the yard cab could be pulled out and used for another load-out job. It was close to quitting time. Koby – as we called him – asked me to double check something on the load. All checked out until I heard him shout, "Blahak, I'm going to kill you!". Koby started chasing Joe around the truck to no avail. He grabbed a five-foot long piece of cottonwood and slung it at Joe as Joe ran for the main building. I was amazed how far he flung it but he missed. Joe had taken grease off of the fifth wheel and pasted it all over the seat, steering wheel and shifting knob. Koby was plastered in gooey grime.

I met up with Joe at the wash basins and he thought that was pretty cool. I grinned a little as we cleaned up. Then Joe said this stuff (GO-JO hand cleaner) smelled like bananas. All of sudden Joe took a proverbial pie in the face. Koby had snuck up on him and had a copious amount of GO-JO in his hand. He got him in the mouth, the nose, the ears and eyes. Koby joyfully danced a jig as he announced "I got you Blahak" over and over. Joe finally recovered and we made it back to the Cadillac where Bobby was impatiently waiting. Well, we assumed the back seat position and closed our eyes as I was tired and Joe was convalescing. The two "G's" of acceleration from the Cadillac just pressed us back farther into the seats and felt good. Windows were down and the rush of air at 65 m.p.h. felt cooling as we headed west back to town on Highway 30. All of sudden cattails were slapping us in the face. I could see nothing other than vegetation slamming the front windshield. Bobby was in the driver's seat laughing his sphincter off. Then he pulled back onto the highway like nothing happened. Joe roared, "What the hell are you doing butt head – why were you in the ditch? You piece of #@!$!" Bobby smirked, "I was down there last night – no problem". Just another day at work.

RUN, JUMP, THROW

In the 1960's, you could run in three open track events plus one relay. You could also participate in all field events. At one meet Joe did all of the field events, winning most of them. He then won the 100, 200 and the 180 yard low hurdles and anchored the 4 x 220-yard relay. He could have been a good decathlete except he probably would not like the high hurdles or mile run. In fact, I don't think Joe would even run the 440. It was just too far! He might have to actually train a little.

RUNNING STYLE

While Joe and I were at the University of Nebraska, we were timed in the 40-yard dash at the conclusion of winter work outs. I felt like I should be producing better times. So I concentrated on Joe's running style as he ran 40's. Joe never ran like Steve Shadle (who had the easiest running motion of any Scotus runner in the 440-yard dash) or like Mike Cieloha (who ran with power and no wasted motion). I would sort of glide through the 40's. Joe would bust out low, dig in his cleats, maintain a forward lean, and just pound the turf like pistons in an engine, smashing and compressing the ground below. Let's put it this way – Steve was a smooth running BMW sports car, Mike had a little more muscle and size like a Corvette, and Joe?

Joe was a roaring, dirt throwing MONSTER truck painted with sponsors of your favorite brands of beer.

Now back to the point. He would bust off some 4.4's. Using his technique, I was able to run 4.5. If it came down to a straight line race from 40 to 200 yards I would take Joe the Jet over Johnny the Jet Rodgers any day. However, throw in a few jukes and hip shakes and Johnny was the king. I did my student teaching at Lincoln East High School in math and also coached track. One day we were running timed 100 yard dashes so I decided to give it a try as I always ran with the kids during practice. I was able to clock a 9.7. But old Joe was not to be challenged. Coach Dean Brittenham, one of the track coaches at UNL, asked Joe to try out for track and gave him a time trial. Joe ran a 9.5 and probably could have done better than that. He always had that extra gear – always.

A TRUE BROTHER

Joe was like a brother. Our lives crisscrossed from the very start. Joe and I were born in the same town, same hospital two days apart. We probably should have been in the same class but he attended St. Anthony's one year after I went to St. Bonaventure grade school. Once we got to high school, we pretty much saw each other on the practice field, the gym or the track every day. Then it was on to the University where we were able to again extend our friendship on the football field. Our oldest sons followed us to Lincoln to play for the Big Red too. Joe then moved on to the NFL and I was playing semi pro ball for the Omaha Mustangs. I received a call from one of the Minnesota Viking scouts and he said they had an injured defensive back and asked if I would fly up for a try out. I said yes. He said they had one guy in front of me to look at first. I asked who that was and he said, of all the people on the face of this earth, Joe Blahak! I just deflated. Well, I never got the tryout as Joe called me afterwards and said he had the best day of one-on-one coverage in his life. He went on to have a fabulous career with the Vikings and he proudly wore his Super Bowl ring as a result.

I moved from Columbus to Lincoln in 2001 (Joe and Diane's city of residence since college) and Joe would get us involved in all of these "free" golf tournaments for charity or fund raising events. This took us to many cities across Nebraska, provided an opportunity to meet a lot of new people and to lend our help for a good cause. Joe's last round of golf was with his son Chad, Biff Roberts and myself at the Nebraska Lettermen's Scramble just before the 2016 Nebraska Spring Game at the secluded Quarry Oaks Golf course. I think he had more fun chortling with the turkeys, looking for deer and observing nature rather than playing golf. He was always quick-witted, was generous in his offers to buy you a brewsky or two, or three, or…and he entertained the foursome. On his day, he could hit them far and was uncanny around the green. Having said that, I believe if Joe had to pick one passion, it would be hunting. Joe would jump in head first and get any and every gadget necessary to track that bird or hunt down that deer. Camouflaged hat, coat, pants, shoes, gloves, rifle, pistol, shot gun, bow, arrow, knife, trap, bait, tree stand, tent, truck, trailer, boat, decoys … you get the picture … Joe was going to get it. Whatever he did, he was 100% in to it!

RANDOM THOUGHTS

Who would Joe say was the most impressive athlete he played against in his life time? I would guess it might have been Walter Payton, the great Chicago Bear running back, "Sweetness" as he was nicknamed.

How did Joe end up at the University of Nebraska? He had full scholarship offers from Notre Dame and Nebraska. Diane was a year ahead of Joe so she was already attending Nebraska. Joe said that if Notre Dame wanted him to play for them, they should offer a scholarship to Diane as he was going to school wherever she was. Diane did not transfer so Joe went to Lincoln – a history changing event.

Strange occurrence – Joe and I each ended up with ten career interceptions at Nebraska but oddly we each hold the single season record for most return yards in a single game at 116 yards; even our total career interception yardage was almost identical! We just could not get out of each other's way!

What makes a group of athletes not only a team but a *championship* team? When a group of guys show up for fall camp football practice, each one is like an ice cube. They all have some talent and fill a position on the field. A leader can come in and start to melt that ice into a fluid group that can interact and blend together. A guy like Joe could take that water and make it *boil*! He could change the water to steam and steam can make a locomotive come to life and move a hundred-car freight train down the tracks at high speed. He had the secret ingredients – talent, infectious personality, persona and an unquenchable desire to win.

Of all three levels of participation in sports – high school, college, and professional – Joe truly enjoyed high school the most. National Championships and Super Bowl rings were noteworthy, but Scotus is where his heart was. He truly cherished the night he was able to present to his high school, Scotus Central Catholic High School, a special football. The NFL gave each Super Bowl participant a gold NFL Super-Bowl-engraved football, for presentation to his high school. Columbus was the place where his heart was. It was the best of times and where his best of friends were made. His impact will last as long as…as we share our memories of him.

Diane warned me, take your ear plugs, so I packed them carefully with my gear. Joe and I always supported the annual Teammates Golf Tournament at the Wild Horse Golf course at Gothenburg, Nebraska. To save on expenses this particular weekend, Joe and I shared a room. The air conditioning was on medium cool and low fan. I was already cold and tucked under the covers. Joe's bed was closest to the A/C and he said, "I'm turning it all the way down and putting the fan on high". "Holy Jesus, I can see my breath," I said. No comment from Joe as he plopped into his bed in boxer shorts and the lights went out. He did not even cover up! A little while later, I heard some snorts and when I finally realized what was going on I remembered what Diane said. So I plugged my ears and covered my head with the extra pillows. Little did I know that this was only the toy lawn mower version of what was yet to come.

In the middle of the night, the 465-cubic-inch-premium-powered-double-hemi-fuel-injected chain saw kicked in. I could not squelch that incessant blare! The glasses in the bathroom rattled on the vanity top. Wallpaper was curling. I got up, dressed and escaped down to the lobby to warm up. I did not know if I should report to the hotel manager that someone was snoring loudly in room 237 or call the police with a domestic disturbance complaint. I had thoughts of just sleeping in the lobby, but all the lights were on, so I went out to the car. I actually did sleep some but at the crack of dawn, I was awakened by someone tapping on the window. A thought of "Did someone else actually report this to the hotel manager and are they searching the parking lot for survivors?" surfaced. As I looked out I saw Joe and I read his lips "I'm sorry". I believe I gave him the one figure salute. How can a man in his sleep stir up so much consternation? After a cold shower and a good breakfast, all was well again.

LAST GOOD-BYE

It was my third night in Boston on an East Coast trip and for some reason I could not sleep. I rolled around and around - then I just got up at 5:00 a.m. Eastern time. I emailed my wife, Linda, telling her my schedule for that day. A few minutes later she called me. Joe had just had a heart attack and passed away. All day my thoughts were on Joe, on all the memories, on Diane and the family as I made plans to fly home for the funeral. The ceremony was well attended by family, friends and teammates.

I was honored to be considered one of the pallbearers. The priest was Fr. Leo Kosch, my cousin. He first read in English and then sang a special song in Latin for Joe at the end of the ceremony. As we placed him in the hearse I was the last one to touch his casket. I stood there for a brief moment – hundreds of thoughts running through my head – then I slapped the lid like the Marines, and said my goodbye. Later in the day I complimented Fr. Leo and said the Latin song was very nostalgic and reminded me of when I was a server for Mass. Joe's family had told Fr. Leo that Joe wanted to be a server, and had memorized all of the Latin verses and prayers but missed the last day of instruction due to an injury.

Ironically, Joe's funeral was held at Sacred Heart Catholic Church in Lincoln, the very same church where Linda and I were married in 1971, with Diane and Joe in our wedding party. Joe's funeral was our first time back to this church. This church was now the site of two major events in my life and I was struggling with competing emotions; however, Joe would have insisted that we celebrate and be happy and not be mournful. At the rosary the night before the funeral, one of Joe's sisters-in-law commented to me that Joe had a little smirk on his face. Old Joe was sending us a message that he was feeling no pain.

I will miss you, Brother Joe.

Steve Wieser

Scotus High School 1966 - 1970

- Four-year football letterman, 1966-1969
- Member of the 1967 state championship football team
- All-State football selection, 1969
- Shrine Bowl participant, 1970
- Three-year letterman at the University of Nebraska, 1972-1974

When I was a little boy in the late fifties we lived in Duncan and my mother and father worked in Columbus. During the day I would stay at my grandmother's house on 18th Avenue by the railroad tracks. In the late summer and fall I would watch the St. Bon's high school football team walk by on their way to practice. I didn't know where they were going but I sure thought they were cool. That is my first memory of Shamrock football. Just a few years later I would be making that same trip to and from our practice field.

Our first practice in the fall we would line up and walk the field looking for rocks and broken glass. I hope the facilities have improved since! Practice back then was always in full pads. Even in the heat of two–a–days you couldn't take off your helmet, kneel or sit, and there was no water during practice. It seems we always had contact and scrimmaged regularly. I don't *think* the coaches were trying to kill us, that's just the way it was.

Speaking of practice, one of Coach Puetz's favorite drills was called "Bull in the Ring". In the drill, one guy stood in the middle of a circle of teammates. Then one by one, Coach would call out a name and the guy in the middle had to fend off blocks in rapid order. Coach loved that drill; us, not so much.

When we were freshmen we practiced in the lot north of the old St Mary's hospital. The Koschs lived nearby and had a freezer in their garage. Larry Holys was able to get instant Gatorade from his dad and we would mix up gallon jugs of the stuff before practice and put them in the freezer. After practice it would be ice cold and we would run over and chug it down. Nothing has ever tasted better since. As a freshman I made the varsity as a kicker. I was so good we didn't even attempt an extra point all year, never mind a field goal. Fortunately, we scored enough and I was able to letter by just kicking off.

My sophomore year we only had about 33 guys on the team and not many more in other years. It was not uncommon to never leave the game. We would play every down, offense, defense, and special teams.

My first game as a sophomore was one of those games. I recall I was playing defensive end and Mark Lueke was at tackle. About half way through the fourth quarter we were looking at each other wondering if the game would ever end. We were exhausted. We swore they were adding time to the clock – not letting it tick down!

That year we had all new coaches, Claire Stramel, Jim Puetz, and Vern Younger. When they saw how few guys were on the team they must have wondered what they had taken on. I'm sure things looked brighter once they realized they had a back field consisting of Bill and Bob Kosch and Joe Blahak. There was a tremendous amount of speed and talent for a small school and we won the Class C state championship.

Throughout my career I played a lot of different positions including quarterback, running back, center, guard, tackle, defensive end, and middle linebacker. By far my favorite was linebacker.

Of the guys I played with three stood out. Bill Kosch was a great player and a great leader. He was relatively quiet, but led by example. The best athlete was Joe Blahak – maybe the best athlete ever at Scotus. But the best football player was Bob Kosch. Bob was ultra-competitive and fearless as well as a great running back. We were undefeated half way through our senior year when Bob broke his arm. We the ended up losing a couple of games. Had Bob stayed healthy I think we would have stayed unbeaten.

I would like to thank our coaches, all my fellow athletes, and all of those who supported Shamrock athletics for the great experience I had at Scotus Central Catholic.

Brenda Grubaugh

Scotus High School 1970 - 1974

- Gold medal winner in the 50-yard dash, 220-yard dash, and Two-time gold medal winner in the 100-yard dash
- Set state record in 50-yard dash, 1973
- First recipient of the Scotus Female Athlete of the Year, 1974
- Shamrock Athletic Hall of Fame inductee, 1999

I started high school prior to Title IX (1972), so the idea of a girls' athletic team was something new to the school. I am proud of what we were able to accomplish at Scotus while I was in high school as well as what women's athletics has developed into at Scotus. As a Shamrock athlete, I was very fortunate to have the support of Scotus during this time.

My dad, Al Grubaugh, had the greatest influence on me becoming an athlete. He helped to start the girls' track & field team at Scotus. He realized the importance of getting girls involved in athletics.

My fondest memory as a Shamrock athlete is winning three events at the state track meet (50-yard dash, 100-yard dash, and 220-yard dash) and setting the Class B record in the 50-yard dash my junior year at the state track meet, which earned us the runner-up trophy. One of my most memorable experiences was competing as a freshman in the first Nebraska girls' state track & field meet.

Some of the best athletes that I competed against were Sondra Obermeier from Aurora High School and Diane Polak from David City Aquinas.

During my four years competing as a Shamrock athlete, I had numerous coaches including my dad, Al Grubaugh, and my brother, Tracy Grubaugh.

Not many people can say that their dad and brother helped coach them during their high school career.

I am most proud of being the first female Athlete of the Year and winning three events (50-yard dash, 100-yard dash, and 220-yard dash) at the state track meet.

Whether you are a female or male, with the right support system you can be successful in whatever you choose.

Dan Steiner

Scotus High School 1971 - 1975

- All-State football selection, 1974
- Scotus Co-Athlete of the Year, 1975
- Shrine Bowl participant, 1975
- Starter at guard on the 10-2 1979 Nebraska football team
- Shamrock Athletic Hall of Fame inductee, 2001

Being a former Shamrock means everything; it's all I thought about all through high school. The coaches, the older athletes, and my brothers – Jack, Mike, and Dave – all had a tremendous influence on me as an athlete.

I can remember taking a shower and using the same towel several times during football two-a-days, and drinking water from the well with my helmet. And, I remember the drills: *Bull In the Ring*, the *Kill Drill*, and *Come and Get Me*. Memorable game day experiences include a trip to Schuyler my junior year and beating a good Schuyler team. I also remember beating Aquinas 7-0 my senior year. My most memorable moment was probably catching a tackle eligible pass against Fremont Bergan in the conference championship game in my junior year.

The best athlete I played with at Scotus was Jim Brock. My brother Dave was one of the smartest and toughest football players I played with. The best athletes I competed against were Tom Vering from Fremont Bergan and Mike Thompson from Omaha Holy Name.

Coach Jim Puetz always had a great halftime speech. He once threw a water bottle at me to get me and the team fired up. It was also fun getting him to tell stories in class. I am most proud of my hard work paying off by getting a scholarship to play football at the University of Nebraska. It changed my life. Those are the life lessons I learned: hard work, loyalty, teamwork, and *never let up* because you may be letting down a teammate.

Ron Mimick and I were both linemen, so we competed together in all conditioning, etc. It made us both what we came to be. We would run ladder sprints - 10 yards, 20 yards, 30 yards, etc. Coach Puetz would always be at the start; I would win almost all races going away against Coach Puetz. When we would come back, Ron would run a little faster. Puetz would always yell, "*Mimick is going to beat Steiner*!" I would get so mad I would try to catch him; sometimes I did, and sometimes I didn't.

Before my senior year of college, I was lifting at Scotus with all the Scotus kids like Bob Heimann and Mark Kurtenbach. I told Jim and Gary Puetz I would buy a 400-pound York Olympic weight set if they would buy a good bench. That summer we all worked hard and the improvements were incredible! By the end of that year they had purchased two or three more sets. They told me several years later that they laughed when I offered to spend $500 on a set of weights. The Scotus weight room has been one of the best in the state for years.

Gregg Grubaugh

Scotus High School 1971 - 1975

- Class B All-State basketball Honorable Mention, 1974
- Scotus Co-Athlete of the Year, 1975
- School record holder for Most Career Rebounds (576)
- Three-Year basketball letter winner at Kearney State College

---

Editor's Note: The story for Gregg Grubaugh was written by his brother, Tracy. Gregg passed away on February 19, 2015. Gregg is considered to be one of the most talented basketball players in Scotus history.

Scotus has a very rich history in athletics, and Gregg, who loved sports in general, was honored and proud to have participated in sports for this school.

Al and Bess Grubaugh, his parents, had a big influence on Gregg. They gave him direction and support all the way through his years, and probably made it to about every game he played in at Scotus. Gregg just loved playing for Frank Spenceri, Jim Puetz, Vern Younger and all the assistant coaches at Scotus, there was no question about that. Basketball was his best sport, and Gregg always said that Frank Spenceri really molded him into the player he was. He made Gregg a fundamentally very sound player, which prepared him to play college basketball after Scotus.

I am not sure if I know what Gregg's funniest moment was, but here is a fond memory that we all shared at Scotus, as they had the best school cafeteria program in the state. No athlete ever went away from the table hungry at Scotus. I do remember a funny moment, not funny at the time, but Gregg liked to tell the story of when he was a freshman, he suited up with the varsity for a couple of games toward the end of the year. Frank put him in the game in the 4th quarter of a close game with Lakeview. Gregg thought he was going to die that night. Jim Pillen probably schooled him, but he survived.

Gregg's most memorable game day experience may have been when Scotus beat Aquinas at the buzzer in district basketball tournament in Gregg's senior year. Gregg and cousin Rick Grubaugh, who played for Aquinas that year, still argue about that one. Also, in his junior year, Scotus beat Lakeview in triple overtime in district tournaments.

Gregg had Frank Spenceri as head coach for basketball, and Jim Puetz as head coach for football and track. He loved it. We're talking about a couple of coaching legends. Scotus was lucky to have them for all those years.

I really think Gregg was just proud to be part of the teams he played on there, and the life-long friends he has because of that. Gregg never really talked about personal accomplishments. He liked talking about the teams, the coaches, and the guys he played with.

It was a special moment for him to be named Co- Athlete of the Year with Dan Steiner his senior year. He really considered that quite an honor.

Ron Mimick

Scotus High School 1971 - 1975

- Class B All-State Defensive End, 1974
- Shrine Bowl participant, 1975
- 2016 *Lincoln Journal Star* Coach of the Year
- 274 career wins and seven state championships as a high school football coach

---

I was always proud to be a Shamrock. I remember growing up watching my brother Bill, Joe Blahak, and Bob and Bill Kosch.

Jim Puetz and Vern Younger had the greatest influence on me.

My fondest memory is beating Aquinas on Homecoming my senior year when we were both ranked in the Top Ten.

My most memorable experience is running in the snow and rain at a track meet and placing second in the 180-yard low hurdles; it helped us win a close meet.

The best athlete I played with was Tom Sobotka. The best athlete I played against was a linebacker from Ord, but I can't remember his name.

It was fun playing for Coach Jim Puetz; the best times were when Jim would get excited about the game or a track meet.

As far as life lessons that I learned while an athlete at Scotus, it was to keep grinding forward. Scotus really was an extension of my faith.

One memorable story was during halftime of a football game when Jim Puetz got excited and threw several water bottles and explained that some of us players wouldn't make the "All-South Side" team. Needless to say, we were more motivated and played much better in the second half.

Dan Martin

Scotus High School 1972 - 1976

- All-Conference running back, 1975
- Shrine Bowl participant, 1976
- Shrine Bowl Most Valuable Offensive player, 1976
- Three-year letter winner at Kearney State College

Being a Shamrock athlete meant being a competitor and giving 100% toward winning the game, races, and events you participated in as a teammate and as an individual. Also, to take pride in being a Shamrock and wearing green.

Coach Jim Puetz and Coach Vern Younger had the greatest influence on me as an athlete. Coach Puetz emphasized being a competitor. If it was at practice or in a game, he made you push yourself to get better and reach for higher goals. As the freshman football coach, Vern Younger gave us a great introduction to the Scotus tradition and competitive ways. Our freshman football team was dominant as we were 6-0 and only had six total points scored on us that season.

A couple of fond memories were scoring my first varsity touchdown in my freshman season in a big win at Grand Island Central Catholic. I scored my last touchdown on an 84-yard fumble recovery, also against GICC. It was the only defensive touchdown of my career, We won the game 31-0 and knocked GICC out of the playoffs my senior season.

My most memorable game day experience was rushing for a record 220 yards and three touchdowns in a 42-14 win at Columbus Lakeview during my senior season.

The best athlete I ever played with was John Fischer. John was an outstanding tight end and defensive end. John was one of the first in-state players to be offered a scholarship to play at Nebraska that year. Beside playing together at Scotus, John and I were both picked to play for the North team in the Nebraska Shrine Bowl. The majority of the players in the Shrine Bowl that year were going to play football in college. Players on the North squad who played at Nebraska were John Fischer (Scotus), Dan Pensick (Columbus High), Kerry Weinmaster (North Platte), Mike Bruce (Omaha Burke) and Tim Wurth (Omaha Burke). Players going to other major colleges were Casey McCormick (Creighton Prep) who went to Notre Dame, Jim Molini (Norfolk High) who went to Iowa, and Frank Taylor (Omaha North) who went to Kansas. John and I both started in the Shrine game and represented Scotus well. I scored the first touchdown of the game, was the leading rusher, and was named the game's Outstanding Offensive Player. John made several key receptions, was the leading receiver, and was in the running for Outstanding Offensive Player as well.

Coach Jim Puetz believed in working hard as practices were tough and very demanding. His practices made you better, tougher, and a competitor. Coach Puetz was hard-nosed, but had fun with it with many good memories.

I am most proud of getting to start at running back for three years on teams that went 9-1, 7-2, and 7-2, and were highly ranked in the state throughout the seasons against a very competitive schedule. Many of the teams we played had some of their best teams during these years.

During my senior football season, we started out ranked #2 in Class B behind Lincoln Pius X. We went to into the Wahoo Neumann game 6-0 and still ranked #2. Neumann was ranked #1 in Class C; they were the biggest Class C school in the state, and Scotus was one of the smallest Class B schools with only a few students' difference that year. We had some injuries to some of our players that hurt us going into the game and some during the game also.

Going into the fourth quarter we were ahead of Neumann 15-13. We punted on fourth down just short of midfield; the snap went over the punter's head. Neumann got the ball in great field possession and scored a touchdown, going ahead 19-15. Right after they kicked off to us the scoreboard and half the lights on the field went out. There was a loud "pop" when it happened. The referees and coaches met at midfield and decided to continue the game with half the lights working and to keep time on one of the referees' hand watches. When the scoreboard went out there was about three minutes and forty seconds left to play; we were out of timeouts. We were passing on every down to save time on the clock. We had moved the ball to just past midfield and had only run about four or five plays. There was a lot of confusion with no scoreboard with time running out.

We got up to the line to run another play and the referee who was manually keeping time blew his whistle and said time had run out and the game was over. Neumann won 19-15. It was a packed stadium with many fans standing along the sidelines. Scotus fans couldn't believe that time had actually run out and we had lost. Neumann fans were cheering loudly and jumping up and down as it was a huge win for them. Neumann won the Class C title that year – the first year of the playoffs.

Scotus was really down after that loss, thinking we had probably lost out on getting to the playoffs. We played David City Aquinas the next game and lost 16-0 on the road; we didn't play very well that night and didn't make the playoffs. We beat Grand Island Central Catholic in our last game of the year 31-0. It was Homecoming, and was a good last game to win; we knocked GICC out of the playoffs. They were 7-1 going into our game.

Life lessons that I learned were to show up every day, willing and ready to work hard, do your best, reach for higher goals, and be a good co-worker and friend. Also, to have fun and enjoy family and friends with good times.

Tom Sobotka

Scotus High School 1972 - 1976

- 1976 gold medal winner in the 120-yard high hurdles
- School record holder in 110-meter high hurdles (14.3)
- Three-year letter winner in football and basketball
- Four-year letter winner in track & field
- Scotus Athlete of the Year, 1976

It was a source of pride representing Scotus. There was a reputation with Scotus such that we would catch the opponent's eye when we took the field and usually get their best shot.

The coaches that had the greatest influence on me were Frank Spenceri and Vern Younger. How to compete of course, but how to do it the right way with honor and respect.

One of my funniest memories as an athlete at Scotus was during basketball practice in the old gym. It was raining outside, there were buckets on the floor to catch the water leaking through the roof, and players were falling down after kicking the bucket with water spilling, and the coach's clipboard and basketball flying into the stands in frustration. I also fondly recall Bull in the Ring drills during football practice, and the first outdoor track practices of the season where you were dropped outside of town about 40 miles away (or so it seemed) and had to jog back. I remember riding the bus into Boys Town for a senior year football game and seeing a large, dark moon rising in the locker room window (we beat them so it turned out well). We spent large chunks of class time in Jim Puetz's history class projecting track team and meet scores for large invitational meets. Vern Younger always called me "ZZZabodka" as he didn't have an "S" in his vocabulary. And there were times when Jim Puetz kicked full coolers during half time pep talks.

A few memories I'd like to forget include the S-Club initiation rites, running track meets at the Knights of Columbus Invitational on the cinder track in the rain, and bologna sandwiches for lunch at away track meets.

My most memorable game day experience was probably going deep for three straight plays at end of first half of Lakeview game senior year. Same call, same play, against the same Lakeview DB. On the last throw, Chris Hoffman floated a perfect ball over my shoulder into my outstretched arms for a long TD to end the half.

The best athlete I played with at Scotus was John Fischer. The best athletes I played against were Dave Liegl from Central City and Scott Poehling from Fremont Bergan.

I remember a basketball game at Omaha Cathedral in my senior season in their old cracker box gym. We were getting beat by a good margin, there were questionable foul no-calls, you would run into the end wall after layups as the gym was so small. The entire game was very frustrating as a player, even though our effort and desire was good. Coach Spenceri subbed me out near the end of the game; as I came to the bench he tried to shake my hand and I blew him off. I then received an extensive tongue lashing (well deserved) about sportsmanship and the ability to be a good loser. That has stuck with me throughout the years.

I am most proud of during my time at Scotus to have the opportunity to represent the school, the student body, and the Columbus community well in the sports that we played.

The life lessons that I learned include hard work, perseverance, believing in yourself, working as a band of brothers toward a goal, respecting yourself, your teammates, and your opponents.

Two final stories: While playing football at Wahoo Neumann our senior season we played without a scoreboard or clock; the time keeping seeming kind of odd at the end of the game, which we lost. During a basketball game at Omaha Cathedral a student manager got locked in locker room for the entire second half of the game; the team got quite thirsty.

Jim Feehan

Scotus High School 1974 - 1977

- Class B All-State football, 1976
- All-Conference football selection, 1976
- All-Conference basketball selection, 1977

I was very fortunate to have parents that were actively involved at Scotus and thus I was exposed to Scotus (St. Bon's) sporting events at a very early age. The highlight of the week was always attending whatever game was in season and if it was an away game discussing the highlights (or lowlights) on the drive home. At the end of the year we attended the athletic banquets and listened to speakers such as Digger Phelps, Gale Sayers, Mick Tingelhoff and Bill Toomey tell their inspiring stories and then getting their autographs at the end of the program. (Yes, this was before sports stars figured out they could get big dollars for public speaking).

This early exposure inspired me to compete and try to emulate those athletes I watched growing up. Sports meant the world to me in high school and it provided me with many great friends and memories.

Frank Spenceri had the greatest influence on me as a Shamrock athlete. He had a passion for winning and doing things the right way. I learned from Frank that the way to succeed was to work hard and master the fundamentals. Though some people did not respond to Frank's style of coaching, I thoroughly enjoyed it.

One of the most disappointing seasons was the 1975 football season. I would argue the class of 1976 was one of the most talented classes ever at Scotus. They had Tom Sobotka, Dan Martin, John Fischer, Kevin Abbott,

Darrell Spulak, and Dan Schaecher yet Aquinas upset us and we missed the playoffs. It was the first year of the football playoffs.

I will never forget February 28, 1977, at the District semifinals and we were playing Seward (in York). Seward had the 6'-5" Bosak twins and a good point guard named Marc Felix. I believe they were rated number two in state and we were down by two points with three seconds to play. I was fouled and had two shots, I made the first and missed the second and we lost by one. Seward went on to beat Central City the following night by a large margin and to this day I believe if we would have won that game we would have gone on to the state tournament (a Scotus basketball team had not been to state in 40 years). I am reminded of this game every year on my birthday.

John Fischer was the most talented athlete I played with or against. Besides being a good athlete he was also a good person.

You cannot mention St Bonaventure/Scotus sports without thinking of Jim and Gary Puetz. They both loved competition and were tremendous motivators. Anyone that played football will recall at least one Jim Puetz halftime rant.

Gary was my line coach at Scotus and as he tells me I was his first All-State football player; to this day I believe it was all attributable to him. I look back at their coaching styles and they had the ability to get the most out of every individual and team – they kept things simple, worked with what they had and more importantly kept it a fun experience.

Though sports were important maintaining high academics was also important if not more so. Scotus can be as proud of their academic legacy as their sports.

I look back on our 1977 senior class and though we were not the most athletically gifted class we were a group of guys that worked hard and cared for each other. We ended the year rated in the top ten for both football and basketball and before the school year began most people thought we would be lucky to finish at .500 in either sport. A life lesson I learned was that good things happen to those who work hard and teamwork matters.

A couple other memories worth mentioning:

Coach Puetz always had some great names for the drills at football practice such as "Bull in the Ring", "Burma Road", "Burma Road with Popper", and the "Oklahoma drill". He would also post the practice schedule and add inspirational quotes at the bottom such as "*Beat the heat with hustle*".

Two-a-days in August and drinking water from our helmets – yikes!

The football Watermelon feed.

The shed with the dummies that reeked of mold!

To break up the monotony of practice Frank Spenceri had us form a circle at half court, hold hands, and move around while singing "ring around the rosie" and then we all fell down.

Coach Spenceri telling Ron Reilly that some people were shooters and others passers – Ron was a passer.

Coach Spenceri getting so angry he broke a clipboard smashing it on the edge of the stage in the old gym – we bought him a steel one at the end of the year.

Once at a basketball practice, Dennis Ryba and Tim Harrington were in the stands watching practice. Coach Spenceri told them to quit "screwing around" which they did for about five minutes. Then they started making noise again and Frank's temper erupted – he began throwing basketballs at them and telling them to leave the gym (cannot quote him as this is a "family" publication).

The uniquely Scotus invention of *football-track*!

Going to football games when I was young and it seemed every year (it was probably only a couple of times but it seemed like more) Omaha Cathedral and Scotus would be undefeated and playing for the state number one rating. As I recall Cathedral got the best of us numerous times.

In the late 1960's, Scotus was playing Schuyler in football. 6'10" Chuck Jura was the quarterback for Schuyler and Bill Kosch blitzed and stepped between Jura and their running back, took the ball and ran 50-plus yards for a touchdown. I was probably nine or ten years old at the time.

Tim Hroza

Scotus High School 1976 - 1978

- All-Centennial Conference running back, 1977
- Scotus Athlete of the Year, 1978
- Shrine Bowl participant, 1978
- Three-year football letter winner University of North Dakota

One of the best things about being a Shamrock athlete was that I got to date some of the nicest, best-looking girls in school!

The coach who had the greatest influence on me was Randy Berlin; he always supported me – in good times and in bad.

Some of my best memories include watching fullback Rex Kumpf get down and dirty while blocking for me ... thanks, buddy!

As far as game days go, I fondly remember watching Jim and Gary Puetz explode after popping off a 50-foot throw to win the shot put in the conference track meet.

The best athlete I played with was Chris Hoffman. Chris could do it all, and with intensity. I also have to mention Pat Novicki; Pat just had raw determination.

After watching an episode of *A Football Life* about Coach Vince Lombardi on the NFL Network, I'd have to say Coach Jim Puetz came to mind a few times. Watching Coach Puetz on the sideline was a classic.

I am most proud of learning about hard work and commitment while a Scotus athlete. Now, I am able to teach my sons that same work ethic, both on and off the field. The life lessons that I learned were determination and dedication; these have stuck with me and have helped me to raise my two sons. It has also helped me as a coach with grit and hopefully, some grace.

My worst football game memory was the Grand Island Central Catholic game. My best memory was a halfback pass to Pat Novicki for a touchdown. As for track, it was probably hanging out with Jeff Muhle after field events while everyone else was working their butts off!

Mike Cielocha

Scotus High School 1975 - 1979

- Class B All-State defensive back, 1978
- Member of two state championship track teams, 1978-79
- Six-time Grand Champion at the state track championships:
  440-yard dash (1977, 1978, 1979); 100-yard dash (1979); 220- yard dash (1979); 880-yard relay (1978)
- Class B state record in the 440-yard dash, 1977 (48.9)
- Four school records in track (100, 200, 440, 880 Relay)
- Captain - University of Nebraska track team, 1983
- Shamrock Athletic Hall of Fame inductee, 1999
- Nebraska High School Sports Hall of Fame inductee, 2005

It was truly a privilege to wear the green of Scotus. I was humbled by the tremendous tradition that Scotus had prior to my participation in Scotus athletics during my high school years. As an athlete at Scotus, I had a competitive attitude to play the best I could every time I took the field or track. Losing was not an option.

I was very fortunate to have some excellent coaches while I participated in sports at Scotus: Jim Puetz, Frank Spenceri, Vern Younger, Gary Puetz, and Randy Berlin. The things that each of these individuals taught me were discipline, dedication, respect, practice hard / play hard, have fun, and *be on time*! Each one of these coaches brought a unique approach to the practice and games. I still consider my coaches some of my closest friends today.

Playing basketball for Coach Frank Spenceri was an experience that I will never forget. Frank had a really strong competitive attitude. He was a great teacher of fundamentals; each practice was a story all by itself. I learned a lot from Coach Spenceri; he was a great disciplinarian. He was like a father-figure to me. Frank is one of my best friends today.

Jim Puetz coached me in football and track. Jim had a tremendous competitive attitude. He had a great sense of humor and always tried to incorporate this into his practices in order to keep things fun. Jim hated losing!

I played with a lot of great athletes during my time at Scotus. That was a huge reason for the tremendous successes we achieved. One of the best athletes that I competed against was Marty Kobza. Even though we did not directly compete against each other in our events on the track, I respected the level of success he achieved. Marty was one of the best track athletes to ever participate in track in the state of Nebraska.

Rick Schumacher

Scotus High School 1975 - 1979

- 1979 gold medal winner triple jump (46'-6")
- Scotus Athlete of the Year, 1979
- Three-year, three-sport letter winner (football, basketball, track)
- Held school record for most tackles in a season (153) for 37 years

I have always been proud to be a Scotus alum. There is so much tradition at Scotus. The success wouldn't be possible if it weren't for all of the hard work put in by the priests, students, teachers, coaches and administration we have had at Scotus over the years. John Petersen and Gary Puetz both retired from Scotus this year (2016). They are the last teachers and coaches who were at Scotus when I graduated in 1979. When I graduated from Scotus, there were only three state championship banners hanging in the gym at Scotus. Now there are forty-four! Faces change, but the success continues. To be part of the success, tradition and Catholic faith we have had at Scotus is pretty special.

My wife Theresa and I are proud to have both of our children attend Scotus. Our daughter Sarah graduated in 2016 and our son Nathan graduates in 2019. I think if you asked both of them their thoughts about Scotus, they would be the same as mine. Scotus is and always will be a special place.

I would have to say my dad LeRoy had the greatest influence on me as a Shamrock athlete. I also was influenced by my three brothers (Jeff '75, Jim '76 and Bob '83). Growing up, we were constantly outside playing different sports depending on what time of year it was (our mom, Alvina, would kick us out of the house). We all knew that Scotus was special and that we were lucky to have the opportunity to participate in sports at such a great school. Our dad taught us to compete and be the best we could be.

He had a great saying that I will never forget. If we were nervous about an upcoming game or competing against some outstanding athletes, he would always remind us that our opponents put their pants on in the morning the same way as we did - one leg at a time. He was trying to tell us that the opponents were human just like us and that we should go out and compete against them and do our best. If our best was not good enough to win, that was OK if we competed to the best of our ability.

The fondest memory of being a Shamrock athlete was in track. I was fortunate to be a part of arguably the best three-year run in school history in boys track from 1977-1979. Our team placed third at state in 1977 and won state championships in 1978 and 1979. During my senior year we were undefeated in five events (the 100, 220, 440, triple jump and the 880 relay). It was nice to have Mike Cielocha compete in four of those undefeated events.

Football also produced a lot great memories for me. Our defense my senior year had six shutouts and it should have been seven. Lakeview scored on us late in the game after we pulled our starters while we were leading 34-0 to ruin the shutout. We gave up 42 points in 10 games that year. We played a six–two defense and blitzed on almost every play. It was a blast. We competed in Class B and ended the regular season 7-2-1. Unfortunately, we didn't make the state playoffs since they only took the top eight teams back then.

I played with a lot of great athletes at Scotus, but Mike Cielocha was the best. Mike was one of the greatest track athletes of all time not only at Scotus but the entire state of Nebraska. He was a super competitor and didn't like to lose at anything.

Another great athlete I competed against was Todd Brown from Holdrege. He was a senior when I was a junior. I triple jumped against him at the state meet when I was a sophomore and junior. I was lucky to witness his state and state meet record triple jump of 50'2.25" which still stands 38 years later. Todd was one of the few people who beat Mike Cielocha in the 100-yard dash which he did at the state meet in 1978.

While I was at Scotus I played for many great coaches. Jim Puetz was the head coach in both football and track. He was a master motivator and got the best out of all his players. Coach Puetz always seemed to come up with ways to motivate and get the best out of all of us. Frank Spenceri was a great fundamental basketball coach. I learned a lot from Coach Spenceri. I was lucky to also have the opportunity to be coached by assistants Gary Puetz, Vern Younger and Randy Berlin.

The one story I have to tell is related to basketball. We traveled to Omaha on a cold Saturday night in January to play Omaha Cathedral. Cathedral was led by John Higgins who has refereed numerous men's NCAA final four basketball games (the one with the good hair). We played horribly that night and got beat. Coach Spenceri knew we needed to work on our fundamentals. When we got back to Columbus, he announced that the varsity would have practice the next morning at 6:00 a.m. It was cold (wind chills in the minus 20's and snow flurries) and as Mike Savage and I were heading home, I developed a flat tire on my car about a mile or so away from home. Not being in a very good mood due to our poor performance and practice less than five hours away, I drove all the way home on the rim. Needless to say, my parents were not very happy with me but Mike Savage was.

We had a tradition after football games and track meets that we won. Pat Novicki, who was a year ahead of me at Scotus, would lead us singing polka songs on the bus ride home. When Pat graduated, we found someone else in our class to lead us in the songs and carry on the tradition. I would be curious how long after we graduated the tradition lasted.

The last story I would like to add is an example of the many ways Jim Puetz used to motivate the football team. Our opponent one particular week was Wahoo Neumann. Our team was watching prior year film of our game against Neumann. We noticed a cheap shot a Neumann player put on one of our Scotus teammates in that game. The player's name was Dave Spicka and he was a junior in the prior year so he was returning to play in the game we had with them that week. At practice the next day, Jim Puetz came up with a drill called "Spicka the Pricka drill" where we all took turns beating up on a tackling dummy with Spicka's name on it. We were definitely ready to play Neumann that week.

Scotus is a lot more than state championship banners and awards. It is a place where students can prepare themselves for the real world after graduation. I couldn't have asked for a better school to spend my high school years. I am extremely blessed.

Bret Kumpf

Scotus High School 1977 - 1981

- Class B All-State basketball selection, 1981
- Member of the 1981 Class B state champion golf team

I am very proud to be a former Shamrock athlete. I always wanted to represent the school well and to play to the standard set by those who played before me. I always had great support from former athletes and fans.

As an athlete, the people who had the greatest influence on me were former players: Gregg Grubaugh, John Fischer, Chris Hoffman, Kurt Kline – and my coaches: Jim and Gary Puetz, Frank Spenceri, and Vern Younger.

One of my funniest memories was being the designated "lead singer" on our away trips on the bus. Our two favorite songs were "Big John" by Jimmy Dean and "Teddy Bear" by Elvis Presley. I had a great chorus of teammates to accompany me.

My most memorable game day experience – no question – was the opening round of the State basketball Tournament in 1981 at Pershing Auditorium in Lincoln.

The best athletes I played with were Glen Kucera, Rick Schumacher, and Mike Cielocha. I remember watching Mike Cielocha at the state track meet in Omaha and how just used to *smoke* by the other runners; Mike was amazingly fast. The best athletes I competed against were Marty Kobza from Schuyler and Russ Uhing from Hartington Cedar Catholic.

Some vivid memories include watching basketball game films in the basement of Coach Spenceri's house. I also remember the halftime speeches of Coach Jim Puetz; mostly when we were getting outplayed(!). I am most proud that our 1981 basketball team was able to break through a long drought and make it to the state basketball tournament. That was a very special team. I also remember making a three-quarter court shot at the end of the third quarter at the state tournament. The crowd was going crazy and my teammates were going nuts. All I was thinking about was "We've got one more quarter to finally win a game at state", so that's what I was saying going into the huddle at the end of the quarter. *I also knew that's what Coach Spenceri would be saying.

I also remember the unbelievable crowd support and real passion of our student body in our quest to get to the state tournament in 1981. We had a very senior-dominated team with the exception of sophomore Mark Brezinski. This team averaged over 70 points a game without a three-point line. Coach Frank Spenceri was a very passionate and knowledgeable coach. The memories, friendships, and camaraderie were like no other.

Our 1981 golf team went from hitting wiffle balls off tumbling mats to winning the state golf title. Two members of that team, Brian Kuta and Tony Schieffer, went on to become golf professionals.

Some of the life lessons I learned during my time as a student and athlete at Scotus were to respect upperclassmen, and also to pass down the traditions they taught us.

Lana Torczon

Scotus High School 1977 - 1981

- Three-year letter winner in volleyball (1978, 1979, 1980) and basketball (1979, 1980, 1981)
- Four-year letter winner in track (1978, 1979, 1980, 1981)
- First team All-State in basketball, 1981
- Honorable Mention All-State in volleyball (1980) and basketball (1980)
- All-conference in volleyball (1979-80), basketball (1980-81)
- Played in Coaches All-Star basketball game, 1981
- Set several school records in basketball, including rebounds in a season (248), 1981
- Member of school record two-mile relay, 1981
- Scotus Athlete of the Year, 1981
- Shamrock Hall of Fame inductee, 2000

Well, unfortunately, I was at the very beginning of the Coach John Petersen era and did not win any district or state titles with him. I was a freshman when Coach Petersen started coaching at Scotus. It did not take long for the girls' volleyball and basketball programs to drastically improve after Coach Petersen's arrival. Opposing coaches started to immediately notice the improvement of the Scotus players' fundamental skills. During this time, basketball season was a challenge because Scotus only had one gym and the girls' varsity team practiced after the boys' varsity team and the freshman and JV girls' teams had to practice at other gyms around town. Thankfully, Mr. and Mrs. Dowd generously donated the money to build the new gym during my time at Scotus.

Upon his arrival, Coach Petersen started implementing summer programs for both the volleyball and basketball players and intramural programs for the elementary students. At the end of every sports season he gave each player who would be returning the next year a list of the player's strengths, weaknesses and improvements that the player needed to make over the course of the summer. Coach Petersen was always available at any time if an athlete wanted to put in extra work and I made sure I took advantage of his extra help.

My sophomore year in basketball was a lot of fun. I had a lot of great teammates. We won our first Centennial Conference tournament crown. I was able to play in what was probably at that time the first meaningful game in the history of Scotus girls' athletics. The Scotus girls' basketball team made it to the district finals in 1979. Unfortunately, we lost in a double overtime thriller at the Platte College gym. The Scotus fans, always known for supporting the boys' athletics, showed up to cheer on the Scotus girls with an estimated 1,500 people in attendance at that game. It was the most exciting environment that I had ever played in during my time at Scotus. We finished the season with 14-5 record which was the best season ever for the girls' basketball team at that point.

My senior season, our volleyball team ended up losing in the district finals in a close three-set match against a highly-ranked Lakeview team. Our 13-4 record that season was the best volleyball record at Scotus at that time. During my senior basketball season, we knocked off No. 1 Wahoo Neumann. In the district semifinals we blew out the number five Class B team in the State. In fact, after the first quarter we were ahead 18-0 and when some of our fans came into the game late that they thought we were getting blown out. Of course, once again we lost to highly-ranked Lakeview in the district finals.

To put in perspective the immediate impact Coach Petersen had on the Scotus girls' athletic teams: the year before he arrived the girls varsity basketball team did not win one game and in Pete's second year the varsity basketball team was already in the district finals game and we should have won! I'm very proud that I played a part in Coach Petersen's efforts to build what would become a multi-generational dynasty.

Following my senior year, I was very honored to be the first female athlete at Scotus to play in the state's all-star game in Omaha. It was a great opportunity to meet and play with the best athletes in the state of Nebraska. Obviously, having only played organized basketball for four years this would not have been possible without the excellent and persistent coaching of John Petersen.

During my time at Scotus, John Kopetzky was the "president" of the girls' booster club and he made sure we had music at our warm-ups, put posters on our doors on game days and that the student body attended our away games. The boys were great supporters of our girls' athletics teams.

My most social sport was track. The big track meets were held all day on Fridays and usually there was a lot of waiting around between events. Therefore, you had a lot of time to meet people from other schools. I enjoyed our coaches Barb Malicky and Dan Mahoney. It was a lot of fun!! My senior year, our 3200-meter relay team broke the Class B record in districts and we qualified for the state track meet.

One of my memories of track was when the long distance girls tried to get away with cutting short a run. The day before a track meet the practice was usually pretty light and usually consisted of a run around Wagner's Lake. I'm not sure who instigated this but as we were running around Wagner's Lake we decided to save some time and make our light practice even lighter by going across Behlen's bridge rather than run around the entire lake. However, unbeknownst to us Coach Mahoney was driving around the lake to check on us and couldn't find us. Yes, we had to do a lot of extra running because of our detour at Wagner's Lake. So much for cutting our run short!

Overall, I loved my time in Scotus athletics and my teammates that I played with throughout high school. I'm proud of my teams' efforts and some of our "firsts". I have really enjoyed watching the successes of the younger generations including my niece Taylor Harsh's three state volleyball championships under Coach Petersen. The work ethic that Coach Petersen instilled in me in high school served me well in college, law school, and as an attorney in Kansas City, Missouri. Keep it going, Shamrocks!

Steve Bonk

Scotus High School 1981 - 1985

- Class B All-State Linebacker, 1984
- Member of the 1984 Class B state champion football team

The 1953 St. Bonaventure football team was undefeated; my dad (Joe) and my uncle (Tom) played on that team – this was before the championship games were played. There is a long legacy of Bonk football players: In 1984 I was on the 13-0 Class B state championship football team, in 1993 my cousin Cody Bonk was on the state championship football team, and in 2015 my son Ross Bonk played on the state championship team. My two sons Kyle and Ross were both selected to play in the Shrine Bowl. Kyle won the Spirit of Scotus award when he graduated in 2013. As you can see we have a long history at Scotus.

I would say the classes from 1977 to 1981 had the greatest influence on me as an athlete. These men are keeping Scotus alive by helping with the Gala, or taking tickets at games, etc. They are involved in the community as leaders and are proud to say that they went to Scotus. They still support all athletics at Scotus.

The best athlete I played with was Jeff Podraza (may he rest in peace). Jeff was not only great athlete, but great friend to everyone. If you talked to him once he would remember your name and hold a conversation like you were best friends forever. The most memorable game as a father was watching my son win the 2015 football championship. As a player, it was probably *any* game against Aquinas. As far as playing for my head coach, Jim Puetz, I was scared to death at each halftime. As a sophomore

I remember a cooler being thrown over my head against the wall. Then some words followed by Van Dyke. Then we ran out as fast as we could. Yeah, I learned to *always keep your helmet on.*

In closing I would like to thank all the Southsiders for making me a better person and athlete: the Novickis, Driefursts, Shotkoskis, Prososkis, and Cielochas. Without playing a baseball game at St. Anthony's School or shooting baskets at Buffalo Park, I would not have been the athlete I turned out to be.

Jeff Podraza

Scotus High School 1981 - 1985

- Three-year letter winner in football, 1982, 1983, 1984
- Honorable Mention All-State & All-Conference football, 1983, 1984
- Longest punt in Shrine Bowl history (76 yards), 1985
- Played on 1984 state championship football team with a 13-0 record and a school record eight shutouts
- Three-year letter winner in basketball, 1983, 1984, 1985
- Led the team in blocked shots, rebounds, and steals, 1985
- Four-year letter winner in track, 1982, 1983, 1984, 1985
- Held several school records in track and was a 1985 state track medalist in 110-meter high hurdles (2nd), All-Class 110- meter high hurdles (5th), long jump (6th), and a member of the 2nd place 4x100 meter relay team (with current school record time)
- Scotus Athlete of the Year, 1985
- Shamrock Hall of Fame inductee, 2000

Editor's note: The story of Jeff Podraza is being written by his very close friend and teammate, Todd Duren. Jeff, along with his two young daughters Jordyn and Taylor, were tragically killed in a car accident on December 18, 2010. Jeff will always be remembered for his high spirit and willingness to do whatever it takes to be the best he could be on athletic field or in the classroom.

Jeff's parents, Ambrose and Helen, had a significant influence on Jeff. Jeff spent a lot of time working on the farm with Ambrose and always wanted to follow in his footsteps as a football player. Ambrose was a great high school football player himself, and often times my dad told me of the legend that Ambrose was when he was growing up in the Monroe/Platte Center/Columbus Area. Jeff was everything to his parents and sister

Stacey, they were always there to support his efforts in sports both in high school and during his football career at UNO. I would also have to say that Jeff's coaches that he played under at Scotus had a big influence on his athletic career, from Frank Spenceri in basketball, to Jim and Gary Puetz in football and Vern Younger in track.

Jeff made every day at practices and during games or track meets fond and memorable. Jeff had a great sense of humor and was always there to make light of a tough practice or a coach's butt-chewing. Jeff was the guy that could always run the fastest, jump the highest and hit the hardest, but was also always there to encourage his teammates to be the best that they could be. He always had a smile on his face and was always kidding around, but never seemed to be the guy to get caught when we were out of line. I would think that Jeff would say that Scotus athletics was one of the highlights of his life, the friends that he made during his high school years, were a group of friends that shared so many memories that it is impossible to give the best. They were all great and we as a group will always share this bond of friendship.

I would have to think that Jeff's most memorable game would have to be stated as his most memorable season and that would be his senior football season. In the fall of 1984, Jeff and his teammates accomplished a 13-0 season which ended in a state championship win over the Gothenburg Swedes. Jeff was a key part on this team, being a captain, offensive and defensive starter, and did all the kicking duties. In fact, Coach Jim Puetz labeled Jeff as "Mr. Versatile". Jeff was the starting fullback, who was a great blocker, runner and very good receiver, in fact he once had a 80-yard receiving touchdown, that just so happened to be a screen pass, but it sure made me look good in the paper (a real stat builder). Jeff was also one of the leading tacklers from his linebacker position, and handled all of the kicking duties, he even had a key 70-yard punt in the state championship game.

I would imagine that if Jeff had to say who he felt was the best athlete that he played with he would have just said that they were all great, guys in his class, and the guys younger and older were all great and played a huge part in making him the athlete that he was. As far as the best athlete that he played against, I would think that he would have said Bump Novacek from Gothenburg. Bump was a big guy with a ton of talent, in fact he played five or six offensive positions against us in the state championship football game.

It's likely that that Jeff's most proud moments during his time at Scotus would be threefold: first: winning the state football championship, second: competing and medaling in the state track meet, and third: being named the 1985 Male Athlete of the Year.

I really think that Jeff would have said that his experiences and influences both from his student and athletic time at Scotus were ever so influential in his success as a student/athlete at the University of Nebraska-Omaha and in his professional career as a pharmacist and consultant to the United States Olympic athletes.

There are so many funny stories that just cannot be printed in this book, so if you would like to hear them, just eavesdrop on the conversation at the table of the class of 1985 at Glurs Tavern during the alumni basketball tournament each year. Jeff is gone, but his memories and stories will be told over and over, year after year.

Bob Klopnieski

Scotus High School 1982 - 1986

- All-Centennial Conference, 1983, 1984, 1985
- Class B All-State selection in football, 1985
- Member of the 1984 Class B State Champion football team
- Shrine Bowl participant, 1986

The year we won the 1984 State Championship was special for a lot of reasons. It all started when were in 7th and 8th grade together. People kept talking about all the talent our two classes had and that we would win a state championship in something. Football was our best sport. It started with Dennis Zowada, our coach then. He was a tough cookie, but treated us fairly. He taught us to give it our all, and you would never fail. It just kept going from there. Vern Younger as our freshman coach, all the way to Jim and Gary Puetz, Randy Berlin and Vern as varsity. They believed in us and we in them. I never lost a football game from 7th to 9th grade, we lost three when I was sophomore and only one as a senior. How many guys can say that? It was a great time.

Two of the best football players that I played with would have to Jeff Podraza and Steve Bonk. Those guys could play! They never took a practice off or a play off during the game. Jeff and Steve played linebacker in our 6-3 that we played, and Jeff played behind me as a defensive end. Any mistake I made, he was there to fix it. Those times are something I will never forget.

Two of the best football players that I played against would have to be Jim Wanek from Aurora and Bump Novacek from Gothenburg. We played both during our run to the championship, and hitting those guys was like hitting a brick wall. I sure hope they felt the same from me.

One story I do remember vaguely is during our undefeated championship season, we were playing Aquinas and was not playing well. Nothing worked on offense that Coach Puetz was calling. So toward the end of the game, Todd Duren, the quarterback, got a call run in to the huddle, and we decided to run what we needed to get things going. The coaches never complained about it, we never said anything, and we ended up winning. That is team unity, from the coaches on down.

On a note about Gary Puetz: Gary always pushed me hard because he knew I could be good and I did everything to make him proud. My father got sick at the beginning of my sophomore year and ended up passing away early November. I remember my cleats broke in like the 7th or 8th game, and Gary ended up getting me a pair to wear the rest of the year. I also remember playing at Aquinas that year and got news that day that my dad was really bad off; I still played the game, but the emotions took over after. Gary found some parents to take me back to Columbus so I could be alone. So I rode in a van with some parents I really didn't know, but Gary took care of me. I will always be grateful for what he did.

Karl Hroza

Scotus High School 1982 - 1986

- Class B All-State football player, 1984, 1985
- All-Class All-State football, 1985
- Two-time gold medal winner in the triple jump, 1985, 1986
- Scotus school record holder in the triple jump (47'0")
- Scotus Athlete of the Year, 1986
- Shrine Bowl participant, 1986
- Shamrock Athletic Hall of Fame inductee, 1999
- 1986 recruiting class – University of Nebraska football

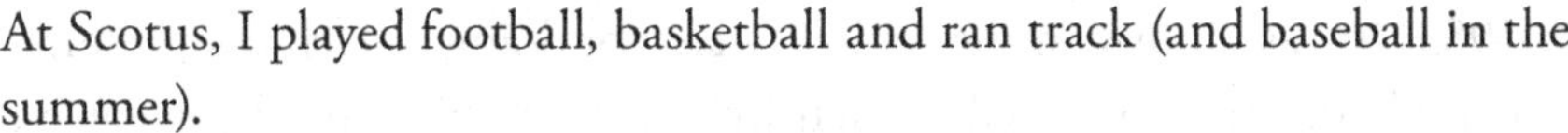

At Scotus, I played football, basketball and ran track (and baseball in the summer).

My favorite coach was Randy Berlin; he was the quarterback coach in football, my JV basketball coach, and he coached the jumpers in track.

My favorite play was probably the Todd Duren touchdown pass against Omaha Roncalli in the 1984 state championship run. It was a down-out-and-up route and he hit me in stride (it was the only time all year). The subsequent running / jumping high-five at the 20-yard line that was perfectly executed truly made the play complete.

My most memorable moment was the 1984 championship run in football and all the motivating characters (conjured up by Coach Puetz): our "Slam Sam" theme from when we played Wood River, the hard hitting Aurora game, the Omaha Roncalli game (the aforementioned TD pass and last minute sack by Jeff Podraza), and finally "Dumping Bump" (Novacek) from Gothenburg.

Instead of elaborating on the numerous memorable moments, I will focus on the few defining and life changing moments encountered in my Scotus career.

The 1980 Junior High football team

My dad and older brother Tim played I-back and I trained my entire previous life to be an I-back and punt returner. Then, one day in the 7th grade, I think it was the first day of practice, and we lined up for positions, when we realized there was nobody at quarterback. The next thing I know, the ball was chucked at me and Vern Younger told me to take the helm. From that day onwards, I was the quarterback.

The 1983 Varsity football team

I learned the biggest lesson in humility at halftime of the Aquinas game in 1983. It was Homecoming and we were not doing so well due to some "internal" distractions. Well, Coach Jim Puetz decided to take it out on the sophomore defensive back who he claimed had a sense of entitlement. When confronted, I told the truth and paid the ultimate price. From that day onward, I was a changed young man with a new direction in life.

The 1984 Varsity Track team

When goal-setting at Scotus, Coach Randy Berlin told us to set them high – but achievable. This was appropriate for a track coach for the jumpers and this later paid off my senior year when the Nebraska football recruiter (Dan Young) came to school one day and I got pulled out of class to meet with him. He said the feedback he had was that I could not jump based on the last summer's camp results. So we went to the old gym, stretched a bit in my corduroys and penny loafers, and stood looking up at the rim. He claimed my vertical was lacking until I stationary jumped up and hung on the rim for a few seconds. This was truly a dunk for a scholarship.

The 1985 Varsity basketball team

Last but not least, I think the hard work ethic and perseverance demanded by Coach Frank Spenceri became a core value, even to this day. He saved a few butt-kickings for me (this actually started in 1978 with my brother), but reinforced that preparation and hard work will be a prelude to great results.

In the end, I became a product of the Scotus "System". I have an All-American dad, endeavored to follow in my big brother's footsteps, and continue to emulate them today as the ultimate Father Figures (and my heroes).

The Scotus education continues to solidify my relationships with family, friends, sport and school.

Pat Engelbert

Scotus High School 1983 - 1987

- Two-time football All-State selection, 1985, 1986
- All-Class All-State football selection, 1986
- Member of the 1984 Class B State Champion football team
- Silver Medal winner in Shot Put at state track meet, 1987
- Scotus School record holder in Shot Put (57'-9")
- Scotus Athlete of the Year, 1987
- Shrine Bowl participant, 1987
- Two-time Second Team All-Big 8 Conference, 1990 - 1991
- Academic All-American University of Nebraska, 1991
- Shamrock Athletic Hall of Fame inductee, 1999

Growing up in Columbus, with three older brothers and several older cousins, I attended Scotus games as far back as I can remember. From intramurals to varsity basketball and football games, our family went to every single one, both home and away, traveling to Fremont, David City, Wahoo, West Point, Omaha, you name it, to watch my brothers and cousins play. As a pre-teen back then, watching basketball games meant going to the "Old Gym" and sitting along the railing with all your buddies, feet dangling down above the court. And football games at Memorial Stadium meant hanging over the wall to smack the shoulder pads of the players as they walked out of the locker room. The atmosphere, the excitement, and the roar of the crowd was intoxicating for a little kid. It was a great source of pride when one of the Engelberts, Heimanns, Kurtenbachs, or Beiermanns made a tackle or basket. There was so much tradition that it was easy for me to think, "I want to be just like my brothers and cousins and wear that Scotus uniform".

I had three outstanding coaches who spent the majority of their career establishing loyalty and tradition at Scotus: Jim Puetz, Gary Puetz, and Frank Spenceri. They each had their own style and approach, but all had a significant influence on me as a person and as a student athlete. Jim Puetz taught me the art of motivation and teamwork. He had an ability to get players fired up for a mundane Tuesday football practice or a rainy day track workout. In addition, he instilled a sense of teamwork in every player. For example, in track, each meet was not a series of individual events, but rather a team competition, where a fifth place finish in any given event was just as important as a first place finish. It definitely established an all-for-one-and-one-for-all mentality.

Gary Puetz instilled in me the importance of having sound technique and being very disciplined. The cage drill, board drill, and fit and drive for the lineman in football, and glide drills, release point and arm placement drills for the weight men in track were done over, and over, and over. No one ever missed a summer workout either, because he would sit in the coach's office monitoring each and every one of us. It was no surprise that he coached numerous all-conference and all-state linemen, as well as state-qualifying and medal-winning weight men.

Frank Spenceri stressed the importance of fundamentals and playing with passion. Footwork, ball handling, passing and shooting drills, jump stops, drop steps, and u-shape follow through shooting drills were the foundation of every practice. Do the little things right and the big things will take care of themselves. His inspirational speeches and quick anecdotes during basketball practices and games are legendary. There were many times that he would mix in a little sarcasm while providing spirited instruction, and you literally had to bite your tongue and look at your shoes so that he didn't see you smiling. More importantly, he taught us that you only get out of life what you put into it, and that good things happen to good people. I truly appreciate everything that each of these men did for me. They have left a lasting impression, and I will never forget them.

In the fall of 1984, I was a sophomore on the state championship football team. Going 13-0, and beating the best teams in Class B, was a feeling

I will never forget. It happened in no small part due to the incredible leadership of the class of 1985. They were a large class with some truly gifted athletes, and some characters, but their commitment, drive, and leadership is what I remember most about that special bunch of guys, and it was contagious. Jeff Podraza, Todd Duren, Steve Bonk, Todd Jarecke, and others in that class embraced the underclassmen and took it upon themselves to make everyone around them better. After each game, the seniors would lead us on a short cheer to mark another victory. Coining a line from "Ghostbusters", we would yell, "We came. We saw. We kicked their..." three times. Funny thing is, I can't remember if we yelled that before or after we prayed three Hail Marys for a safe trip home.

No disrespect to any other teammate, but Karl Hroza, class of 1986, was the best athlete I played with at Scotus. There was nothing he couldn't do. He could play any position in football or basketball, and compete and place in every track event if he wanted to. His tenacity and competitiveness were unmatched. He had a way about him that you just knew it was going to be all right because Karl wouldn't have it any other way. He instilled such confidence in all those around him. He definitely had that "It" factor.

I look back fondly on my years at Scotus. It was a tremendous experience made possible by the strong support and example of family, the dedication and loyalty of the coaching staff, and the solid foundation that is the Scotus student body, especially the Class of 1987. I feel very fortunate to have been a small part of it.

Kelly Nicolas

Scotus High School 1983 – 1987

- Class B All-State volleyball, 1986
- Class B State volleyball champion, 1987
- Two-time Class B All-State basketball, 1986-1987
- Scotus record holder for most career points in basketball (1,075) and steals (310)
- Scotus Co-Athlete of the Year, 1987
- Shamrock Athletic Hall of Fame inductee, 1999

"Go, Go, Go, Go, Go, Go, Go, Go, Shamrocks, Shamrocks ... Goooooo Shamrocks!! Cheers, Cheers for old Scotus High, to us the memories will never die!" These words were the beginning of our fight song at Scotus Central Catholic High School in Columbus, Nebraska and I can still hear our fans and cheerleaders singing the words before our games. These words being shouted out before our games, with a full crowd supporting us, made me so excited and proud to be wearing Shamrock uniforms, even though they were green, yellow, and white! Our fight song truly sums up my four years as a student-athlete at Scotus. Cheers to the class of 1987's numerous academic and athletic accomplishments, to the friendships we all formed, and to the beautiful memories we created and that we will all hold near and dear that will never die.

With that said, I am proud to say that I was a student-athlete at Scotus Central Catholic High School because a Shamrock athlete to me is one who exemplifies pride, confidence and integrity, as well as portrays great sportsmanship. If it weren't for my parents, Harold and Nina Nicolas, I would not have had this wonderful opportunity and I wouldn't be the person I am today. My name is Kelly Incontro (Nicolas). I attended Scotus from 1984-1987. I was a varsity starter in volleyball and basketball all four years and was also a member of the track & field team all four years.

During my years at Scotus there were so many incredible memories like our repeated trips to Lincoln for state volleyball and to Omaha for state track, when our volleyball team earned the title of Class B State volleyball champs in 1986 and again in 1987, our summer camps we attended, the close nail-biting basketball and volleyball games against Hartington Cedar Catholic (my favorite team we played), our Dairy Queen treat from Mr. Mahoney the entire week before the state track meet (except our senior year but we won't say why that was taken away), when I was selected as Co-Athlete of the Year my senior year along with Kelli Martin, and our amazing following by our Scotus fans. My fondest memory at Scotus was the friendships I formed as some of these same friends 28 years ago are still a part of my life today creating new memories that will never die.

By attending a reputable school with strong values and a tradition of athletic excellence with phenomenal coaches and extraordinary support from the faculty and fans, this truly set the foundation of our competitive nature. In fact, the class of 1987 was so competitive and driven that practices and games during the week weren't enough for us. I loved it that my teammates were all very competitive and strived to be the best we could be. Our class would call Coach Petersen many weekends and during the summer months to ask him to open the gym and give us more volleyball and basketball playing time. He not only opened the gym for us on weekends but he chose the teams and always stayed to play with us. As we got older, so did Coach Petersen, and it was getting more difficult for him to keep up with us on the weekends, especially our senior year! Our class would like to think that we were just getting stronger and quicker on the court vs. Coach Petersen slowing down as the years passed! His wife, Marilyn, was so patient and accepting of the time he spent with our class and always had ice bags waiting for him when he returned home from our weekend scrimmages!

Coach John Petersen was definitely the most influential to me throughout my years as a Shamrock athlete. He coached me in two of the three sports I played for Scotus and he definitely strengthened my fundamentals as an athlete. He challenged me to be the best I could be on and off the court, instilled leadership qualities in me through my positions as setter and point guard, taught me to never give up, and prepared me to play volleyball at the collegiate level. He made playing sports so much fun. In fact, I realized later in life how important it was to have had a talented coach that focused on perfecting fundamentals, conditioning, and lifting weights so that is why I decided to coach my two daughters so they too could have the same opportunities that Coach Petersen gave to me.

While coaching volleyball for my two daughters, Jordyn and Taylor, and their friends at the YMCA and St. Wenceslaus Catholic Grade School in Omaha, I incorporated a lot of Coach Petersen's coaching techniques into my own style of coaching and even found myself preaching some of the same things to my two daughters and their friends like "*Never miss a serve when it's game point or after a timeout!*" I even had my team run suicides which I thought made no sense when Coach Petersen had us running them in high school; however, later in life I quickly learned the value of conditioning, especially the older we get!

In conclusion, my years at Scotus not only provided me with four years of athletic excellence but it strengthened my faith as a Catholic and shaped who I am today. Attending a Catholic High School provided me with a strong religious foundation that I continued to build upon while raising my two daughters and when joining the St. Wenceslaus parish in Omaha. I thank God every day for the friendships I formed when I attended Scotus Central Catholic High School because a handful of these same friends, especially Paula Smith (Bator), along with my strong Catholic faith and support of my husband J. Incontro, assisted me through the most difficult time of my life, the tragic loss of my two beautiful daughters Jordyn and Taylor in December of 2010.

Mary Fehringer

Scotus High School 1984 – 1988

- Class B All-State volleyball, 1987
- School record holder in high jump (5'6")
- Scotus Athlete of the Year, 1988
- Shamrock Athletic Hall of Fame inductee, 2002

As a 3rd grader playing softball against a group of phenomenal athletes that made up the Pizza Hut team, I never imagined I'd have the skill or the confidence to play alongside such amazing players. Gradually, and met with much resistance, my dad was able to keep me playing any sports that included a ball and had me running his neighborhood-formed track meets against the boys.

Eventually, I found myself part of the Shamrock volleyball, basketball, and track teams playing and running with those same great athletes from the Pizza Hut softball team from years earlier.

The first time I took a basketball chest pass as a freshman from Kelli Martin (and then promptly had the ball stolen from me by Kelly Nicolas) I knew I was in for quite an athletic education. The women from the class of 1987 taught me as well as the rest of my class teammates what winning and success felt like. They were unstoppable on both the volleyball and basketball courts and they took me right along with them. I can honestly say that I would not have been half the athlete I was without their showing me what success felt like.

They had the raw talent that I got to practice with daily, they had the confidence to understand what it meant to make the second string feel as much a part of the win as they themselves felt and they were fun. These are some of the funniest people I have ever competed with making the practices, the games and the long road trips anything but monotonous. I was always in awe that I got to "ride that train" with those same grade school softball players that utterly intimidated me - both in 3rd grade and again at high school practices.

At all times, Mr. Petersen, yet another person I was completely intimidated by, was there to keep it organized and demand that everyone involved step it up a notch. I remember one practice junior year where he sat our second team down apart from the first string and explained to us that we were the best competition our better half had and that we needed to push them at all times so as to get them ready for the few times they met a team that could compete with them.

This speech was made in a way that instilled so much confidence in ourselves and it built solidly enough to carry us through not only that volleyball season, but for the rest of our high school careers. I would attribute this confidence boost to the reason that I decided to see what high jump felt like starting that spring of junior year. Having success at an individual event was definitely a change, but just as satisfying. I am grateful Mr. Petersen this opportunity to stretch and try something I did not have the confidence to try my first two seasons of high school track.

The whole process of developing from the green, immature athlete to the experienced winner is a life lesson applicable in so many avenues of adult living and giving a shout out to the class of '87 teams seems most appropriate.

Becky Puetz

Scotus High School 1985 - 1989

- Four-Time district champion in shot put
- State runner-up in shot put (1988), state champion (1989)
- School record holder in shot put (42'3")
- Member of state volleyball championship team, 1986

Looking back after many years I would consider being a Shamrock athlete as a member of an elite society that exemplifies hard work, determination, and dedication.

As an athlete, John Petersen had the biggest influence on me in volleyball and basketball, and Greg Bauer in track. Playing for Coach Petersen was very intense! By far, he was the toughest coach I ever had. He respected all of us but knew how to push us without going over the edge. I might not have always *liked* Mr. Petersen, but as I look back through my own experiences, I always respected him as a coach and how he ran his programs.

One of the fondest memories that I had as a Shamrock was the day that I won the state championship in girls Class B shot put. My most memorable game-day experience was probably any time that the team played Lakeview or Columbus High. It seemed as if the intensity of play always increased because we knew the girls playing across from us.

The best athlete I played with as a Shamrock was Camille Sobota.

I am most proud of being a four-time district champion in the shot put, finishing 4th at the state track meet my sophomore year, being state runner-up my junior year, and being state champion in Class B in the shot put my senior year.

I always loved Scotus and what it stands for; it was *my school.* I continue to feel a sense of pride and accomplishment when I reflect on my time at Scotus. I learned to work hard and that things are never handed to you no matter who you are. Everything is earned and lost on a person with hard work and dedication.

Travis Brock

Scotus High School 1986 - 1990

- Class B All-State football, 1989
- Scotus Athlete of the Year, 1990
- School record holder for best field goal % (65.2%)
- Shrine Bowl participant, 1990

If I could sum up my experience as a student-athlete at Scotus, the word that comes to my mind first would be tradition. Growing up in Columbus, I knew about Scotus' tradition way before I started high school. I remember listening to my dad (Tim Brock), my uncles (Dan and Jim Brock), and my Grandpa (Bob Brock) talk about their stories of Scotus' tradition as I was growing up. It was an honor to be an athlete at Scotus. I enjoyed playing with my friends and representing Scotus athletics in the time I was there from 1986 to 1990. Even more so, I am proud to be part of the Scotus family and athletic tradition that continues today.

I had many great influences in my life while I was at Scotus. Most were positive and some were difficult. I would not change anything that occurred during those times because they helped shape the person who I am today. The person who I am greatly appreciative of during my time at Scotus was Gary Puetz. Coach Puetz believed in me when I didn't at times believe in myself. He was a type of person who you respected as a mentor, and he wanted the best for you. I remember the great respect my classmates and I had for Coach Puetz. He was a coach you would die for because you didn't want to let him down. Gary is one the big reasons that I got my act straight and went on to UNO on football scholarship. Today, I still tell people without Coach Puetz, I don't know where I would be today. I had other great role models such as Jim Puetz, Frank Spenceri, Merlin Lahm, and Vern Younger who helped me and challenged me to face my obstacles and become a better person.

I have so many great memories playing football, basketball, and track at Scotus. I played in many events with and against many great athletes. One event I will never forget is when I was a senior and we were playing Fremont Bergan at their house in football. We were both ranked high and it was the last game of the season. We were in Class B at the time and Fremont Bergan was C-1. They had a very good team including two future NFL products in Zach Wiegert and Brad Otis. The story goes, some of my other senior classmates and I were traveling in the school van to the game when something occurred. The van either broke down or something occurred that made us show up late to the game. All I remember is running to the locker room to get my equipment on while the game was beginning.

The first half we got our butts kicked. I think we were down 14 or 21 points at halftime. I remember Jim and Gary Puetz were not too happy with our performance and telling us we had a half to salvage the game. Our quarterback at that time was Tom Fehringer and I remember him saying we were going to come back and win the game. That pumped me and the other lineman up that we needed to take control of the line of scrimmage and fight our way back. So what we did like most of the Scotus football teams do in crisis, we played one down at a time, the hardest that we could. It happens that we took control of the game and inched our way back and were in striking distance of taking the lead. We were down seven points and took the ball down around the 10-yard line of Bergan with little time left in the 4th quarter. I remember we had a penalty and it took us back around the 15 or 20-yard line. We had one play left because it was 4th down and little time on the clock. Then the play I will never forget occurred. Tom Fehringer took the ball and dropped back and threw an amazing pass to Dean Valish in the back of the end-zone to win the game with no time left.

I remember the place going wild, people running on the field, but the funniest thing occurred which I still laugh about today is watching Coach Jim Puetz run full speed for at least 60 yards to grab Dean Valish in the back of the end zone. He was moving and moving fast! I mean he looked like he ran a 4.4 at 60 yards. I didn't think coach Jim Puetz had it in him to run that fast. We beat a great team that day against odds of winning. To me that is what Scotus athletics is about. Competing at a high level against any odds and having the mentality you are still going to win. Today I am old and slow, but I still think no matter what I do I am always going to put in great effort and never quit attitude. I owe this to the tradition of Scotus athletics.

In terms of other Scotus athletes having an impact on me, well, the list is too long. I grew up and played with most of my teammates since I was little. I never wanted to let them down and we were a competitive bunch with and against each other. One Scotus athlete that was a role model for me was Pat Engelbert. Pat was not only a great athlete, a great student, but an outstanding person. Pat always has a smile on his face and always asks how you are doing. I used to love to play against Pat in the alumni basketball tournament because it was all-out war. I think we lost a couple classmates in those battles on the court. Pat was a role model on and off the field of play. He was the extension of the Scotus tradition that was passed to him, to other players, and down to other players like Steve Soulliere, Travis Bock, Tom Fehringer, Brad Hatcher and I during my time at Scotus.

I had other great role models in my family such as my dad who always taught me to never quit and my uncles Dan Brock (Shamrock Hall of Fame inductee) and Jim Brock who were outstanding athletes at Scotus themselves. (Later, my younger brother Drew Brock who was an all-state lineman in football at Scotus also). I feel playing for Scotus is bigger than me. It is a tradition that will continue long after that I am gone. I have been privileged to have won many awards while at Scotus and may still have some records left, but the thing I will always remember is the classmates that I played with and the times that we had to contribute to the Scotus tradition. Scotus athletics has taught me the principles of work ethic, integrity, and relentlessness in the things that I do in my current life. It also has made me humble that life is not all about me, but about learning to give back to other people. Especially, those people who are going through their own life obstacles.

Coach Merlin Lahm would give us sayings every week during basketball season to help us reflect on what we were doing but more importantly the lessons of why we were learning them for our future. I still have these today but the real story is that I didn't always like Coach Lahm at times. Especially when he made me come in the morning and he ran me until I couldn't run anymore. The fact is that Coach Lahm taught me a hard lesson that if you want something in life you have to be willing to dedicate yourself to it. You can't go through life blaming other people and things, and thus you need to be an active person in your life not a bystander. It was one thing as a young man to read inspirational sayings of wisdom and another thing to experience sayings of wisdom. I want to thank Coach Lahm for trying to make me a better person, even though at the time I did not understand it. I know now for a fact it made me a better basketball player and human being.

Recently, I had the privilege to watch Scotus win another state championship in football and play for a championship in basketball. It brought back some of these memories that I am describing here. Being part of Scotus is being part of a family that continues to grow year after year. I always love to hear the names of the athletes because there is always a connection from the past to the present and then to the future. Who knows maybe someday there may be a Brock playing for Scotus again! God help us all! I want to thank all of the coaches and teachers at Scotus who had a significant influence in my life. I hope I can guide people as you help guide me.

Kristi Sobota

Scotus High School 1987 - 1991

- Two-time All-State volleyball player, 1989, 1990
- All-State basketball player, 1991
- Member of the Class B state volleyball champions, 1990
- Scotus Athlete of the Year, 1991
- Shamrock Athletic Hall of Fame inductee, 2001

I enjoyed my athletic career at Scotus, and over the years it has meant so much to me to know that I am a part of a great tradition of athletics where not only winning but also good sportsmanship has always been emphasized.

Coach John Petersen was a phenomenal coach and teacher. He always stressed how sports are learning lessons for life. I have often relied on these lessons throughout my life, during my education and training as a physician, and as I have faced different trials in my life. One thing he emphasized was discipline. "*No discipline seems pleasant at the time, but painful. Later on, however, it produces a harvest of righteousness and peace for those who have been trained by it.*" Hebrews 12:11 (NIV)

There are far too many good memories for me to be able to write them all down. Two great memories stand out in all of them. First, I was a freshman on the first Scotus basketball team that made the state tournament. Second, as a senior I was a member of the volleyball team that were undefeated state champions! One funny memory actually came after I had graduated. I was in medical school when my youngest sister, Heidi was in junior high. One weekend I went to watch her play in an 8th grade tournament. Two of the Scotus 8th graders let a ball drop between them, and I literally flinched and my first thought was "Oh no! They didn't go after the ball, 30 pushups!"

My most memorable game day experience was playing in the 1990 volleyball state championship game. We finished a great season, and were able to beat the team that had knocked us out of the tournament the year before. Having Coach put the medal around my neck and hoisting the championship trophy is one of the best experiences of my life.

The best athlete I played with at Scotus was my friend and classmate, Megan Tooley. She had great quickness and mobility, and also had great hops!

Playing for Coach Petersen was a wonderful experience. He was passionate about the sports he coached and worked hard to make us better. He would always say his job was to make practice tougher than anything we would see in a game, and if we were not getting something correct in a drill, or not performing a fundamental skill wrong, we stayed until it was right ("Missed supper again, Mom. Sorry!") But again, he cared about us, not just as athletes but also as students and people. He held us accountable for our play, schoolwork, and behavior on and off the court. I remember him saying that sports are a lesson for life, and the things I learned both on and off the court from him have helped me through tough times, and showed me how working hard toward a goal is always rewarding. One thing in particular he would say I would like other young athletes to hear: "There is a difference between being confident and being cocky". I became a better person for having played under him and his assistant coaches.

I am proud of being part of the 1990 state championship volleyball team. We had a great team, and everyone played a part and understood their role on the team. As I look back now, I don't think about the early morning weight room sessions or long practices, I think about the fun we had on the court together and what we accomplished as a team.

Through my athletic career, I learned self-discipline. I learned to step outside my comfort zone and challenge myself to improve. I learned teamwork and leadership. These have been invaluable throughout my medical training and career.

There are simply too many great memories from my athletic career for me to pick one. Again, my fondest memory is winning a state championship. "My friend smiled and shook his head. 'I play the game for the game's own sake,' said he." Sherlock Holmes, "The Adventure of the Bruce-Partington Plans" by Sir Arthur Conan Doyle. This quote says it all. I played sports because I love sports.

Jesse Kosch

Scotus High School 1989 – 1993

- Two-time Class B All-State in football, 1991, 1992
- Scotus Athlete of the Year, 1993
- Football Shrine Bowl participant, 1993
- Soccer Shrine Bowl MVP, 1993
- School record holder for career rushing yards (3,454)
- Member of three football National Championship teams at the University of Nebraska
- Third-team All-Big 12 punter, 1997
- Named to the Nebraska All-Century football team, 2000
- Shamrock Athletic Hall of Fame inductee, 2007

Editor's Note: Jesse and his father Bill combined have all five National Championship rings (1970, 1971, 1994, 1995, 1997) as players on the University of Nebraska football team. They might be the only Father-Son duo to hold this distinction.

Being a Scotus athlete meant trying to continue the success of being one of the best athletic programs in the state. As an athlete, my dad, Bill, had the greatest influence on me. Also Jim Puetz who was my head coach at Scotus.

My most memorable game day experience came in my sophomore year in a Homecoming game against Wahoo Neumann. I was recovering from an injury, and Coach Puetz told me in the cafeteria in the pregame walk-through, "Get ready; you're going to play tonight." I was really nervous, but we ended up winning. A memory I'd like to forget was signing the petition to start up a soccer program at Scotus. Once certain people found out, it became a little uncomfortable.

The best athletes I played with were Jeff Herdzina and John Hain.

I am proud of being able to stay out of trouble during my years at Scotus(!). Also, through my years at Scotus we were able to bring football back as a State contender, and we were able to become a soccer power.

I came to learn that you can forget sleep – in the winter when it snowed, Coach Puetz would give me a 3:00 a.m. wake-up call to get out and start shoveling, so Steve Beiermann and I would be a little late to school sometimes. I also learned that you can't have success by yourself; all your teammates are very important.

One final memory: The last time I represented Scotus I was invited to play in the 1993 Soccer Shrine Bowl. It was the first time I played and did not know one person on the team. Our coach for the North team didn't ever know who I was. I remember he was putting out the starting lineup and was looking for a midfielder and asked if anyone was left-footed; I raised my hand. At first I was very nervous and was trying to adjust playing with people I have never played with previously (I was the only player not from Omaha or Lincoln).

Once I got settled in I made a play and scored the first goal of the game. We won 4-3 and the coolest part was after every score they would announce all goals scored and your school. So seven times the fans heard "Jesse Kosch from Columbus Scotus"; probably half the people had never heard of Scotus. I played pretty well and at the end of the game both teams met in the middle of the field and I didn't even know this, but over the loudspeaker I heard, " ... the 1993 Soccer Shrine Bowl MVP ... from Columbus Scotus ... Jesse Kosch!".

That was a special ending to my career as a Shamrock.

Keri Stopak

Scotus High School 1989 - 1993

- State track gold medal winner 100m dash, 1993
- State track gold medal winner 400m relay, 1993

Being a Shamrock athlete meant being very proud to be part of a great school and athletic institution. Coaches Mr. Mahoney and Mr. Grubaugh had the greatest influence on me as an athlete.

I graduated right after the 1993 state track meet; it was a very memorable weekend! My best memory was winning the gold medal in the 100-meter dash at the state track meet.

The 1993 4x100 meter relay team was a great group of athletes; we also won the gold medal that year.

I am most proud of maintaining good grades while a student at Scotus. The life lessons I learned were determination, teamwork, and faith.

Brandon Drum

Scotus High School 1990 - 1994

- Two-time All-State football, 1992, 1993
- Member of the 1993 state champion football team
- Scotus Athlete of the Year, 1995

Coach Scott Miller taught me a lesson. A lesson that took me years to appreciate but has helped guide my adult life. Ray Bradbury tried to teach me the same lesson at about the same time, had I just done the assigned reading in English class as I was supposed to.

"You're afraid of making mistakes. Don't be. Mistakes can be profited by. Man, when I was young I shoved my ignorance in people's faces. They beat me with sticks. If you hide your ignorance, no one will hit you and you'll never learn."
Fahrenheit 451

The 8th grade boys football team mustered every day in full pads outside the north entrance. It was singular trepidation, the wait before the sprint to the practice field. We were to round the corner and cross 15th Street under the strict guise that being run over by a passing car was forbidden by the coaching staff. Then two blocks south and a hard left behind Speicher's house, cut through Hanover Square and traverse the deep ditch that ran adjacent to the Union Pacific tracks then up and over the hellacious embankment to safety.

Each player prayed that a well-timed coal train would be passing and as such, extend the time we were expected to make the run. It sucked, but it became routine and made us hard. The hard that only comes from small-town Nebraska. That hardness that becomes a thread throughout your life and is always waiting underneath your skin for when you may need to call it up to the surface.

Coaches Miller and Salyard drove to the practice field. Practice field? It was actually the vacant lot next to the varsity practice field, full of ankle high pigweed stubble that someone mowed down once or twice during the fall. They were always waiting there with stopwatch in hand, there was no way to cheat it, no faster route.

I remember that generally everyone made it in time, that was of course unless you were sitting in detention. A thirty-minute detention, if memory serves me, could be awarded after three tardies or grievous misbehavior. I had been accused of both on occasion, but on this particular day it was a third tardy that resulted in my first detention of the school year. I had missed muster, and subsequently the run. After changing out I set off walking to practice, walked the entire stretch up to that embankment where I sprinted over to give the impression that I pined for my sins. Not a soul gave me so much as a second look. Miller ignored my late arrival, my teammates seemed indifferent and practice drudged on. I joined in just as drills were ending.

It was a hot day. That fantastic Nebraska humidity that hits you like a screen door when you step outside. It too, made us hard. We learned about gaps, the two gap, the three gap, gap responsibility and the huge gap between adolescence and adulthood. I believed that if I worked hard I would be forgiven. I wanted to be as great a lineman as Pat Engelbert, Travis Brock and Matt Naughton. I was going to earn jersey #70, the number those great seniors had each worn in turn. Eventually I forgot about my detention, that exceptional gift of teenagers, to completely disregard everything except the here and now.

Unfortunately, Coach Miller had not forgotten.

Scott Miller hailed from a faraway place, the Sandhills maybe, I honestly don't remember. What I do remember is he wore a cowboy hat in his free time. That was scary because nobody in Columbus wore cowboy hats.

He didn't teach at Scotus, he was the P.E. teacher for the three Catholic grade schools and he drove a gigantic Dodge Ram Charger 4x4. All of this combined with his six-foot frame added to the quixotic that was Coach Miller.

After practice he swiftly laid out my punishment. I was to run from the water fountain to the nearest building at the end of the varsity practice field, touch the fence and run back as fast as I could. It was a good 150 yards one way. "No problem", I thought. Killer Miller took up his stopwatch and off I went. Now 300 yards is no joke. In full pads on grass for a 14-year-old, you're looking at maybe 45 seconds. I ran as fast as I could and no one has ever accused me of being fast. Touching the fence, I spun around. On the way back a terrible thought crossed my mind. It was a hell of a lot easier running 300 yards then the daily sprint to the practice field, maybe detention wasn't so bad. "This was all right, less than a minute of putout and only the fun parts of practice, I could do this every day!"

I got back to the cowboy and collapsed onto that itchy grass tasting blood. "Fifty-three seconds," he announced. "Now you're gonna do two more gassers just as fast or faster." he said. "And for each one you don't make in time you're gonna do one more."

Now if I was a writer I could keep pulling you into the suffering I experienced, the vomit, the blood I pissed the next day, the blight that was Coach Miller, but I can't. This was my mistake, one of many that I've made and tried to learn from. We all have them and without the exceptional teachers, parents, coaches and teammates that have helped each of us learn from our mistakes we wouldn't be as hard as we are. I ended up doing 17 gassers and didn't even get a ride back to school. Miller made me walk. The most embarrassing part was that as I walked back through Hanover square, I sat down on the end of the slide and fell asleep. I was awakened by Coach Miller honking his horn and flashing his headlights over an hour after we had left the field.

Thank you Scott Miller for the lesson I learned that day in 1990. The lesson, that perhaps Miller himself has never learned, has at least helped me do some good in this world.

When you make a mistake, own it.

Jeff Herdzina

Scotus High School 1990 - 1994

- Two-time All-State football running back, 1992 - 1993
- Two-time All-State soccer, 1993 - 1994
- Member of the Class B state champion football team, 1993
- School record holder for most points scored in a football season (225) and most points scored football career (309)
- School record holder most rushing yards season (2,181)
- School record holder for most soccer goals game (5), season (33) and career (91)
- Shrine Bowl participant, 1994
- Scotus Athlete of the Year, 1994
- Winner of the Leo Peary Award at UNO, 1996
- Voted Outstanding Back at UNO, 1997
- Shamrock Athletic Hall of Fame inductee, 2004

I was proud to carry on a rich athletic tradition and represent Scotus and the Columbus community through success on and off the field.

All of my coaches, from junior high through high school, had a significant impact on me as a player.

One of my fondest memories was scoring all six goals in a 6-0 win over Gretna. My most memorable game day experience was a double-overtime victory over Beatrice in the football playoffs.

The best athlete I played with was Scott Sobota. The best athlete I ever played against was Chad Kelsay from Auburn.

Coach Puetz expected to win every game – and so did we. This passion and intensity were unbelievable. After we won the state championship, Scott Sobota picked him up and carried him off the field.

I am most proud of our 1993 state championship in football; a 13-0 season record.

Today, I use the competitiveness I learned at Scotus to succeed in the business world. I apply those leadership skills to lead my staff to do their best each day.

JoDe Cieloha

Scotus High School 1990 - 1994

- Two-time All-State in volleyball, 1992, 1993
- All-State in basketball, 1993
- Scotus Athlete of the Year, 1994
- School record holder for blocks in a season (74) and blocks in a career (174)
- Shamrock Athletic Hall of Fame inductee, 2004

When you are young and playing for Scotus, you take the opportunity for granted. Scotus has such a deep tradition of success, you realize after you have graduated how fortunate you really were to grow up in Columbus and attend Scotus.

Coach John Petersen had the greatest influence on my Scotus athletic career. Mr. Petersen knew how to push his athletes to work harder than most, and the fundamentals are where it started. Coach Petersen is someone who you constantly wanted to please and who you respected immensely.

Honestly I can't single out only one fondest memory while at Scotus. There are too many positive memories to single out just one, that is an accomplishment in itself. The memory I'd like to forget is our team losing the state volleyball championship game my senior year in 1993 to Grand Island Central Catholic. We were winning and it should have been a done deal. GICC slowly kept creeping back and the momentum changed. We lost after being in the lead 11-2, and it was the hardest loss I have ever dealt with.

Even though I'd like to forget part of the game, our championship volleyball match against GICC in 1993 is something that I will always remember. I knew going into that game it was my last volleyball match playing for Scotus and that was emotional in itself. Even though the outcome was a loss, big picture it was a celebration of a great career at Scotus for my fellow teammates and myself.

The best athlete I played with while at Scotus would have to be Kristi Sobota. Even though I did not play volleyball with her as I was a freshman when she was a senior, I did play basketball with her. I always admired her work ethic and her humble approach to her success. Kristi was who I strived to be like after she graduated. The best athlete I played against would be Kelly Luther from Grand Island Central Catholic. GICC was a volleyball powerhouse and Kelly went on to play college volleyball and was always a tough competitor.

Playing for Coach Petersen was a true honor. He was so demanding and intimidating, but he has a way of maximizing potential out of his athletes. I recall a junior high volleyball practice in the old gym, and people would start whispering that Coach Petersen was in the stairwell watching us and the nerves would kick in. He was a legend for as long as I can remember at SCC, and I feel very fortunate to have been coached by him in back to back seasons of volleyball and basketball. Coach Petersen pushed his athletes on a daily basis as he expected so much of us, but that is what made us successful as individuals and teams. I have so many positive memories of high school and playing for Coach Petersen, it's really hard to single out one memory.

Reflecting on my time at Scotus, I think I am most proud of the work ethic I learned while playing at Scotus. My years at Scotus taught me a work ethic I still carry on today whether it's with my family, career, or anything I do.

Life lessons I learned while at Scotus would be to always give your all in whatever you do. Work hard and be a good person. These are lessons that I'm trying to instill in my children now that I'm a parent, and the same reason we are sending them to a Catholic grade school in Omaha. With my experience at Scotus being such a positive one, my husband and I are trying to develop a solid Catholic foundation for our boys as well.

Sam Graus

Scotus High School 1992 - 1996

- All-State football, 1995

Obviously I grew up in Columbus and first attended St Bon's in grade school. Back in the day it was cool to go to Columbus High. I was not really happy with my parents' decision to send me to Catholic schools. I had a brother who went through the public school system and I thought the world of him. I remember going to CHS basketball games and loving every bit of it. That was where I wanted to be.

Needless to say, my parents made the decision that I needed to stay at Scotus. I entered Junior High. As all did, with all my friends. Football started in the fall and I joined. I went through a few practices and felt this was not for me. I walked off. I was not in for the up-downs in the middle of a sandbur patch. Mr. Miller and Mr. Salyard were the coaches at the time. Again I walked off. I did later regret my decision. Later that year I was in a serious accident while playing basketball in the old gym. I did not know at the time or even care that I would play football again.

As my freshman year approached I thought I would give football a try again. I made no waves. Coaches probably thought there was no reason for me to be out there. I think the same happened my sophomore year as well. During that year Scotus won the Class B state championship. I was no part of the team even though I received a letter for playing in a certain amount of games.

Enter my junior year. As always, Scotus had a good number of kids out for football each year. I was at the bottom and the only hope I had was playing JV and that is all I did. During the off-season I worked my tail off in the weight room to get ready for my senior year. I ended up being an all-state selection that year.

My senior year, we entered the year with little familiarity. We did not get along with the class below us. To make a long story short, we bonded and had a better year than expected. To this day some of my best friends are from the class behind me. Nothing can replace the experiences that I had at Scotus.

Who had the greatest influence on me as an athlete? Gary Puetz - I can't say enough about this man. It took a while for him to believe in me and to give me a chance. There is no way I would have accomplished what I had without him.

My fondest memory was walking off the field after our last game in Wahoo. We were told we never should have been there, but we were. We had no continuity on our team from the start. We as seniors gelled with the classes below us made a serious team to deal with. My favorite game day experience was the pre-game meal senior year. Thin crust cheese pizza - no sauce - split with Chris Langan. I also had to have my white Neumanns (gloves) for every game. Ironically I lost them before our last game.

Life Lesson: don't give up, work for what you believe. If you work hard you can achieve anything.

Chad Mustard

Scotus High School 1993 - 1996

- First team All-State football, 1995
- First team All-State basketball, 1996
- Member of the state championship football team, 1993
- Scotus Athlete of the Year, 1996
- Shamrock Athletic Hall of Fame inductee, 2006
- Finished his college basketball career as the 7th leading scorer for the University of North Dakota
- Member of the 2001 Div-II University of North Dakota national championship football team
- Played five seasons in the NFL with Cleveland and Denver

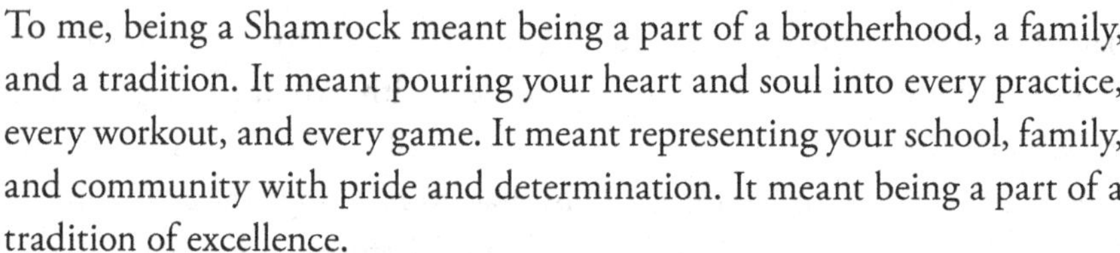

To me, being a Shamrock meant being a part of a brotherhood, a family, and a tradition. It meant pouring your heart and soul into every practice, every workout, and every game. It meant representing your school, family, and community with pride and determination. It meant being a part of a tradition of excellence.

My father and my brother Chris had the greatest influence on me as a Shamrock athlete. Ironically, that influence took place and played a significant role in my life long before I ever wore a Scotus uniform.

Growing up around their passion for competition and their examples of hard work and dedication pushed me to be the best I could be. My brother was an amazing athlete in high school. He was a fierce hitter on the football field and played with the same ferocity on the on the basketball court. He unfortunately was injured most of his senior year, but had a great career. My father was as fierce in the stands as a fan. I never knew anything but to be "all in" and to go as hard as I possibly could.

Come to think of it, I may have been the least physical Mustard to play football at Scotus. My little brother Craig loved to hit people too! I don't remember loving that part of the game. I just loved winning; I loved putting it on the line with my teammates to get the win. I loved chasing victory - I still do.

One of my fondest memories as a Shamrock was winning the district final in basketball in 1996 over Wahoo Neumann to go to state. It had been a goal of ours for years, since junior high at least, and we had finally accomplished it. We had an experienced team and took it to them pretty good. It was so gratifying to do it with such a great group of guys.

The memory I would most like to forget came in our very next game. In the first round of the state tournament we met Wahoo High. It was a #1 versus #2 match-up. We played an extremely hard-fought game, with neither team really playing their best. I was fouled late in the game and had a chance to give our team the lead. I made one of two free throws to tie the game and we eventually went to overtime. As it goes, we lost that game on a tip in at the buzzer in overtime. Heartbreaking stuff! Wahoo went on to cruise to the state title over the next two days. It was very tough for me to swallow (if you can't tell).

It may seem strange, but some of my favorite times as an athlete at Scotus were my trips to the state track meet. I qualified my junior and senior year in the triple jump, placing my senior year with my last jump being my career longest. More so than results themselves, I enjoyed the experiences of the state track meet. It was a social atmosphere where you could relax and enjoy a year's worth of hard work with your teammates and your fellow competitors and even some of your rivals. I tripled jumped my senior year in the morning of day one and was able to enjoy the rest of the meet knowing I had put a wrap on my high school career. It was surreal, but very gratifying.

Some memorable games:

1993 state football championship vs. Hastings Adams Central
1995 Homecoming shutout win vs. Battle Creek

1995 playoff loss vs. Wahoo (final high school football game)
1995 home basketball game vs. Grand Island CC (91-81 win) led to #1 rank in C-1
1996 district basketball final win vs. Wahoo Neumann
1996 state basketball tournament loss vs. Wahoo High

There were some great athletes during my time at Scotus, but I don't recall any better than Jeff Herdzina and Scott Sobota from the 1993 State Championship football team.

All my coaches were great (Jim and Gary Puetz, Vern Younger, Pat Brockhaus, etc.) But I had a special bond with coach Merlin Lahm, my basketball coach. So much so, that I joke that I grew up and "became" him (I currently teach math and coach high school basketball myself). That surely is not an accident. Merlin had a calm, confident sensibility about him that made you feel like you were going to win. He did things the right way and put value in that and it made us as players do the same. He was serious and some would say strict, but with my teammates and I, he connected on personal level. We worked hard, but had a ton of fun too. He was our leader, but we knew he was standing right next to us as we worked to achieve our goals. He made a difference and in turn it helped us raise our level of play. We had a very special group and fell just short of reaching our ultimate goal of a state championship. I'm not sure Merlin ever got enough credit for that. He saw we were a special group even at a young age, and cultivated that into one of the best seasons in school history.

I look back all the things my teammates and I accomplished on the football field, the basketball court, and the track and there are just so many things to be proud of. But far and away I am most proud of the relationships I have with my teammates: Chad Gonka, Kelcey Krings, Nate Karges, Joe Dierks, Jason Cumberland, Sam Graus, John Vyhlidal, Luke Fendrick, Pat Sokol, Eric Kloke, and the list goes on and on. We have been out of high school for 20 years now and when we get together and it's like we left Scotus yesterday. I may be wrong, but I'm not sure that happens everywhere else. I believe it more about what Scotus is, than who we are. I love these guys!

I have to tell the story about the night "Pearl" (Coach Merlin Lahm) took us cruising in the school van after we went to team camp in Norfolk and went 6-0. I'm not sure who talked him into it, but we made two loops around before we got back to school. He might have even laid on the horn a little bit just to top things off.

Below is an excerpt from Chad's Scotus Athletic Hall of Fame acceptance speech. Chad was playing for the Denver Broncos and was not able to attend in person:

Greetings from Denver. I wish I could be there in person, but my "older, little" brother will have to do. I hope this finds the Scotus community doing well. I would just like to say few things with regard to tonight's award.

First, I would like to say that it is a great honor for me to be inducted into the Shamrock Hall of Fame. I will take great pride in being in such an exclusive group of Scotus athletes, coaches, and boosters.

More importantly I would like to thank all of those who played a part in the success I had here at Scotus. Thank you to my teachers, you helped lay a foundation of knowledge and faith that I will carry with me throughout my life. Thank you to my coaches, I learned valuable life lessons from you; not only from the way they taught and coached, but also from the way you lived your lives. So much so that you have inspired me to become your colleague in the education and coaching professions. Thank you to my teammates; this is truly your honor as well. My intensity and will to compete didn't always make me the easiest person to be around, but you stuck with me and we succeeded together. And last, but not least, thank you to my family. You provided me great examples of hard work, dedication, love, caring, and sacrifice that I needed to be the person I was here at Scotus and who I am today.

And as I finish up, let me just say to the current student-athletes of Scotus Central Catholic: Appreciate and value the athletic, scholastic, and faith experiences you have here at Scotus. There are advantages that you have that I know I took for granted during my time here. As I moved through college and into my professional career, I quickly found out how far ahead of "the game" I really was, both in the classroom and on the court and field. In the coming years, you too will leave here and see that you're at a great advantage because of the teachers, coaches, and teammates that you had while you competed here.

Congratulations to all the award winners tonight. Once again, thank you very much for this honor.

Go Shamrocks!

Nick Puetz

Scotus High School 1993 - 1997

- All-State football, 1996
- Member of the 1993 state champion football team
- All-Conference football selection, 1995-1996
- Football team captain, 1996
- Sertoma Athlete of the Year, 1997

Having a father and uncle who taught and coached at Scotus, you grow up eating, sleeping and breathing Scotus. However, the extended family you gain through your athletic experiences was a reward that I hadn't anticipated. I formed long lasting friendships with people who share a passion for competition and camaraderie. I still count many of these people as some of my closest friends today.

Unequivocally, my father Gary was the greatest influence on me as an athlete. I learned the game (both football and track) from him, I got to play for him and he helped put me in a position to succeed well beyond high school. Getting to play for my father was the greatest experience of my athletic career.

My fondest memory wasn't of a singular event, but a season as a whole. My junior year (1995), we had only two returning starters and a handful of letter winners, so no one was expecting much from us on the field. In addition, we had a junior and senior class that historically hadn't seen "eye to eye" on things. However, the summer leading up to that season, key leaders from both classes started to spend more time together and by the time two-a-days came and went, we were one gelled group (on and off the field). Long story short, we went on to a 9-2 season and ended up ranked in the top five in the state.

My most memorable game day experience was: the food. For about a 24-hour cycle, it seemed that the offensive linemen did nothing but eat. It started the day prior to the game where all the offensive linemen would have a punting contest and the winner ("longest" kick) would get his dinner paid for by the rest of the linemen. After the walk-through, we would all head off to Valentino's. That restaurant had to have lost money every day we came in. The morning of game day, many of the offensive linemen would get together for breakfast and then came the pregame "snacks" after school. It was like an eating contest three hours before the game. It is beyond me how we were able to function out on the field! I don't know what we were thinking, but somehow, we managed.

The best athlete I played with at Scotus was Chad Mustard. He dominated on the football field and basketball court and was a state qualifier in track. He went on to become and All-American basketball player at North Dakota and then found his way to the NFL where he played for several years.

The best athlete I played against was a close call; between Battle Creek, David City Aquinas and Wahoo Neumann, there were some incredible athletes running around the field. I would have to give my nod to Paul Fujan of Wahoo Neumann. He was elusive, had speed and was a great competitor. Fujan was the best running back in the state, in my opinion.

Getting to play for my uncle was a great experience. It was interesting as I always knew the Jim Puetz that you get on the family side of things, which was a little less intense than the Coach Puetz we all knew that walked the sidelines. The one thing I appreciated more than anything was that I was treated no different than any other player on the team. I had to earn my playing time, just like everyone else. The other coach from whom I learned a lot was my long and triple jump coach, Merlin Lahm. The triple jump wasn't a natural skill set for me and Coach Lahm had to take a lot of time to coach me through the basics. Coach Lahm taught me a great deal about balancing high intensity while having a lot of fun along the way.

From a team perspective, I am most proud of the great friendships that I formed while I was at Scotus and our team's accomplishments during the

1995 football season. On a personal level, being selected to the All-State football team during my senior year was very fulfilling as I was chosen at the position that my father had coached me at.

The life lessons I learned were how to apply attitude, confidence and hard work to achieve goals and competitive spirit.

This isn't a story about competition, but it is pretty funny. I didn't play much on the varsity football team my sophomore year. We made the playoffs and were playing at Gretna. The student section at Gretna was right on top of the visiting team's sidelines and their student body was ruthless. Well, somehow the student body figured out that I was the coach's kid and they ripped into me the entire game. "*55 you must really suck; your dad won't even play you*!". That was a long game, but we won!

Joe Puetz

Scotus High School 1997 - 2001

- All-Conference football selection, 1999-2000
- Honorable Mention All-State, 2000
- Football team captain, 2000
- Lifter of the Year, 1999-2000
- Babe Ruth Award winner, 2001

Being a Shamrock athlete was special ... specifically football. The Friday routine before games is something that I will never forget. From waking up and putting on the jersey to breakfast in the cafeteria with members of the team, to Mass and pregame meal. I probably shouldn't say this but I don't think I ever learned anything in class on game days just being so excited to get to the field.

The greatest influence on me as a Shamrock athlete was my dad, Gary, and my uncle, Jim Puetz.

I can't remember who we were playing, but we were winning by like three touchdowns and driving again. Earlier that day at Mass, we read Exodus (3:8), where God promises to take the Israelites out of slavery in Egypt to a "...good and spacious land, a land flowing with milk and honey."

We were around the 30-yard line and the QB, Eric Hinze, called a running play in the huddle and Drew Brock just erupted and said something along the line of "Let's take this bitch to the land of milk and honey". We just kind of looked and him and burst out laughing. I'm pretty sure we scored on that play which was fitting.

We beat Lakeview (I believe) 42-14 my senior year. The previous year at track meets they talked trash all the time and were convinced that it wasn't even going to be a game. We came out and crushed them at their field. Needless to say ... "We came, we saw, we kicked their ass" ... was the loudest I can remember.

The best athlete I played with was Thadd Recek. The best athlete I played against was Matt Herian from Pierce (especially track; he would win the shot, disc, and the 100).

Playing for my coach was intense; when the head coach is your uncle and his main assistant is your dad (who was also the Athletic Director) it can be pretty crazy. Listening to Jim and Gary talk refs was hilarious. Before our first game (Hastings St. Cecelia Blue Hawks) when I was a sophomore, someone cut the ropes at the practice field. Jim found a feather nearby and said it was a Blue Hawk feather and starting ranting about how Saint Cecelia was trying to sabotage us. Little things like that happened all the time which was always funny.

My senior year was really hard. I blew out my knee after our second game (thankfully it was after Lakeview so I was able to take part in that ass kicking). I was able to come back and compete in track at a pretty high level and just missed state (Although if we were in a different district I would have made state easily). To be able to get through that experience was a proud moment.

My experience was a lot different than most. When you play for your dad and uncle and a lot of your family is involved in the program it is pretty special. Going to Scotus is also why I think our alumni are so dedicated. I always have people who didn't go to Scotus ask me why we talk about high school so much and it's because they didn't have the experience that we had. When you have a small high school with a dedicated faculty like we had it's hard not to form great memories. To this day a lot of my teammates are some of my best friends. It just isn't that way at a lot of places. When you have friends that you went to college with from another high school who know the names of a lot of Scotus faculty, that shows you the impact and it's pretty unique.

I also caught three passes in one football game ... I can't be sure ... but we thought that may have been a record at the time.

Jon Brezenski

Scotus High School 1994 - 1998

- Two-time All-State soccer, 1997,1998
- Member of the 1997 state champion soccer team
- Football letterman, 1995-1997
- Basketball letterman, 1995-1997

Being an athlete during my era at Scotus was really special. We were successful in many of our sports – boys and girls – during the 1990s. Being able to compete in state tournament games and attend so many great games for our basketball and volleyball teams were so much fun. Wearing Scotus apparel in the community and around the state was special because people took notice and knew about Scotus. To this day, people remember a lot of our games which took place during the 1990s and when they find out I was a part of some of those teams, it's always fun to reminisce about certain football games or soccer matches.

Gary Puetz and Vern Younger had the greatest influence on me as an athlete. Gary was in charge of our strength program during my years at Scotus. He was always so well-organized and pushed us to maximize our potential in the weight room. Vern Younger was the first coach to teach me what it takes to be tough and disciplined. I never wanted to let him down. I always say Vern was the 'unspoken' key to our football success during the years he coached at Scotus because he molded you as a freshman to prepare you for the next three years of football.

My favorite memories are related to our 1997 and 1998 soccer teams. Our teams were so close during the years of 1997 and 1998. We were fortunate enough to win the 1997 state championship and were runners-up in 1998. Our bus rides and time together off the field were always fun. To this day, during our Scotus Alumni Soccer Tournament, we can recollect about all of our old stories and they seem like yesterday. The closeness of those teams is what I have tried to instill in our current soccer program and to understand the importance of the Scotus soccer family.

The 1997 Class B state soccer championship is a great memory, and heartbreaking at the same time. It was a #1 vs. #2 showdown against our rival, Blair. We fell behind 1-0 in the middle of the first half. With about 20 minutes to go, we scored two goals in a one-minute span to take the lead 2-1. We were also able to hold on and win Scotus' first state soccer championship! Unfortunately, that same night, our close friend and teammate, Christopher "Chip" Kaup, passed away. His death is still tough. I think of him every day.

My most memorable game day experience is tough to narrow down, but the final four games of the 1997 football season were great memories, and heartbreaking at the same time. We defeated Lincoln Pius X 14-9 in Columbus. Pius X was ranked #1 in Class B and was undefeated. We were starting to hit our peak after a rough 2-2 start. We forced five turnovers in the game to defeat Pius, who ended up finishing the season as the Class B state champs. In the playoffs, we defeated Wahoo 40-10 and then went up to Norfolk Catholic and beat them 28-21. Our season ended in the quarterfinals after a tough loss to the eventual champion, David City Aquinas, 31-30 on a last-second field goal.

Tom Rogers ('99) was the best athlete I played with. Tom was intense and smooth in all his athletic movements. He was a solid football played and excellent soccer player. He was so smart and knew how to use his body so well in both sports. Kyle Ringenberg from Elkhorn was the best athlete I played against. Kyle was a stud for their soccer team and in our 1997 state semifinal he made some unbelievable saves in our match. He was like a man amongst boys. We were fortunate enough to get a free kick past him in the match to defeat them 1-0 and advance to the championship match. He ended up playing football at Nebraska as a tight end.

Jim Puetz was my football coach and I wanted to play for Jim because he had a way of connecting with us as players. You wanted to play hard for him because he cared about you as a person. He was so organized. He had all our practices written out and posted for us to see during the day. Our practices were so efficient and we knew what was expected of us each day. I really think his organization and motivational skills as a coach were his greatest attributes to the success of the football program.

Jim was afraid of snakes. I recall at least once every year the seniors would try and find a small snake to scare him. I believe it was my junior year in 1996 when one of the seniors put one in their helmet and when Jim picked it up he took off running down the practice field to get away from it!

Fr. Wayne Pavela was my soccer coach from 1994-1997. We knew 1997 would be his last year and we wanted to send him out on the right note by winning the championship. Nineteen ninety-seven was the first year soccer was split into Class A and Class B. The smile on his face after our championship was something I will never forget.

I am proud we were able to win a state championship in soccer in 1997 and also the runner-up finish in 1998. We also had successful football and basketball teams. I was blessed to play with some very good athletes. I was not overly gifted as one of them, but I worked hard and pushed myself and our teams. I was named the captain of our football team in 1997 and soccer team in 1998, so I felt blessed to earn my teammates' trust. Jim Puetz always told me, "You aren't the biggest guy, but you are 155 pounds of *mean*."

If you want something bad enough, you have to put in the work to achieve your goal. We were always taught to work hard. Our coaches instilled discipline and confidence in us and I have been able to carry those lessons in my life. I have been fortunate to achieve many of my life goals so far and I always think back to the messages I received from my coaches at Scotus as a foundation for my professional life.

Kim Rickert

Scotus High School 1994 - 1998

- All-State volleyball, 1997
- All-State basketball, 1998
- Three-time state volleyball champion, 1995 - 1997
- Three-time state basketball champion, 1996 - 1998
- Shamrock Athletic Hall of Fame inductee, 2011

Being a Shamrock athlete meant hard work, dedication, and discipline. If you wanted to be lazy, the gym or track was not the place for you. It meant striving to be the best version of you and developing amazing friendships and memories that will last a lifetime.

Without a doubt, no questions asked, John Petersen (head volleyball and basketball coach) and Scott Miller (assistant basketball coach) had the greatest influence on me. I credit much of my success to these two gentlemen.

My fondest memory would be hugging Coach Petersen and Coach Miller one last time as I received my 1998 state basketball championship medal. Knowing it was all over, I couldn't have asked for better coaches and experiences I had for four awesome years.

A memory that could be funny now, but I wished it never happened at the time would be oversleeping for a morning basketball walk-through my senior year. We had a Saturday afternoon basketball game that day and I will never forget it. I obviously missed the home phone ring (cell phones barely existed) and I slept until noon. When Pete finally got a hold of me and I heard the tone of his voice, I knew I was dead meat. Needless to say, I didn't start that game and maybe saw the court in the fourth quarter. Wow, Pete was so mad at me that day, but I believe by the end of that year, he was over it.

The 1997 volleyball district final against Grand Island Central Catholic is the most memorable. Ranked #1 and #2 in the state, no wild card at that time, it made for one heck of a district final. We had played each other three times already that season (them having won twice and us once). It was still the old-fashioned scoring and it went to three sets. I served the game-winning point, which was pretty amazing! Mrs. Tooley was not there due to the adoption of her son, Toby. We all said prior to the game, we would win it for her. Little did we know we would actually complete the task.

Man, I played with a lot of amazing athletes and to pick one is pretty hard. Kristie (Korth) Brezenski is someone that comes to mind right away. Being in the same class as her, we played on many championship teams together and she always found a way to push me to be a better athlete whether she knew it or not.

The best athlete I played against in volleyball was Jenny Kropp (GICC) and in basketball was Brandy Trofholz (Schuyler).

Words to describe playing for John Petersen are truly an honor and very special. I am not sure there are any other coaches out there quite like him. You wanted to make him proud and have him consider you the best squad he ever coached. He knew exactly what to say and when to exactly say them. I have a slew of memorable experiences with Coach Petersen; however, the one that pops out at me is when I tore my ACL the end of my sophomore year. He rode down to Lincoln with my mom and me to the orthopedic clinic to get the dreadful diagnosis. The fact he rode along with us not only meant he cared for me on the court, but off the court as well.

A few things I am most proud of as an athlete at Scotus is starting all four years for the varsity basketball squad, earning one runner-up state basketball medal, followed by three state volleyball and basketball championship medals.

Kristie Korth

Scotus High School 1994 – 1998

- Two-time All-State Soccer, 1997-1998
- All-State volleyball, 1997
- Three-Time state volleyball champion, 1995-1997
- Two-time state basketball champion, 1997-1998
- Scotus Athlete of the Year, 1998
- School record holder for season assists in soccer (28) and career assists in soccer (58)
- *Lincoln Journal Star* Female Athlete of the Year, 1998
- Shamrock Athletic Hall of Fame inductee, 2008

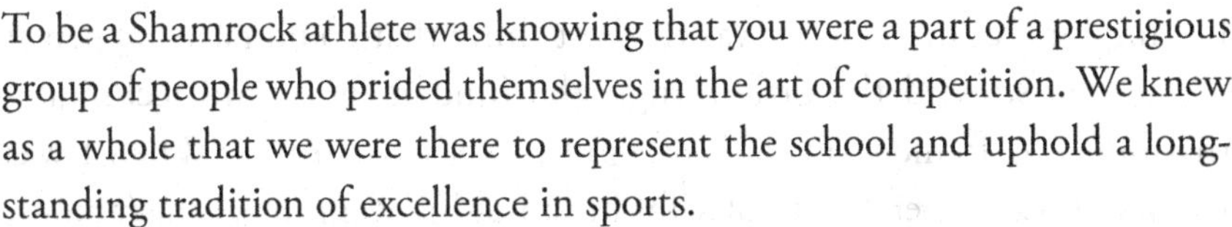

To be a Shamrock athlete was knowing that you were a part of a prestigious group of people who prided themselves in the art of competition. We knew as a whole that we were there to represent the school and uphold a long-standing tradition of excellence in sports.

All the Scotus coaches had a great influence on me, but I have to say that Coach John Petersen had the greatest influence. He taught me that nothing was going to come easy and that all success came with a price. A price you had to work for and dedicate yourself to, one that came from perseverance, self-control, a positive attitude, and a great team. A team that worked together, believed in themselves and their capabilities, and busted their butts to achieve a common goal. He didn't let us slack off, he expected perfection, and we came to expect it from ourselves.

There are many memories that still come to mind, but a couple of my favorites were the 1997 Grand Island Central Catholic volleyball district final where we beat them (#1 ranked) in three sets to get to state which was a major upset! Another was the 1997 district final basketball game against North Bend where we were behind the entire game (Stacy Rosche kept us in the game by shooting the lights out) – we won in the final seconds to get to state. Beating Battle Creek all four years at state basketball (1995 was a big upset) was memorable. Each state championship was fun and special.

The best athlete I played with was Shauna Greiner. She was the lone senior on the basketball team my sophomore year. She always worked so hard and pushed herself to get better and better. I remember her always staying after practice to shoot around when I was dead tired and starving, trying to get out of the gym as fast as I could. I always tried to keep up with her in conditioning drills and always looked up to her. I loved being her teammate!

Tiffany Volk from Battle Creek and KC Cowgill from GICC were both awesome opponents in basketball. Jenny Kropp and Heather Budd were two volleyball opponents that were fun to play against as well.

Playing for Coach Petersen was the best thing that could have happened to me. He stressed the little things, the fundamentals and techniques that built the foundations of successful powerhouse teams. When I was younger I was so nervous to play for him; I didn't want to get the famous, "*What the hell are you doing*?!?" Petey face. If you did something wrong at practice or in games, you did not want to look his way because he was going to let you know! But that only pushed us to do more things right; to constantly adjust and better ourselves, pushing out of our comfort zone to be able to compete and succeed at a high level. We all trusted him and had a love and respect for him that we knew we had in return. My most memorable experience about John Petersen was just hanging out after our championships, talking about the highs and lows of the season.

My favorite memory was when we were practicing basketball in the old gym and Coach Miller was showing us how we need to box-out. He was going to box out Kim Rickert and in the process a small can drops out of his pocket and rolls down the court – it rolls long enough and far enough that it got everyone's attention and we just stood there and watched it as it rolled down to the other side of the court and dropped down, which opened the lid of the can and chewing tobacco fell out all over the floor.

Mr. Miller just calmly said, "Coach, keep the girls all down there while I clean this up." We were all laughing so hard. I also remember pre-game rituals in volleyball: Jewelia Grennan and Steph Kruse would do "Mary Catherine Gallagher" skits and "Spartan Cheerleader Cheers" from Saturday Night Live.

I am most proud of my teams and my fellow teammates when I was at Scotus. We all pushed hard and expected great things from one another. We had great camaraderie, we played for one another, we pushed each other at practice, we forced ourselves to be at our best at the right time and never look back. We didn't have one "star" player – we had a team that came through when we needed it the most. The life lessons I learned while at Scotus were to never settle on being good enough at something. There is always time and there are ways to make yourself better at anything you do. Never stop striving to be the greatest you can be.

Jewelia Grennan

Scotus High School 1995 - 1999

- Two-time All-State volleyball, 1997, 1998
- All-State basketball, 1999
- Four-time state champion in volleyball, 1995-1998
- Scotus Athlete of the Year, 1999
- Shamrock Athletic Hall of Fame inductee, 2012

To me, being a Shamrock athlete meant hard work, determination, teamwork, and camaraderie among my teammates. The greatest influence on me was Coach John Petersen.

A memory that comes to mind is during my sophomore year, I was playing volleyball and was put against a senior middle blocker in a tough middle drill. I was so frustrated (and so was Coach Petersen). I accidentally rolled my eyes at him...*never again did that happen.*

My most memorable game day experience came at the state championship game my junior year. We played Grand Island Central Catholic – the place was packed and loud! Also, during my sophomore year at the state basketball tournament I made a shot at the buzzer and got fouled. I was all alone at the Devaney Center and I made the shot (even though I was never a good free throw shooter).

There are so many great athletes I played with: Carmen Burbach, Rhea Wemhoff, Kim Rickert, Kristie Korth, Sara Kunneman, Steph Kruse. The biggest rivalry I had with opponents was with Jenny Kropp from GICC and Kati Blacheter from North Bend.

Coach Petersen was amazing. So were Coaches Miller, Tooley, Blazer, and Dusel. They showed us what teamwork was all about.

I learned many lessons I carried on in life through playing sports. I learned about balance by playing all sports and still being expected to do well in the classroom. This has continued in all my life experiences. I thank Scotus, my teammates, and coaches for showing me that hard work and dedication will pay off. They set the standard that I now take with me for the rest of my life. ***Go Shamrocks!!!***

Stephanie Kruse

Scotus High School 1995 - 1999

- Three-Time state volleyball champion, 1996 - 1998
- Two-time state basketball champion, 1997 – 1998
- State soccer champion, 1998; runner-up, 1999
- All-State volleyball, 1998
- All-State Honorable Mention basketball, 1998 - 1999
- Two-time All-State soccer, 1997 – 1998
- NSAA All-State basketball game player, 1999
- Shrine All-Star soccer game player, 1999
- Shamrock Athletic Hall of Fame inductee, 2012

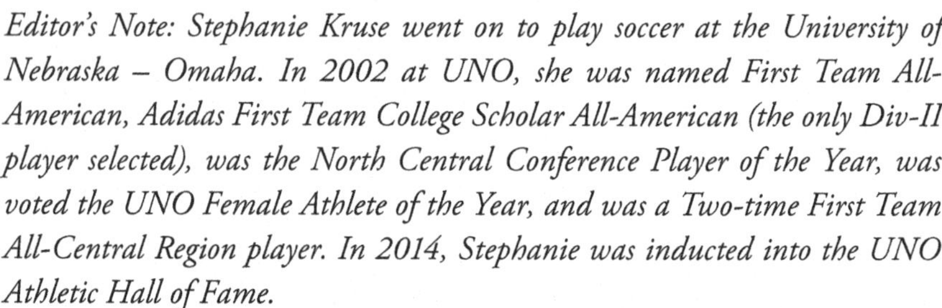

Editor's Note: Stephanie Kruse went on to play soccer at the University of Nebraska – Omaha. In 2002 at UNO, she was named First Team All-American, Adidas First Team College Scholar All-American (the only Div-II player selected), was the North Central Conference Player of the Year, was voted the UNO Female Athlete of the Year, and was a Two-time First Team All-Central Region player. In 2014, Stephanie was inducted into the UNO Athletic Hall of Fame.

Growing up, I always wanted to be a part of any athletic activity. I remember watching my brother play sports with his friends in the backyard and him playing basketball one-on-one with our dad, and so desperately wanting to have them ask me to join. As a girl I would go to Scotus games and want to follow in the footsteps of players such as Shauna Greiner, Amy Kuhlen and JoDe Cieloha. They were legends as far as I was concerned.

Sports are an ongoing theme in my life and I feel fortunate to have had the ability at Scotus to be involved in not only multiple sports, but also other activities. Students don't always get that luxury and instead are forced to specialize way too early. I distinctly remember a time at Scotus where I had flag corps practice in the morning, went to class all day, basketball practice after school, and then rehearsal for the play *Oliver* later that night. Being involved in so many activities gave me the opportunity to test my skills in a variety of areas.

Attending Scotus has developed my character and taught me about dedication, all while helping me learn how I can be of service to others. Many teachers and coaches have impacted the students that have come through these doors; one in particular is John Petersen. He asks much of players even when they may not fully understand why. You just have to trust and be led. For instance, I didn't know why Coach Petersen wouldn't let us look up our stats. I didn't know why we had to sweep the bus after away games. I didn't know why he would praise the person for going across the court to pick up the volleyball while others had a water break first. Now I realize all of these were to take the focus off the individual and put it back on the team; working as a unit and creating chemistry, all while developing character.

Scotus provides instant credibility due to the dedication of the teachers, coaches and staff. When I graduated from high school, my college coaches told me they knew I would be a well-coached and disciplined individual having come from Scotus. I always found that to be such a compliment. Coming from a smaller school, I took for granted many things that I see now are so fundamentally important to creating community. The unity at Scotus in undeniable and I am proud to say that I graduated from here. Throughout life I've realized that this sense of connectedness that I grew accustomed to in high school was not other people's experience. When it's all said and done I believe it's not about the actual sports here at Scotus. It's about how being involved in sports developed my character and created the relationships that I still have to this day.

Words can't express how thankful I am to my parents for their support through the years. Their decision to send me to Scotus is one for which I will always be grateful. Scotus has meant a great deal to forming my identity. You don't get to choose your family or sometimes even the high school you attend, but God has truly blessed me with both.

Tom Rogers

Scotus High School 1995 - 1999

- Two-time All-State football, 1997 - 1998
- Two-time All-State soccer, 1998 – 1999; named to the soccer Super-State team, 1999
- Down Under Bowl (soccer) player, 1997
- State champion soccer team member, 1997
- Shamrock Athletic Hall of Fame inductee, 2013

As a Shamrock athlete, I formed some great friendships, and many of those people are still close friends today. We all took a lot of pride in competing for each other and the Shamrocks. Scotus had a long tradition of athletic excellence, and it was great to be a part of that and make our mark.

The greatest influence on me as a Shamrock athlete was my father, John Thomas Rogers. He was a great athlete, which motivated me to improve and to make him proud. He spent countless hours taking me to and from games and practices as well as working with me one-on-one.

We shared lots of great bonding/shenanigans on the bus rides to and from games. I would love to forget some heartbreaking loses in the football state playoffs to David City Aquinas and Norfolk Catholic, and soccer state playoffs to Blair and Omaha Roncalli.

My most memorable game-day experience was winning a soccer state championship in 1997. I'll never forget Chip Kaup. I played with and against a lot of great athletes during my time at Scotus. I can't really single one out.

I played for several different head coaches, and they were all unique and great in their own way. The one thing they all had in common is that they really cared about the people that played for them. It wasn't just about the game or the win.

I always loved competing in athletics at Scotus. I always thought about winning state championships or awards, but really looking back on it, the things I remember most are the relationships and the experiences I had with my teammates and coaches. All my athletic achievements were a part of the team.

The life lessons I learned were to work hard and play hard.

Heather VanAckeren

Scotus High School 1996 - 2000

- Two-time All-State volleyball, 1998 - 1999
- All-State soccer, 2000
- Four-time volleyball state champion, 1996 - 1999
- Two-time basketball state champion, 1997 - 1998
- State soccer champion, 1998
- Scotus Athlete of the Year, 2000
- Shamrock Athletic Hall of Fame inductee, 2013

Being a Shamrock athlete not only required day-to-day physical commitment, but also meant having a positive attitude. It not only meant that I had to have mental integrity, but I also had to hold myself accountable for my behavior. It helped ingrain in me the value of teamwork, sportsmanship and respect of others.

Coach John Petersen had the greatest influence on me as a Shamrock athlete. He was a coach that not only got his athletes to believe in themselves, but he was also a great life teacher. He was a coach that not only taught us the skills, techniques, and strategy of the sport(s), but also looked for opportunities to teach us about the importance of positive attitudes. From teaching us about winning, losing, and good sportsmanship, he also taught us rebounding from failures and setbacks, and trusting your teammates. I have been able to carry those important lessons well beyond my high school career thanks to my time at Scotus.

With the teams that I was a part of, we had such great camaraderie between the same group of girls, year after year, season after season. In 1997, my sophomore year, we were traveling from Columbus to Omaha to play Skutt Catholic. Our middle blocker, Jewelia (Grennan) Wagner, was sick with mono and the coaches were discussing who would play her starting position. The discussion must have been consuming Mrs. Janet Tooley and Mr. John Petersen's thoughts because he failed to stop at the railroad tracks, and got pulled over. We went on to win the volleyball game and I vividly remember Stephanie (Kruse) Kros served 15 straight points to win one set!

Throughout my high school volleyball career, our rival was always Grand Island Central Catholic. In 1997, we needed to win against them in order to make it to the state tournament, and it was played at Grand Island. The gym was packed to maximum capacity and the overflowing crowd made their way to the commons area of the school. Before the days of live streaming on the internet, Twitter and Facebook, the school officials needed to put a video camcorder in the main gym and have it play on TVs in the commons area/hallway so that the overflowing crowd could watch it!

I am most proud of the teamwork on the teams I played on. I was fortunate to win seven state titles in my high school career (volleyball 1996, 1997, 1998, and 1999, basketball 1997 and 1998 and soccer 1998) and I would have not been able to do that without my teammates and the teamwork that was involved.

Jeff Kosch

Scotus High School 1997 - 2001

- All-State running back, 2000
- Scotus Athlete of the Year, 2001
- Shrine Bowl participant, 2001

Being a Shamrock meant instant pride and honor to play to the best of my ability in upholding high athletic standards. The hope of continuing to add to the tradition built by all Shamrock athletes who came before me.

My brother (Jesse) had a significant influence on me, but my dad (Bill) took the cake. I remember going to nearly all of my brother's sports events and his success helped provide a vision for me, something to shoot for. I obviously never was able to see my dad play sports, but continuously heard stories about him from several people in the community. That coupled with my dad having a vigorous spirit for Scotus athletics in general left me no choice but to realize that I needed to give it my all in every sport. He never forced anything upon me, but I just knew that if I did not play hard, it would let him down. I took great pride in my dad's and brother's success at Scotus and wanted to essentially keep that success going when I was playing.

My fondest memory is winning the Class B state soccer championship my senior year (2001). We had nine seniors in my class who essentially all played club soccer growing up. So, to know you are playing your last game ever together and will never all play 11-on-11 again; to go out on top was a great feeling.

I didn't play much with him given a two-year difference in age, but Thadd Recek was probably the best athlete I played with. He was probably the closest person around me in age who had the best chance to be an All-State athlete in three different sports, a great measuring tool of all-around athleticism. Tom Rogers would be right there with Thadd as well. The best athlete I played against is a tough question, but I would say either Matt Herian from Pierce or Mike Stuntz from Council Bluff St. Albert. Herian was solid in every sport and made it look easy...throwing the shot put and running 100 meters in track was pretty impressive. I played against Mike Stuntz in soccer and he flew past me during the game and I could not believe how fast he was. He later in college threw the famous Black 41 Flash Reverse Pass to Eric Crouch to beat Oklahoma in 2001.

Winning the state soccer championship was a very proud moment, but I also take pride in knowing that I honestly gave it my all in every sport and departed with no regrets. I loved to compete and truly enjoyed every minute of it. I moved back to Columbus in 2012 and have since assisted Jon Brezenski with boys soccer. I'm proud to now represent Scotus from a coaching standpoint and hope to carry on the tradition of athletic success on the field as well as teaching life moments to athletes when necessary off the field.

I will never forget a story during freshman football practice. My first time playing football was in junior high so I learned as I went and did some nice things. When freshman year rolled around I realized that I could be a pretty good player and then it started going to my head... the pride started swelling up a bit. During one freshman practice we ran an offensive play (I was the running back) and I got dropped for a four or five-yard loss. I was furious on the way back to the huddle and stated, "*Come on line you need to block better*!". Vern Younger (our coach) immediately busted in the huddle, grabbed my facemask, pulled it right to his face and absolutely chewed me out. This was probably the best thing that ever happened to me. I was starting to get a little taste of arrogance as an athlete and then Vern humbled me and brought me back down to earth. From the point forward I tried to stay grounded with sports. I would like to think if my dad was the coach then he would have done the same thing Vern did. He wasn't the coach so Vern did his job. I really am grateful for that day.

Parents make a great financial sacrifice with the hope of their child receiving a solid education. The parents and the school provide the opportunity, so it's up to the student to maximize the experience. I learned this early on and will always be thankful that my parents allowed me to attend Scotus. There are several great high schools throughout the USA, and Scotus truly is one of them. My mom taught at Scotus for around 20 years, so I had an appreciation for teachers in general. Also the teaching continuity and longevity (also with coaches) is fascinating. Teachers and coaches come to Scotus, they enjoy it, give it their all and stay for decades. That alone is an extremely big reason on why Scotus continues to have a consistently high level of success in the classroom and on the field/court. Finally, God should be at the center of life, and being able to learn about God at Scotus and develop a lifelong relationship with Him is the most important thing I learned.

Molly Engel

Scotus High School 1997 - 2001

- State cross country individual and team champion, 2000
- Scotus Athlete of the Year, 2001
- Shamrock Athletic Hall of Fame inductee, 2013

Janet Tooley and Dan Mahoney had the greatest influence on me as a Scotus athlete. Coach Tooley always had the toughest track workouts that pushed the limits. Her workouts allowed me to peak by the end of the track season. She expected a lot on the track, but she was also very caring and inspiring. I always wanted to run well for her. Rain or shine, she was always out on the track yelling out splits when I ran a race, letting me know where timing was at. I remember a crazy windy rainy meet we had in Wayne, NE. Most people were taking shelter or in a building, but Coach Tooley was on the track in pouring rain and blistering winds yelling splits. Her track workouts really prepared me to compete at the collegiate level.

Coach Mahoney also had a huge impact on my life and running in college as a coach. He would drive us out to the country to make sure we trained on the most challenging hills to prepare our legs for some of the more challenging courses. One of my most fond memories was when we won the school's first girls cross-country team title in 2000 in Kearney. Our third and fourth runners edged out a few Gothenburg runners to seal the title. It was crazy and so close! On the way home in our school van, he started playing "We are the Champions" by Queen. Just relishing in the moment of letting all that hard work sink in and realizing we just won a state title was a great feeling.

My senior year in cross country was also the most memorable because I won the Class C state individual title and we won the team title. It was the first year in Scotus school history for winning the individual and state title. Just the feeling of knowing on the home stretch at the state meet you are going to cross the line first is a pretty emotional experience.

The best athlete I ran against in high school was Alice Schmidt from Elkhorn who was the state record holder in the 800 meters. She went on to the University of North Carolina to run track and then competed for the U.S. in the Olympics in the 800 meters. In cross-country, the best athlete I ran against was Amanda Kuca, from Lincoln Lutheran. She was the state runner up in the 2000 state cross country meet. She also competed professionally for a few years in the steeplechase in her post-college years.

A story that has to be told: During my freshman year at the state track meet in Omaha, we were neck-and-neck with Elkhorn for the state class B title. There were only a few events left. Renee Boman and I were competing the 1600-meter run. We were running through laps 2-3 of the race 1-2 in front of everyone. We ended up placing 1st and 4th, with Renee winning the race and me 4th. We were competing against Alice Schmidt from Elkhorn and Kathryn Handrup from Aurora, who both ended up as NCAA Division I runners. This race was just loaded with talent. I honestly didn't think I could medal but I just found the courage within me to compete. Elkhorn ended up winning the class B state track title, and Scotus girls were runner-up.

Scotus track and cross country taught me many life lessons. First, hard work is necessary to achieve your goals. Second, I learned to always set goals and plan for how you will achieve them. Last, I learned that adversity builds character and will strengthen mental toughness. These coaches and sports gave me discipline and a strong work ethic in my collegiate years and as a professional nurse. I am very grateful to them and Scotus athletics for setting me on the right path.

Meghan Pile

Scotus High School 1998 – 2002

- Three-time All-State volleyball, 1999 - 2001
- Three-time All-State Soccer, 2000 - 2002
- All-State basketball, 2002
- Basketball state champion 1998; runner-up, 2002
- Three-time volleyball state champion, 1998, 1999, 2001
- Two-time soccer state champion, 2001, 2002
- Scotus Athlete of the Year, 2002
- School record holder for career digs (695)
- Shamrock Athletic Hall of Fame inductee, 2014

Editor's Note: On teams that Meghan Pile competed on at Scotus, the overall record was 248-36, six state championships, and four state runners-up. Meghan made it to the state finals all four years in both volleyball and soccer and once in basketball. At the collegiate level Meghan played soccer for UNO; she made it to the Final Four all four years with one national runner-up and one national championship, was an Academic All-American and captain of the Soccer team her senior year.

Being a Scotus athlete is a badge of honor. It comes with a lot of memories and life time friendships that grew from a shared bond of sweat, hard work and a love of competition. It is impossible for me to walk back into that gym without a beautiful sense of nostalgia.

I know this name is going to be a recurring theme, but I would be lying if I said any other name than John Petersen as the biggest influence on me as an athlete. He was a perfectionist on a mission. He spent countless hours nitpicking, fixing, adjusting every step we made, every swing we took, every ball we passed practice after practice. He and his staff of coaches

(Tooley, Blaser, Luchsinger, Dusel-Misfeldt) were unstoppable. It was an honor, a privilege and the hardest work of my life to play for them. They shaped me not only as a skilled and well-rounded athlete but (unknowingly at the time as a high school adolescent) they prepared me for life outside of the sheltered-safe walls of my parent's house.

When I was an incoming freshman – fresh out of 8th grade - Coach Petersen asked me to come to the varsity's YMCA volleyball league game. I, naïve as any other 14-year-old, figured I would watch. To my great surprise he started me in that game and (to my great fortune) every game after that. Thank goodness for Stephanie Kruse (Kros), Jewelia Grennan (Wagner) and Heather VanAckeren (Diederich) who were literally pulling my shirt to get me in position. I was a baby deer frozen in bright headlights. The terror and astonishment on my face when he told me I was playing must have been remarkable!

Coach Petersen was always looking ahead, trying to spot potential and shape talent to build his program. He also encouraged the older players to push, mentor, and help the up-and-coming players. I was very lucky to play with a lot of great players and I learned from each of them. I always hoped that I was able to influence some of those younger girls who grew up watching Scotus volleyball just like I did. He created a legacy that so many young people wanted to be a part of. Today, I'm happy to say I (as well as many others) contributed to that insurmountable success.

This story is relatable to many of the athletes and other Columbus kids that grew up in our small familiar town. The fall volleyball season of 1999, my sophomore year, started the same as always, two-a-days for two weeks before school began. However, prior to the start of the school year there may have been a large party in a cornfield outside of Columbus that was raided.

As a punishment for my attendance at the party (I was not ticketed) my parents made me call Coach Petersen and tell him my whereabouts. Quite possibly the most terrifying call I have ever had to make. Looking back, I think my parents had it right, but at the time I cannot say I agreed. As a punishment for my attendance at the party Coach Petersen said that I needed to stay after every two-a-day practice and do extra. The extra was to be determined by him. Also terrifying. The fortunate part of the story was that I was not alone. One other lucky player was also part of the joint punishment/torture!

For two weeks we practiced for four-plus hours a day (morning and afternoon) and then after all our teammates left we put on a fresh-dry t-shirt, filled up our water bottles yet again and braced ourselves! We did drills that were meant for groups of three or four with just two people, we ran, we jumped, we set, we hit, we blocked, we dove, we did anything he said as soon as his whistle blew. I can honestly say tears were shed, sweat ran off of us, and exhaustion seemed like a kind word for what we were feeling.

Though the two weeks passed quickly and the season began. Coach Petersen never spoke of it again. Although, I always felt like there a bond was made during those extra practices. It was a punishment of course, but it turned out to be one of the most memorable experiences I had in that gym. My sophomore volleyball season was one of my strongest. I have always attributed it to those extra hours spent nearly one-on-one with the best coach I have ever had the pleasure to play for. And we ended the season with a state championship.

As the state tournament drew near the seniors decided we wanted to find a way to bond during our last practices. So for a couple weeks we planned out what we were going to wear. Each day the seniors would find a way to match – all together or we partnered up. One day all the seniors would wear green shirts and black shorts, the next we would wear all black, then red and so on. It got to be hilarious because the coaches would comment, "Wow, a lot of black shirts today." But they never seemed to catch on to the actual trend. It was becoming difficult to come up with new ideas but we had a lot of fun with it.

The last day before state was our big reveal. We had screen printed an old picture of Coach Petersen on a white t-shirt and all the seniors wore it.

We had all the other players dress alike too, a big obvious, fun-loving joke for practice. Of course we had a lot laughs at that last practice and we still remember like it was yesterday. We gave those shirts to our parents and they wore them when we won the State championship that year (2001).

The funny thing is that most of my vivid memories are from playing volleyball at Scotus. After high school I went on to play soccer at the University of Nebraska-Omaha. I was by no means the most skilled or best soccer player on the field, but I believe that all the skills I practiced playing three sports in high school made me a good athlete and thus a better soccer player. In 2005 my final season at UNO we won a national championship.

The privilege to be an athlete at Scotus shaped my future. It created a bond of lifelong friendships through shared experiences. It was the sorority I never joined in college. It was more than the big wins and the tears that were shed after tough losses. It created a belief that success can be achieved through hard sometimes tedious work and the power of a team working towards a common goal. It gave me a foundation for a successful future.

Laura Dolezal

Scotus High School 2000 - 2004

- All-State volleyball, 2003
- All-State soccer, 2004
- Scotus Athlete of the Year, 2004
- Three-time state volleyball champion, 2001-2003
- Two-time state soccer champion, 2001 - 2002

Being a Scotus athlete was the pride of wearing the Shamrock uniform knowing the great tradition of the school, and the challenge to continue this great success. The attitude of winning and the confidence of success were engrained in the program.

All the coaches through their hard work and dedication to the school were very impactful. Overall, I would say it was Mr. Petersen's drive for continuous improvement and excellence was the most impactful on me as an athlete. The expectations of Coach Petersen were very high. The challenges...blood, sweat, and tears...but the rewards of success were unbelievable not only on the court, but also lessons learned that last a lifetime. I am most proud of the success of our teams and the school. The teamwork that was the foundation of success. The attitude of winning was instilled in us.

My most memorable game day experience was during one of our district soccer tournament games, I was injured and was hospitalized for several days. I was unable to play in the remaining district tournament and state tournament due to being in the hospital. Our team made it to the finals and I was released from the hospital a couple hours prior to the start of the championship game. We drove directly from the Omaha hospital to the state tournament field in Lincoln, arriving just minutes before the start of the final game. When we arrived at the game, the entire Scotus team left the field, ran out to the parking lot, and helped me onto the field so I could watch the finals from the sideline. That was absolutely amazing! What an incredible act of caring and support from my team.

There were so many great athletes at Scotus, but overall I would say Meghan Pile was the best athlete I played with. The best athlete played against was Jordan Larson.

The lessons I learned were about hard work, teamwork, and continuing to improve. This applies to athletics, the classroom, and the business world.

Ann Beiermann

Scotus High School 2001 - 2005

- Two-time All-State volleyball, 2003-2004
- Four-time volleyball state champion, 2001-2004
- Scotus Co-Athlete of the Year, 2005

John Petersen had the greatest influence on me as a Shamrock athlete

One of my funniest memories was when Coach Petersen locked the keys in the bus and in order to get in, we had to open the tiny side window and send Taryn Ketter through that window.

My most memorable game day experience was playing with my sister, Renee, by my side in the 2003 state volleyball championship game; winning was amazing.

The best athlete I played with Laura Dolezal. The best athlete I played against was Jordan Larson.

Coach Petersen demanded perfection. Everything started with fundamentals. He taught me more about life through sports—if you work hard and do things right, good things happen.

I am most proud of during time at Scotus being a part of four state championships and a part of the volleyball winning streak.

Heidi Sobota

Scotus High School 2001 - 2005

- All-State volleyball, 2004
- Two-time All-State soccer, 2004-2005
- Three-time volleyball state champion, 2001-2003
- State basketball champion, 2004
- State soccer champion, 2001-2002

Being a Shamrock meant being part of a great tradition, and it meant that I got to be a part of something that meant so much to the school. All three of my coaches greatly influenced me, especially Coach Petersen.

Some of the funniest memories were joking around with teammates at the hotel during state tournaments. We got to just hang out and be ourselves.

One of my most memorable game day experiences was when we came from two match points behind to beat Lincoln Lutheran in the conference championship. That kept the consecutive win streak alive.

The best athlete I played with was Jamie Tooley. She was a great all-around athlete in all her sports. The best athlete I played against was Jordan Larson in volleyball and basketball.

Having three different head coaches for different sports was interesting. It was a fun dynamic trying to figure out each ones' "quirks" and how to address them. My most memorable experience was seeing Coach Petersen get teary-eyed after we lost in five sets in the state championship match in 2004. I thought I would never see that.

I am most proud of the work ethic that I learned and continue to use every day in a world where work ethic is lacking with many people. There are so many life lessons I learned; a big one is that playing a role is hugely important in life. You may not always be the center of attention, but everyone has an important role.

Coach Petersen was our freshman basketball coach, and we used to practice in the mornings before school quite a bit. One day at morning practice, we were working on an inbounds play. The girl that was supposed to inbound the ball kept going underneath the basket and Coach kept yelling at her to stop doing that. Finally, Coach Petersen took the ball from her and threw the ball at the backboard; he was trying to show why you shouldn't inbound from under the basket. Well, after he threw it, he turned his head and the ball came straight back and hit him in the face. It hit him so hard that it bounced his glasses off. We were all mortified of what was going to happen next, until he finally laughed, and we all realized it was OK to laugh too.

Jamie Tooley

Scotus High School 2002 - 2006

- All-State volleyball, 2005
- Three-time state volleyball champion, 2002, 2003, 2005
- Gold medal triple jump, 2006
- Scotus Athlete of the Year, 2006
- Scotus Athletic Hall of Fame inductee, 2016

I was fortunate to represent Scotus in volleyball, basketball and track from 2002-2006. Because my mom, Janet Tooley, coached at Scotus, I grew up around Scotus athletics. As a young fan, I witnessed years of athletic success at Scotus and looked forward to my time playing for the green, white and gold.

When that time came, I was led by some of the best coaches in the state including Coach Petersen, Coach Tooley, Coach Wickham and Coach Lahm as well as their respective assistants. These individuals strived to make every practice and game/meet a teaching moment. Sometimes the lesson included laughter, sometimes tears and sometimes a heck of a lot of running. There are many great memories with each coach but a few that stand out include Coach Petersen blaring Kelly Clarkson's "Breakaway" over the loud speaker during conditioning, Coach Tooley's Good Friday Relays, Coach Wickham's half-court shot to get out of conditioning, and Coach Lahm's penny drills. The reason Scotus is so successful academically and athletically is because of coaches like these. They will forever hold a special place in my heart for everything they taught me.

The prep for games and meets is something I won't ever forget. Each game day started with Mass in the chapel as a team and a quick meeting after where the nerves of excitement for the upcoming competition would begin. Each organization had their respective t-shirt to wear on game days instead of the traditional SCC polo and posters on our lockers from the cheerleaders reminded us between each period that a game was fast approaching. The bus rides were always something to look forward to with our Hail Mary and Queen of Victory chant, pitch and 'Koopa-Troopa' card games, as well as plenty of goodies to eat from the parents. The singing and dancing in the locker room and the donning of our uniforms made the prep for each game special.

In my time at Scotus I played on one state championship basketball team, two state championship volleyball teams, one state runner-up volleyball team, and earned an individual championship in the triple jump. That success is largely due to the coaches I have previously mentioned and the teammates I was lucky enough to play with. Every day at practice we strived to make each other better. We were so competitive that practices became a battle where the loser would come out more motivated to work harder and win the next drill. I think that the Scotus girls' athletic program has been so successful because of that competitive spirit and hunger to win. The memories made with my teammates over my four years are enough to fill their own book. I will never forget driving home on the bus after winning the state championship in volleyball my sophomore year and realizing that not a single athlete on that bus had ever lost a volleyball game freshman through senior year.

Talk about an impressive feat. I remember the track teams' after-practice breakfast with enough food to feed three teams. The post-game celebrations at Runza, the basketball scrimmages at the YMCA during Christmas break, and the laughs during practice when someone shanked a ball into the ceiling fan are all things I remember fondly. Of course it is impossible for me to forget my senior year of volleyball when we came back from a 9-13 deficit in the fifth set of the state semi-final game and would eventually go on to win the state championship.

I will always look back fondly on the years I was a Scotus athlete. At the time it seemed like athletics were all life was about. However, I now know that the sports I played were not really what life was all about, but more so the lessons I learned while playing them. All of the laughter, tears, puke and sweat were more than worth it for the memories made and lessons learned. I am truly grateful for my time as a Scotus athlete and for the coaches and teammates I was able to share that time with.

Jen Haney

Scotus High School 2002 - 2006

- All-State volleyball, 2005
- All-State soccer, 2006
- Two-time volleyball state champion, 2003, 2005
- Basketball state champion, 2004

I took a lot of pride in being a Shamrock athlete. It was and still is something that I am and always will be proud of. When I was a student at Scotus, I was proud of all of our past success in female athletics and just wanted to keep up the tradition, not only for the program, but for me and my team.

Mr. Petersen had the greatest influence on me as an athlete. He not only was an outstanding volleyball coach, but an amazing teacher. Through coaching, he told us that in order to be successful, the most important things are to have a great work ethic and a great attitude. He would always talk about how important attitude was and that in order to be a good athlete, you needed to be "coachable". I have found that all of those principles have proven true not only in sports at Scotus, but they have carried over to real life as well. I still have my *"Attitude is Everything"* keychain on my key ring over 10 years later! I believe that Mr. Petersen has molded so many of his players into successful volleyball players as well as people of great character and great success.

One of my fondest memories as a Shamrock athlete was at Briar Cliff volleyball team camp we would always dye each other's hair in the dorms. It became a tradition at that overnight team camp every year. Our senior year, before the season started, we made a deal with Mr. Petersen that if we won state, he had to let us dye his hair. We were somewhat of an underdog that year so Mr. Petersen agreed to the deal. Sure enough, we beat Lincoln Lutheran in the state final and Mr. Petersen was no longer gray after that!

We played against Jordan Larson in the state volleyball tournament in 2004. She played for Logan View and went on the play for Nebraska and now Team USA. I am most proud of our tradition, and I am proud to have kept that tradition alive while I was there. I am also proud of being the FIRST libero to ever play at Scotus!

Liz Hadland

Scotus High School 2003 - 2007

- State runner-up in volleyball, 2004
- Two-time state volleyball champion, 2005- 2006
- Two-time All-State volleyball, 2005- 2006
- *Lincoln Journal Star* All-Star Game participant, 2007
- School record holder for most assists in a game (55)
- Scotus Athlete of the Year, 2007

I never fully realized what it meant to be a Shamrock athlete until I was no longer one. At the time, those long practices, weight lifting, conditioning, and summer open gyms were simply part of the job. You showed up because you had to in order to play, but looking back I now realize it was much more than that. Being a Shamrock athlete means having a strong work ethic and dedication toward the sport in which you love. It means being respectful of your coaches, fellow teammates, and the opponent. Shamrock athletes are part of a family, and keeping tradition alive is one of the most important parts.

I realized at a young age what that tradition was, especially when it came to the volleyball court. We lived next to the Tooleys, so early on I was exposed to what Scotus volleyball was all about. Then, came grade school and junior high where I would watch games from the bleachers and dream of being one of the girls on the court. They worked relentlessly toward their goal of winning that state championship at the end of the season.

Our 2005 and 2006 teams were fortunate enough to keep that tradition alive. Coach Petersen and Coach Tooley had the greatest influences on me as a Shamrock athlete. Coach Petersen taught me more than anyone ever could about the game of volleyball. When that man talked, you listened. He always gave each of us players respect; and for that, I will always have enormous of respect for him. I realize now that he taught us far more than simply about the game of volleyball. I learned a great work ethic, leadership, how to be a team player, and that in any situation in life - attitude truly is everything!

Looking back on all the great memories throughout my years as a Shamrock athlete, I'd have to say the most unexpected one came after our senior class won the volleyball state championship. All of the coaches, however, lost a bet they made with our team. We had decided the summer leading up to our final season that if we won state, they would all have to get a tattoo. They must have been thinking this was not our year, or they needed an excuse to get that tattoo they'd secretly always wanted. Maybe it was a little bit of both. The state tournament came around in November, like it does every year. Somehow we pulled it off against Grand Island Central Catholic after being defeated by them twice earlier in the season. That meant each and every coach on the staff would be getting a tattoo of his or her choice. I will never forget Mr. Petersen rolling up his sleeve and showing our team the new ink on his arm. The coaches all kept their word and got their tattoos. Now they'll never be able to forget the class of 2007!

My most unforgettable moment from my career at Scotus would have to be winning the state championship my junior year. It was the first time I had ever experienced a level of joy that great. Working so tirelessly towards a goal and actually attaining it is an overwhelming feeling. Our team was the underdog. The streak of 115 wins in a row was broken in the state championship the year before by Lincoln Lutheran. We were there to redeem ourselves. We had lost to Lincoln Lutheran twice before in the season. In the championship game, we fought and came away with the win. I got to share that moment with teammates whom I had been playing with since junior high. We all envisioned one day getting to hold that first place trophy up high and celebrate. That was the day that made all of our hard work totally worth it.

Playing in high competition games, you get to face talented athletes. The best athlete I ever played against while attending Scotus would undoubtedly be Jordan Larson. It is neat to watch her play for team USA now and get to say that I was on the opposite side of the net in high school.

During my time at Scotus, I am most proud of keeping the volleyball winning tradition alive. I looked up to the older girls when I was little and wanted to be just like them. I wanted a banner hung in the gym with my playing years on it. I wanted to go to state, win championships, and reach that final goal. As a team, we put in long hours and worked hard. We proved that no matter how lofty your goal is; you can achieve it if you are dedicated.

My favorite times with my teammates were not always during the big games when everyone was watching, but during our every day practices where no audience was there to watch. Those were the times we became better players and closer teammates.

Now being out of high school for almost ten years, I have learned a lot and evolved as a person. I have realized that some of my best attributes came from my parents, family, friends, and the fact that I attended Scotus during my most impressionable years. I have learned to always keep my faith in all facets of my life, that hard work honestly does pay off, and that the relationships you create with others are to be treasured. I am so thankful to have had the chance to be surrounded by such remarkable teachers, coaches, and peers during those years. It was a special thing to be a Scotus athlete, and that opportunity is one that I will never forget.

Chase Beiermann

Scotus High School 2005 - 2009

- Two-time All-State soccer, 2008 - 2009
- State soccer champion, 2009
- Scotus Athlete of the Year, 2009
- School record holder for goals against average for a season (0.650) and career (0.863)

All three of my siblings went to Scotus where they were athletes of multiple sports. Being the youngest in my family, I tagged along with my parents to all their games and watched from the stands. When I was in grade school, I particularly remember going to the football games. I looked forward to seeing the sea of green and gold and couldn't wait to wear one of those myself someday.

Hands down, the biggest influence on me was Jon Brezenski. Looking back, he came in as a relatively young coach, but there was no question that he demanded our respect. The great thing about that demanded respect was that you earned his respect right back. Brezenski's first year of coaching soccer was during my freshman year at Scotus, and man, did he make us work hard. He expected us to bring our best every day, whether it was a warm-up, a practice, a game, or even just a meeting. Not only were we challenged to be physically enduring, Brezenski taught us how to be mentally tough. He rallied us as a team, but also as individuals, and each of us was held accountable for our actions.

I believe his attitude set the atmosphere for our team, which in turn brought us closer as a team. In fact, we weren't a team, we were a soccer family. Our team won state soccer my senior year. Although we had some serious talent on the field, it couldn't have been brought together without Jon Brezenski. We believed. We won games that year as a direct reflection of Coach Brezenski's character and commitment to the program.

After graduating from Scotus, I followed Coach Brezenski's path and played soccer at Briar Cliff University. He continues to be a role model for me today and I am grateful to have gotten the privilege of having Jon Brezenski as my coach.

My fondest memory is winning state soccer in overtime versus Columbus High.

The memory I'd like to forget is dropping a wide open pass off a hitch and go route versus Lakeview during a game as a sophomore. We ended up losing a close game that night … and it was our Homecoming. Not the way you want to send your seniors out. I remember being miserable and sick to my stomach that whole weekend.

It's hard to choose the best athlete I played with. The guys in my class were all athletic. Everyone had a great work ethic and loved to compete. Our small guys were feisty and always in your face. Our big guys were bruisers and were actually some of our fastest sprinters. You honestly didn't want to run sprints next to our lineman in football because they could beat you (as a back).

The one person that I knew well and played against in football, basketball, and soccer was Jordan Paben from Lakeview. We grew up playing club basketball and club soccer together. Paben and I were always eager to compete against each other in high school after being teammates during our younger years. He had the size and athleticism to always be able to make a memorable play.

Jon Brezenski was my greatest influence in soccer. Jeff Ohnoutka was my greatest influence in basketball. Coach Ohnoutka knew how to coach and pick teams apart. He was able to give us a game plan that prepared us for what we were going to see every game, no matter the opponent. During practice, he would challenge you with constructive criticism to help you become better. When you met that challenge, Ohnoutka was right there to celebrate with you. I will always remember his enthusiasm and excitement coming into the locker room, especially after a win.

I am most proud of our state soccer banner and the group of guys that put it on the wall. That was the last game our class played as seniors and there is nothing sweeter than going out on top. It was a complete team effort that grew from four years of work. I am incredibly proud of the program and the direction it is going. The boys have won state soccer the past three years, a football championship last fall, and basketball is knocking on the championship door. After graduating, it was my turn to support from the stands and I have learned that anytime Scotus wins state, it's a victory for the whole community.

It's always a great day to be a Shamrock.

Katie Beiermann

Scotus High School 2005 - 2009

- All-State volleyball, 2008
- Two-time All-State soccer, 2008- 2009
- Scotus Co-Athlete of the Year, 2009
- School record holder for most blocks in a game (9)
- Three-time volleyball state champion, 2005, 2006, 2008

My name is Katie Beiermann, I attended Scotus Central Catholic High School and I played for Scotus beginning in the fall of 2005 through the spring of 2009. I played four years of volleyball, basketball, and soccer; and loved every minute of it.

I remember being in elementary school and going to watch Scotus volleyball games. If you weren't there on time, chances are you probably missed most of the game - they were just that good. When you are that young and watch those players they are like celebrities to younger kids. You watch them on the court, you learn their names and the positions they play. Then, before you know it, you are someone's celebrity and everyone is watching you.

I don't think I knew to what extent how successful Scotus' program was, because I grew up around it. I didn't realize that our program was so solid and smooth compared to other programs just 20 minutes away. Coaches used to tell us there was as target on our back whether we were ranked No. 1 in the state or not ranked at all. There aren't many people in Nebraska that don't know what Scotus is. They might not exactly know where Columbus is, but they know the Scotus name. It is usually followed by a discerning look or them rolling their eyes. I loved getting those reactions because it makes you proud of where you came from and the tradition that goes with it.

I would say the biggest culture shock for me when I went to college was seeing how different college programs are run. Things were not run as smoothly and the hard work that you have been surrounded by for the past four years is gone. You see people running around half-speed and it bothers you. You have been taught to give it your all, all the time. What is the point in doing something if you aren't going to do your best? These are college programs that you are now participating in and they just don't measure up to Scotus. It really makes you miss and appreciate your high school athletic experience.

A large portion of the success is due to the coaches. We had some of the greatest coaches out there. I always thought to myself, "If the coaches aren't yelling at you, you should be worried". Luckily I never had that problem. Beginning with coaches: Jane Dusel, Gary Luchsinger, Julie Blaser, Janet Tooley, John Petersen, Sean Wickham and ending with Kevin Stout; I learned something from each coach and I will always remember each and every one of them.

I was pretty close with all of my coaches during my high school years, especially with Mr. Petersen. Mr. Petersen is somewhat of a magician. When you least expect it, he will pull something out of his sleeve and amaze us all. I know this because I've seen it done on multiple occasions. Mr. Petersen and I got very close during my high school experience. During my freshman year, he was my volleyball coach, basketball coach, and geometry teacher. My sophomore he decided to really bring the heat when he was coaching me in volleyball, he also *conveniently* moved up to the JV basketball coaching position that year, and I was assigned to his Study Hall in school. The rest of my high school years I think he was tired of yelling at me, so he moved onto other players. I have heard from a lot of players that he got soft in his last couple years of coaching. However, I do not remember any moment during my experience that would lead me to believe he was being soft on us, and I wouldn't have wanted it any other way.

There is an overwhelming support system in place at Scotus and I don't think people realize how impressive it is. Many college teams talk about how hard it is to play football in Memorial Stadium, because of the Husker fans. That is how important Scotus fans are to this school's program. The Dowd Activity Center is not an easy place to serve on game point, or shoot a free throw when you have fans screaming in your ear. It isn't an easy place to play on any night. You learn a lot when you play at Scotus. Mental toughness is something that probably is the biggest takeaway for me. It is something that transfers into everyday life and is constantly being put to the test. That includes the ability to handle pressure, keeping your composure, being able to think on your feet, and most importantly the habit of working hard. So for that, I would like to say thank you.

There is a reason people say Scotus is a legacy. Success after success upholds that name. Out of it all, I was blessed with some amazing relationships with many players and my coaches that will always be there. I am very privileged to be able to say I attended Scotus Central Catholic High School and that I loved every minute of it.

Sami Spenner

Scotus High School 2005 - 2009

- All-State volleyball, 2008
- Two-time volleyball state champion, 2006, 2008
- Member of state champion track team, 2009
- Scotus Co-Athlete of the Year, 2009
- School record holder for long jump (17'7¾")
- Gold medal winner 400m relay, 2009

Growing up in Columbus, I always knew I was going to attend Scotus Central Catholic once I was old enough. Unlike some kids in my class, I was excited to get started there and dive into the realm that is high school athletics. Scotus has such a rich history of success and tradition that I couldn't wait to be a part of it. Being a Shamrock athlete meant the world to me from the very beginning, and it meant being a part of an amazing legacy that will live on for years.

It's hard to say who had the greatest influence on me only because I had so many great coaches, role models, and teammates. I would definitely say that John Petersen probably had one of the greatest influences just because I had him as a teacher and a coach of multiple sports growing up. He was the coach you wanted to play for, even if he was the scariest person in the world when you were a kid at volleyball and basketball summer camps. Every coach that I encountered in my experience at Scotus played an enormous role in who I am today.

I would also say that some of my role models growing up had some influence on me. My two most memorable role models were Laura Dolezal and Kristie (Korth) Brezenski. I grew up hearing stories about how hard those athletes worked and how great they were, and I wanted to be just like them. One of my most memorable game-day experiences was probably running out onto the court with the crowd on their feet and the band playing. Every time we stepped foot on the court it was a sense of euphoria just knowing we had such an amazing and large support system behind us. I would also say that when we had home games, we would run up and down the halls and run into the weight room and blare some music to get us pumped. That was also something we used to do that always stuck out to me.

The best athlete that I competed with while at Scotus was probably Katie Beiermann. We were co-athletes of the year our senior year. I grew up with Katie, as she lived right across the street from me. She was the only one that stuck it out for basketball with me all four years, and she was always my partner when it came to partner drills at practice.

I had the most amazing coaches throughout my time at Scotus, and competing for every single one of them was something I lived for. I wanted to be a great athlete and I knew that to do that, I had to impress my coaches. I wanted to be the best not only for myself, but for them. I wanted to make them proud, and I wanted them to talk about me and my team for years to come just as they had always talked of the great teams that came before us. They are the ones that got me to strive to be the best that I could be. I will say that some of my most memorable experiences with my coaches was probably any time a state championship was won. Seeing them at their proudest moments were some of my proudest moments.

Some of the things that I am proudest of are my state championship titles - volleyball 2006 and 2008, and track & field 2009. Achieving the status of state champion was always a euphoric feeling, and will always give me goose bumps when I think back to them. They were truly a statement of the hard work and determination our team put into the year. But it wasn't just the trophies and awards that made me the proudest. The camaraderie I had with my teammates through the years is something that I will always be proud of. We were always there to support each other and cheer each other on, which I feel like you don't see a whole lot these days.

Life lessons that I learned? "Attitude is everything." –Coach John Petersen. That statement has been more prevalent in my life that I would have imagined back in the day.

Some of the best/funniest memories I have are as follows:

Any of Coach John Petersen's quotes. At the end of the year, before state volleyball, we would take a white T-shirt and write our favorite Petersen quotes all over it and wear it to practice.

The time that our volleyball team was getting chewed out by Coach Petersen during a particularly bad practice and Coach threw a volleyball backwards with so much force (he did this while still facing us) that it landed in a ball cart on the other side of the cart. It took everything we had not to bust out laughing at the great feat we had just witnessed for fear that we would have to run more suicide lines.

The amount of clipboards that Coach Wickham broke during the basketball season. But also the amount of excitement he displayed during some of our best games. He jumped higher than the athletes themselves!

Coach Dean Hefti getting tripped by a soccer net and saying, "Damn booby traps!"

When I was a freshman, our basketball coach was Coach Petersen, and at the end of the season we had a party. Just the freshmen girls and Coach Petersen. By the end of the night we were making fun of all the things he would say to us, especially how he always said we ran around the court like we were walking on egg shells. And also how he always used the analogy of herding chickens when teaching us to play defense.

Monica Boeding

Scotus High School 2006 - 2010

- Two-time All-State volleyball, 2008, 2009
- Two-time state volleyball team champion, 2008, 2009
- School record holder for game kills (26) and career kills (835)
- School record holder for most career 3-Pointers (51) and co-holder of record for most 3-pointers in a game (5)
- Member state track championship team, 2009
- Gold medal winner 400m relay 2009 and school record holder in that event (49.76)
- Scotus Athlete of the Year, 2010

Being a Shamrock athlete gave me a great sense of pride. Being part of such a tradition-rich program, and continuing the tradition with great people was a great experience.

Coach John Petersen had the biggest influence on me as an athlete. My funniest memory was when Coach Petersen was upset about something we did at practice. While he was yelling, he drop-kicked a volleyball that landed perfectly in the ball cart across the gym. He was angry so we were trying to had to stay serious, but it was hard not to laugh.

My most memorable game day experience was winning state volleyball in 2009. We were the underdogs that year and the five-set match was surreal. We had worked so hard that year, and so many people had already counted us out. It was an indescribable feeling.

The best athlete I played with was Sami Spenner. Her athleticism and ability to adjust to new challenges was amazing. Sami was a great athlete and friend, which made it all the more fun to watch her succeed. The best athlete I played against was Brea Muhle from Lakeview. It was a great rivalry, and fun to play someone with her athleticism so frequently.

Playing for Coach Petersen was a challenge and a blessing all in one. He never settled for less than your best, and instilled so many values in me such as: discipline, hard work, perseverance and of course, "*Attitude is Everything.*" It's hard to pick one experience, but I think the way he cared about all of us on and off the court through the years and after we were done being a Scotus athlete was truly amazing. I remember one time I had gotten sick at a tournament so my parents had to take me home early. I had slept for 24 hours straight, but Coach Petersen had called my mom to make sure I was doing okay.

I am most proud of the success my teammates and I found on and off the court. It is great to see the people you spent so much time with use all we learned at our time at Scotus to succeed in life.

I think the first life lesson was all learn is how important time management is. If you want to succeed as a student-athlete, you have to master that. Also, the most important life lesson I learned was that you can't count yourself out of anything. If you don't believe you can achieve your goals, you are setting yourself up for failure. You have to believe in yourself, and never lower your expectations because of other people.

Since I don't talk about track much, I think that winning the 4x100 relay at state track with my teammates Amber Ewers, Sami Spenner, and Ashley Paprocki was a great memory. I had competed in individual events at state track all through high school, but never found that kind of success on my own. To share that kind of success with my teammates just made it that much more memorable.

Though most of my memories from Scotus athletics came from volleyball and Coach Petersen, I want to say something about the basketball program as well. Up until my senior year, I thought I was going to pursue basketball in college instead of volleyball. Coach Sean Wickham is another coach that had a great impact on me. You could see his passion for the game when he coached, and he helped make the game what it is today. Though the love of a sport comes from the athlete, sometimes a good coach just makes it stronger.

All the coaches I had at Scotus through the years helped shape me into the athlete and person I am today. It is truly a blessing, and not all athletes are fortunate enough to have as many coaches as Scotus that love the sports the way they do, and care for the athletes the way Scotus does. Striving to make us all the best we could be. It was a fast four years as a varsity athlete, but it was a great four years.

Amber Ewers

Scotus High School 2007 - 2011

- Placed in 13 events at state track meet in her career
- 2008: 400m relay (3rd), 100m dash (4th), 200m dash (5th)
- 2009: 400m relay (1st), 100m dash (4th), 200m dash (5th)
- 2010: 100m dash (2nd), 200m dash (2nd), 800m run (7th), 400m dash (1st place and All-Class gold medal)
- 2011: 100m dash (3rd), 200m dash (6th), 400m dash (1st)
- Scotus Athlete of the Year, 2011
- Member state track championship team, 2009

Being a Shamrock athlete meant being involved in something bigger than myself. It gave me the opportunity to participate in activities that went beyond the scope of myself, my goals and education, and even the school itself.

The coaches and my teammates were what made Shamrock sports the enjoyable and successful activities they were in my experience. My parents ran, sometimes literally, through both the good and the bad. At times I think they were more nervous than I was! But they were always there, and attended almost every one of my meets. My teammates and coaches gave me motivation to push my limits and come to practice every day with a smile on my face, even when I absolutely dreaded the workouts. All of my favorite sports memories involved my teammates, and I particularly remember taking younger teammates under my wing. I would drive them to and from practice and try to calm their nerves before races. I was rewarded much more in this relational aspect than I was in accomplishments from the sport itself.

One of my fondest memories is praying before running the 200m at State with my competitors in the pouring rain. We huddled in a circle and were able to find fellowship in faith, keeping in perspective what really mattered before we competed against each other. Another funny memory was after a cross country meet in Kearney in which we rolled down one of the larger hills.

My two most memorable experiences were state track 2010 and 2011. In 2010, our 4x100m relay team won, and Sami Spenner and I went one and two in the 200m, and I won the 400m. We won state as a team, which was an incredible experience.

My junior year (2011), I ran the 100m, 200m, 400m, and 800m. I placed in the 100 and 800 and won the 200 and 400. My 400 time unexpectedly gave me the All-Class gold medal, which was a huge surprise to me.

The best athlete I played with was Sami Spenner. She went out for track her senior year, when I was a sophomore, and competed outstandingly. In our college years when she transferred to UNO and competed in track for them, I was able to compete against her as our schools were in the same conference. She is an incredible athlete, but even more impressively a humble and gracious person with whom I was blessed to compete with, and even against.

One of my most memorable experiences of Coach Tooley in track is her yellow rain-suit, her epic itineraries before state meets, her distinctive yelling voice, and her passion for the sport. Her voice and the voice of my parents were the only voices I could hear while running a race. I would usually be coming around the last curve of the 400 and hear her motivational yelling. She wasn't all-consumed with success, but cared for us and our well-being, as I found out to a greater extent when I was injured and couldn't compete.

The image of Coach Lahm riding his bike alongside us during cross country practice, yelling out times. Traveling to random, in-the-middle-of-nowhere country roads for practice that Mr. Lahm would find on Google

Earth was a sign of his dedication to our practice excellence, though usually dreaded in the moment. His technicality of finding our pace time, E-pace, T-pace, R-pace, not only illuminated his mathematical side, but also his commitment to making us the best runners we could be.

I learned numerous lessons from my time at Scotus, many of which I am still discovering. Through sports I discovered the meaning of discipline and dedication, and how to be confident, yet exercise humility. I found that generosity and giving of myself allowed me to come out of a self-focused world and that leadership is about leading by example toward a greater good. I learned that suffering is finite, and that at times our comfort must be sacrificed for the good of something better.

During my time as a Shamrock athlete, I began to discover how our faith intertwines with many aspects of sports and that God is involved in even the seemingly insignificant events of our lives. Praying before meets and races in high school started a routine in my life which carried throughout my college career.

Particularly during my senior year, I learned that there is much more to life than school and sports. At the beginning of my senior track season, I found out that I had a potentially career-damaging stress fracture in my foot. I competed in the last four meets and was able to be successful at my last state track meet. This experience, although frustrating at the time, gave me the opportunity to grow as a person and realize that my identity was not dependent on what I did.

One of the funniest, and most embarrassing stories from my cross country time was at my first meet. Being a sprinter, I got nervous as the gun went off and sprinted the first 800 meters almost as fast as I could. Needless to say I was ahead by a substantial amount after the first 800, but after this realized I had another two miles to run and was forced to slow down so I could finish. I learned my lesson and didn't sprint out again, but was entered in the 800 a few times during track season.

At the time I didn't realize how incredible being a Shamrock athlete was, but looking back I continue to see how blessed I was to have this opportunity! It has continued to show forth in who I am as a person and even where I am today. There is no doubt in my mind that I would now be who I am or where I am if I had not participated in Shamrock athletics, and I will be forever grateful to the opportunities I had while attending high school at Scotus!

Jordan Chohon

Scotus High School 2008 - 2012

- Two-time All-State volleyball, 2010 - 2011
- Three-time All-State soccer, 2010, 2011, 2012
- Two-time state volleyball champion 2009, 2011
- School record holder career assists (2,322) and career serving points (681)
- Scotus Athlete of the Year, 2012

To me, being a Shamrock athlete meant you were a part of a family.

A great memory was winning a state championship in volleyball my sophomore year and pulling off the upset. However, my favorite memory was winning the state volleyball championship my senior year when we went undefeated.

A funny story about Coach Petersen: one time I remember him drop-kicking a volleyball when he was angry and everyone (including Coach Tooley) couldn't contain their laughter. What made it even funnier was that the volleyball landed on a ball cart.

The best athlete I played with was Tiffany Haney; she is an amazing competitor.

The greatest influence on me as an athlete was Coach John Petersen. I absolutely loved playing for Coach Petersen in volleyball and for Coach Kristie Brezenski in soccer. They are intense, but I loved the pressure!

During my time at Scotus, I tried to be hard working, a good teammate, and a leader. I learned all of these by competing in athletics.

Once a Shamrock, ALWAYS a Shamrock!

Morgan Benesch

Scotus High School 2009 - 2013

- Four-time All-State in cross country
- #3 finish in the state cross country meet in 2009, and #2 finish in 2010, 2011, 2012
- Member of the state cross country championship team, 2012
- School record holder for home course – 4K (15:13:00)
- School record holder for state course – 5K (14:57:00)

To me, being a Shamrock athlete was much more than just competing for myself. It was about bringing pride to the Scotus community and continuing a tradition of hard work and success. It was about winning with pride but learning to lose with grace. To me being a Scotus athlete was about working your hardest every day, and having fun doing it.

Coach Lahm had the greatest influence on me; he believed in my potential more than I did and taught me to go after my aspirations whole-heartedly.

My most memorable race was running at our home cross country meet my senior year. I had never beaten Marissa DeWispelare, someone I had battled against in nearly every race since junior high, and I was running stride for stride with her down the home stretch. I edged her out at the very end to win the race and break the school record for the Lutjelusche course with a time of 15:13, which was over 20 seconds faster than I had previously run at our course.

Although there were many fantastic athletes that I was blessed to be able to have as teammates, the one that stands out who really pushed me the most was Amber Ewers. She led by example and really showed me what hard work and leadership was about. We pushed each other every day at practice and it paid off.

The best athlete I ran against was Marissa DeWispelare from Aquinas. From junior high track to even competing in college now she has always been one of my toughest competitors to face. She's an exceptional person to be able to compete against and have that history of racing with.

Running for Coach Lahm and Coach Tooley was a great honor. They were two coaches that helped me to realize my potential and pushed me daily to reach it. They taught me accountability, desire, determination and humility through their actions. The lessons I learned from them go way beyond the sport of running and are qualities that will help me to be successful in my future career.

I am most proud of helping lead our cross country team to a state championship my senior year. To work so hard for something from our freshman to senior year and finally have it pay off was very rewarding. The bonds and friendships I made with my teammates and the journey it took us to get there will be memories that last a lifetime.

Being an athlete and a student at Scotus taught me about hard work. In order to be good at what you do, you can't just sit around and wait for it to happen. You can't depend on others to bring the success. You have to be willing to give all of your focus and attention to excel in whatever the sport or subject may be. It taught me how to be a leader through leading by example. In order to except your teammates to give 100% of themselves to the team, you must first show them that you yourself are willing to go above and beyond for the sake of the team.

Cody Zimmerman

Scotus High School 2010 - 2014

- All-State football kicker, 2013
- Three-time All-State soccer, 2012, 2013, 2014
- Member of the state champion soccer team, 2014
- Holds three school records for assists: game (4), season (18), career (35)
- Scotus Athlete of the Year, 2014

Being a Shamrock athlete was very special; it was special being a part of a team and competing with your best friends on the field.

Coach Jon Brezenski had the greatest influence on me as an athlete. I played for Coach Brezenski my whole life; he always pushed us to be our best.

Wining the state soccer championship my senior year is my fondest memory. The atmosphere before the championship game was memorable.

The best athlete I played with was Ryan Fuchs. The best athlete I played against was Brock Fitzgerald (Lincoln Pius X).

The life lessons I learned while a Shamrock athlete were time management, how to communicate with teammates differently as a captain, and how to control my emotions.

I'll never forget the feeling of embracing my fellow teammate and friend, Ryan Fuchs, and Coach Brezenski after winning the state soccer championship my senior year. It was something we had all worked for since about the age of ten and it finally happened after all the hard work we put into it!

Emily Kosch

Scotus High School 2010 - 2014

- Two-time All-State soccer, 2013, 2014
- Member 2011 state volleyball championship team

For me being an athlete at Scotus was something to be proud about. It meant that you put a lot of hard work, dedication, and teamwork to play sports that you love.

My coaches played a big part on me as an athlete at Scotus. I think in any sport your coach influences you to be the best you can be and to work hard, and I definitely had those influences from my coaches at Scotus.

I would like to forget the feeling of losing my last volleyball game my senior year. It was a horrible feeling of sadness and frustration, and something that has pushed me to never feel that way again. That feeling/memory has made me work much harder in anything I do now.

I remember riding the bus to state soccer, I believe it was my junior year. Scotus had just gotten a new bus and we took it to state. Well most of the girls got their own seat and I remember at one time we were driving on a bunch of bumps, and girls were literally flying out of their seats and hitting their heads on the ceiling. It was pretty funny.

My freshman year in soccer, we played against two great Skutt players, Mayme Conroy and Liz Bartels, together they were amazing. I remember standing next to Mayme, at one point while we played them at state, and

I think I had to look up a whole foot, she was just giant and an awesome player!

I played for two great coaches, Coach John Petersen and Coach Kristie Brezenski.

Playing for Coach Petersen was tough, you had to be mentally checked into practice at all times. Practices were always intense but they were really competitive and fun.

The most memorable experience I have from Coach Petersen was when he got really upset with us one day at practice and kicked a volleyball and it hit the ceiling. It was pretty scary but once it hit the ceiling it was also really hard not to laugh.

Playing for Coach Brezenski, every day was a learning experience. We were always learning new drills, and different ways to play on the field. It was really fun and I credit her coaching to helping me become the soccer player I am today.

I am most proud of my teams' accomplishments throughout my years at Scotus, in both sports that I played. For volleyball, that entails first at districts for the three years I was on varsity, and first, second, and fourth place at State. For soccer, we were also first at districts all four years I was on varsity, and we made it to state all four years as well. I'm also proud of the lessons I learned through playing these sports; teamwork, sportsmanship, respect, communication, and how to have fun while being competitive.

Being a student athlete takes a lot of time management and dedication, both to school and the sports you're playing. I learned through Scotus how to manage and balance being a student and an athlete. Other life lessons I've learned are teamwork, communication, and respect. All of these, which you learn through sports, are also things we learned in the classroom at Scotus.

A story that I talk about a lot when I think of playing soccer at Scotus is one of the best games I ever played in, and that was my senior year against Pius. Our head coach, Coach Kristie Brezenski couldn't make it to the game so we had the boys head coach, Coach Jon Brezenski coaching us. The weather that day was horrible, windy, rainy, and cold. We didn't start off too well and at half time we were down 2-0. Second half we came out and played amazing and ended up winning 3-2. It is one game I will truly never forget, mostly because it was being videotaped so I still have the recording of it.

Grant Lahm

Scotus High School 2010 - 2014

- Two-time All-State basketball, 2013 - 2014
- Member of 2015 state runner-up basketball team
- Scotus Athlete of the Year, 2015
- Holds seven school basketball records: points scored season (587), points scored career (1,970), three-pointers game (8), three-pointers season (105), three-pointers career (300), three-point % Season (49.0%), three-point % career (46.0%)
- Member of school record 1600m relay team (3:25:67)

It was an honor to be a Shamrock because Scotus has such a rich athletic history. Schools were scared when the saw Scotus on their schedule.

My dad, Merlin Lahm, was the greatest influence on me as an athlete. He pushed me to be the best I could be since I was a young age. One of the best lessons he taught me was, "There are only two things you can control: your attitude and your effort."

I'll never forget jumping into Garret Shanle's arms after winning the state semifinal game in basketball against Wahoo Neumann. After that, we both ran into the student section and Coach Ohnoutka had to get us out.

My favorite player to play with was my brother, Derek Lahm. Even though we didn't get along all the time, he always had my back.

Coach Ohnoutka was great. He truly loves all his players and always goes out of his way to make sure his players are comfortable. I was blessed to play in the Nebraska Coaches Association All-Star game with Coach O as my coach (I got to call him "Jeff" for a weekend).

I am most proud of my work with future Shamrocks. I loved working with kids and youth basketball and football camps. I'd like to think I got kids excited about going to Scotus.

One thing I learned while an athlete at Scotus, is that people are always watching you so you have to act with class. At games or even outside of Scotus activities, there are kids who look up to athletes so you always have to have high character and reflect the image of your school well.

My senior year of basketball, we were playing Grand Island Central Catholic in Grand Island, and I believe Jackson Kumpf found a Mike Wazowski costume (from the Disney movie "Monsters, Inc.") on their stage in the gym. We snuck it on to the bus before the coaches came on and we thought we'd get away with it. The minute Coach O came on the bus he said, "If that damn costume is on the bus, you guys are going to run all day tomorrow." Jackson ran it back as fast as he could.

After every game, I would find Morgan Putnam and give her a hug. Morgan has Down's Syndrome and is the sister of former teammate Miles Putnam. I just loved that, after every hug, she just had the biggest smile on her face. She was our #1 fan, and I love you Morgan!

Payton Chohon

Scotus High School 2010 - 2014

- Two-time All-State volleyball, 2012-2013
- Member of the state champion volleyball team, 2011
- Two-time All-State soccer, 2013-2014

Being a Shamrock athlete meant having good character on and off the court. And, to work hard at everything you do.

One of my fondest memories is winning our district final game in basketball my sophomore year. A memory I'd like to forget is losing 5-1 to Omaha Skutt in the semifinals in soccer my senior year. Although we lost my junior year against Kearney Catholic in volleyball, we all played amazing. Everyone thought they'd blow us out.

The best athletes I played with were Jordan Chohon or Kara Moore. The best athletes I played against were Liz Bartels and Sadie Murran.

The greatest influence on me as an athlete was Coach John Petersen. Playing for Coach Petersen was intense, but fun. Coach Petersen would sometimes chew me out one moment and then tell me "Good Job!" the next. I am most proud of competing at state in all three sports I played.

One lesson I learned as an athlete is time management, and also how important team chemistry is. The relationships we formed with one another were also important.

Alec Foltz

Scotus High School 2011 - 2015

- Super-State soccer player, 2015
- Starter on three-time state champion soccer teams, 2014-2016
- First-ever Scotus gold medal winner at state wrestling (145 lb.), 2015

Shamrock athletes have always maintained a high standard of excellence and success. I wanted to uphold that standard and make the school proud of me. I took great pride in being a Shamrock and always wanted to represent my school's colors to the best of my ability.

My soccer coach, Jon Brezenski, taught me the most about being a Scotus athlete because, as an alumnus, he knew exactly what it meant. He was a great role model, and knew how to get the most out of his athletes while at the same time making it fun. He genuinely cared about his athletes as people first, and athletes second.

A fondest memory is driving to state soccer and listening to loud music on speakers in the bus, and once we got close to Morrison Stadium, listening to the song "Waving Flag". The ride down to Omaha is very exciting and talkative, but once the song starts playing, the bus is silenced and everyone begins to sharpen their focus on the task at hand.

The Kearney Catholic football playoff game, my junior year was memorable because it was a half day of school, and we played at 3:00 p.m. The whole school was buzzing with excitement and even though we lost, it set the tone for next year's state title.

The best athlete I played with was classmate Jake Bos – he was a great all-around, natural athlete. He pushed all of us to be better. The best opponent was Trevor Nichelson from Ashland-Greenwood. I competed against him on the football field and in wrestling. He had potential to go D1 in either sport.

All of my head coaches were very devoted to the sports and players they coach. They cared about their players and drove my teammates and me to be the best we could be.

I am most proud of representing my school and wrestling team in the "Parade of Champions" at state wrestling - walking out of the dark tunnel in the Century Link Center in Omaha while thousands of people are shouting and clapping. There is no other feeling like it!

I learned that hard work pays off! I also learned that sometimes you have to overcome obstacles such as injuries or loses that get in your way of success. When it doesn't work out the way you wanted it to the first time, you have to change the way you approach it and try again.

Participating in sports to me wasn't always just about the sport itself, but rather, being a part of a team and the brotherhood and loyalty that developed between my teammates and me.

When wrestling for my state title, I faced an opponent who I had previously wrestled two other times. Beating a tough opponent twice is never easy, but beating him a third time, I knew would be a real challenge. Coming out of the match victorious is a feeling of accomplishment I'll never forget!

I'm proud of being part of a class with amazing athletes. I think, as a class, we make our mark, a lasting impression on Scotus!

I want to thank my parents for always supporting me in everything I ever did at Scotus and all the benefactors who helped make my success possible. And to the future Scotus athletes – keep the great tradition going!!!

Marcus Dodson

Scotus High School 2012 - 2016

- State wrestling gold medal winner (160 lb.), 2016
- All-State football linebacker, 2015
- Member of the state championship football team, 2015
- Member of the three-time state champion soccer team, 2014, 2015, 2016

I remember transferring over to Scotus my 8th grade year. I was in the student section cheering for the state championship volleyball team. It was hype. It was then I started to bleed green. Ever since I've loved to compete for my school, and to be part of something bigger then myself.

As far as the most influential person on me, it was a combination of my coaches and my teammates. They pushed me to be better every year. Some of my football teammates' 'interesting' pregame rituals were pretty memorable. I can't talk about them here, just know they were pretty funny. I'd like to be able to forget them, but some things you just can't unsee…

My most memorable game day experience is winning state football and getting to play at Memorial Stadium was my most memorable experience. The atmosphere was insane. I felt so small playing in such a big place. It was a humbling experience.

Jake Bos is hands down was the best Scotus athlete I competed with. It's easy to make yourself better when your practices are five times harder than the games. I had to find a way to take Jake down in wrestling or tackle him in football, every single day. It just made me better.

Vincent Thatcher, a 145-pounder from Crete was the best athlete I competed against. At 5'2 he was practically a mini Hulk. It was my freshman year. I felt it was impossible to wrestle someone as strong and explosive as him. I still have nightmares...

Each sport had its own coaching personality. In football it was serious business. Coach Linder was a business-like head coach. We all knew our jobs and executed them. Coach Krienke had some golden one-liners.

In wrestling my dad was the head coach. It put a little extra stress on the sport. All of our wrestling coaches were always very passionate about the sport and they went to great lengths to get us where we needed to be.

In soccer, Coach Brezenski was a good mix of fun and business. He let us have a little more fun because he knew we played better when we were having fun. Of all the sports I looked forward to going to soccer practice the most. Under him we had fun but we knew when we needed to get serious.

Honestly it's too hard to decide between winning state football, state wrestling or state soccer as to which I am most proud of. Winning state football and soccer was amazing because of the teams' chemistry. We had been together for so long and to achieve our ultimate goal and go out on top with my friends was an unbelievable feeling of accomplishment.

State wrestling was more of an individual goal of mine. I had dreamt of earning that gold medal since I was really young. Winning state wrestling took the most discipline and mental toughness to achieve and it was the most gratifying.

There were lots of life lessons I learned at Scotus, a few are: You have to take risks to succeed; you can't just play it safe all the time. You need to learn from your mistakes, not let them drag you down. Make friends, it's more about who you know, not what you know.

My first ever varsity football game I played in, we were playing Aquinas. I sacked the quarterback and I got really excited. When I got off him, the ref put his hand up to signify fourth down. I thought he was going up for a high five, so I high-fived the ref and it was caught it on film. I've been made fun of ever since.

In eighth grade many of our coaches and the upperclassmen said that my class wasn't going to amount to anything in high school. We went on to win multiple state championships and earn many other awards and medals. It felt good proving them wrong.

THE COACHES AND BOOSTERS

Marc Wolfe

Scotus High School – Class of 1978

- Football Clock Operator 1982 - Present
- Basketball Clock Operator 1984 - Present
- Volleyball Clock Operator 2005 - Present
- Track Finish Line Worker 1979 – Present

For me, what it means to be a Shamrock Booster is to support the school and to continue the traditions that came before us. The greatest influence on me was probably my dad, Wayne Wolfe. He joined the Shamrock Club and helped at events long before I was in high school.

My most memorable game day experience was being the clock operator for the first NSAA state football championship game vs. Gothenburg in 1984. Another was the 2015 state football championship game vs. Norfolk Catholic. A great football game just to be at, besides getting the win. A memory I'd like to forget is the loss to Aurora in the district basketball final in 1975. The '75 team was a great team that didn't make the State Tournament. There were also the losses in the 1977 football season to Schuyler and Wahoo Neumann; the Schuyler game was tough because we let it get away, and the loss at Neumann as we had a win taken away in many forms.

I think the best Shamrock athlete I ever saw was Glen Kucera. He was an outstanding three-sport star. Glen could have played either football or basketball at the next level. For the girls' athletes, I would say Kristie Korth. Once again, Kristie was an outstanding three-sport star, and may have been one of the best defensive players I have seen in basketball, as opponents had an extremely difficult time getting the ball up the court on her. Kristie had outstanding instincts and quick hands.

The best opposing athlete I have seen play against Scotus was maybe Wes Eikmeier in basketball from Fremont Bergan. He was a great scorer, but also a very good team player. He went on to Iowa State before transferring to Colorado State to finish his career.

I am most proud of participating in the continuing success of the athletic programs. There have been very few down years, and maybe the current success over the last two years would be the highlight. Having the boy's teams finish in the top 10 in every sport in 2014-15, and the girls only miss out in two sports would top the list, with the run continuing in the 2015-16 year.

Al Niedbalski

Scotus High School – Class of 1971

- Co-founder of the Alumni basketball tournament, 1984
- Longtime Shamrock Club member and officer
- Scotus School Board member and President
- Public address announcer for football, volleyball, and basketball, 2001-present
- Shamrock Athletic Hall of Fame inductee, 2016

For me, being a Shamrock booster means most simply, being able to give something back to an institution that had given much to me. It also meant that I was helping to provide a good foundation for my children, who are now also alumni.

Frank Spenceri has had the greatest impact on my role as a Shamrock booster. He is the one who got me involved first with the Shamrock Night, then the Gala, and finally as a committee member on the Alumni basketball tournament.

My favorite memory comes from my days as a member of the football team – in fact, there are many stories that could be told. One I remember is, after football practice one day, Bill Kosch somehow started up a little motorcycle that Jim Shonka would drive to school, and drove it up the steps, and into the locker room, then just sat there, revving it up. Took a long time for the blue haze to clear the room.

My most memorable game-day experience was during my freshman or sophomore year, we were playing at Pawnee Park late in the season. I think the opponent was Omaha Cathedral. Back then, the light poles were still situated inside the running track, next to the field. It started snowing about kick-off, and really snowed hard, so much so that you could not see the stadium, or the fans, because they were behind the light poles. Late in the game, two white pigeons who had become disoriented by the storm, saw the lights, and landed on the field. All you could hear from behind us, because you could not see them, were the fans yelling: Look, it's the Holy Ghost!

Without a doubt, the best Scotus athlete was Joe Blahak, followed closely by Bill Kosch. Joe was a natural; strong and fast. He could do about anything, whether it was football, basketball, or track. I think at one time, he held at least six event records in track. He made everything look so effortless. Bill, on the other hand, had to work hard, but he was not averse to it. No one worked harder at his game than Bill did. He may not have been as natural a talent as Joe, but with all of his effort and work he put in, he was just as effective and successful.

Best opposing athlete? Probably Chuck Jura and Gene Harmon from Schuyler. Aquinas always had some nice athletes also, but none come to mind.

As the public address announcer, I take pride in being able to highlight the accomplishments of all Scotus students, whether it is football, volleyball, golf, track, as well as fine arts, such as dramas, musicals, speech, and so on. I try also to be very aware of how my efforts present the image of Scotus to our visiting guests, from wherever they may be from.

One story that I want to relate just happened this past year: There is a young man, Ryan Mustard, who as a junior in the summer of 2015 was representing Scotus at Cornhusker Boys State. While playing flag football at Boys State, he tore his ACL, just prior to his senior season on the football team.

I was recuperating from knee replacement surgery, and would go to physical therapy early, so as not to interfere with work. Every time I would pull up at 6:30 in the morning, just before the physical therapy clinic would open, there would be Ryan, sitting in his car, waiting to work out before going to school that day. Ryan's rehabilitation progressed to the point to where he was allowed to suit up for the last home game of the season. When the score got to a comfortable level, and it was late in the game, Scotus was merely running a few plays to run out the clock. On about the last play, Coach Tyler Linder sent Ryan in the game, to play the safety back in the victory formation.

I was the public address announcer, and, knowing how hard Ryan had worked to get to that point, I could not help myself: "Now entering the game for the first time this season, Number 55, Ryan Mustard!" The crowd cheered, and Ryan raised one fist as he ran on to the field. After the game, I went down to the field to congratulate him, and his mother walked up to me, and gave me a hug. "You didn't have to do that." Janell Mustard said.

Yes, I did.

I still do the public address announcing at the volleyball and basketball games, and my partner at the scorer's table is Marc Wolfe, who runs the clock. Like all Scotus workers, we are all volunteers, and do not get paid. So, our running joke is that when a Scotus player comes to the table to check into a game, we ask them for 25 cents, because that is the only way we get paid for our effort.

One night after a game, I happened to be parked next to Tom Pillen, whose daughter Paige played on the team. As we were getting into our vehicles to leave, I told Paige, "Nice game." She said thank you, and then turned to her dad, and said, "Oh yeah, Dad, you owe Al 75 cents!"

Dean Soulliere

St. Bonaventure High School

Athlete 1950-1954

Coach 1959 - 1965

- Member of the undefeated football team, 1953
- Head coach undefeated football season, 1964
- Head coach for state track runner-up, 1963
- Head coach for state track champions, 1964
- *Lincoln Journal Star* Coach of the Year, 1965
- Shamrock Athletic Hall of Fame inductee, 1999

Coach Cletus Fischer had the biggest influence on me as an athlete. He was very tough and had great personal credentials as he had played for the University of Nebraska and also professionally. We all would do anything he asked. One day in scrimmage, one of my fellow teammates hit me and knocked out my front tooth. When Coach Fischer asked me what was wrong with me, I showed him my missing tooth. He merely looked at me and said, "Now you LOOK like a football player".

Perhaps my most memorable times playing were when we went undefeated in football and I was the quarterback. Coach Fischer even had us on a train to go to Sidney to play the final game. Basketball was great fun and I scored 34 points in a game with Lincoln Cathedral and that record stood for quite some time.

Life lessons from athletics are many. You learn discipline, dedication, teamwork and then you must learn to handle the losses as well as the victories. I feel that you learn to set goals and learn what it takes to achieve them. The friendships and camaraderie are priceless.

Upon graduation from Scotus, serving in the Army and graduating from college, Father Timothy Healy came to me and offered me the coaching job at St. Bonaventure if I would be the assistant coach the first year. My wife, Colleen and I had contracts to teach in California but found the idea of returning to St. Bon's as a coach very appealing.

The first year that I was head coach was difficult as we only had a few returning football players. I had to talk several boys into even coming out for football and track. Bill Backes was a standout that year.

We continued to get better each year until we were undefeated in 1964 and became St. Bonaventure's first undefeated football team since 1953, which was coached by Coach Fischer. Competing in Class B, the Shamrocks finished third among 64 schools in the final state ranking, and we were the top scoring team of all 11-man classes, scoring 322 points that season. We were also the Central Catholic Conference champion.

The *Omaha World-Herald* named senior Keith Johnson to the Class B All-State team and senior Mike Shonka was named honorable mention. The *Lincoln Journal Star* recognized seniors Keith Johnson, Ty Jarosz and John Iossi as honorable mention.

That same year, Columbus High School had their first undefeated football season since 1944. The Columbus community sponsored a banquet attended by more than 700 guests to honor both teams. Since I also played on the undefeated 1953 Shamrock team, I received a special honor; and the Columbus community showed its appreciation by sending the head coaches and spouses to the Cotton Bowl game in Dallas to watch Nebraska play Arkansas.

The greatest influence on me as a Shamrock Coach was Coach Fischer. He was very disciplined and always pushed us to be better. He believed in rules and was always consistent and enforced them. One of my classmates said that he was afraid to even "set his pencil down wrong on his desk", but we also had a lot of fun.

Competing against Holy Name and Aquinas were always the most memorable at that time. We were all very happy in 1964 when we beat Aquinas 6-0.

I coached many wonderful, talented athletes and am reluctant to single out any individually, but Larry Liss, Dave Kudron, Bill and Dave Backes, Ty Jarosz, Bill and Mike Shonka, John Iossi, Larry Kretz and Tony Weidner were among them. The athletes were not only talented, but they seemed to have an extra competiveness and discipline.

Perhaps my most memorable experience as a coach was when we were undefeated in football and state champions in track. Our track team had been runner-up at state in 1963.

Watching the boys perform, trying to figure out the best way to get points, praying that the hurdlers didn't trip, the dead heat finishes were all extremely exciting. Winning the Class B championship and having two gold medal winners in Larry Liss and Dave Kudron along with the valuable contributions of every other runner was exhilarating.

I am very proud that so many of the athletes went on and competed in college.

I am also very proud of the fact that at that time, our Shamrock Club was able to attract top speakers from around the country to speak at our Athletic Banquet. I remember one of our meetings in 1964 when we discussed who we should get. I suggested we get "The Best" who happened to be Johnny Unitas. I went home that night and asked my wife, Colleen to write him a letter. I endured some teasing about hearing from "my Buddy" when one day we actually received his positive response. He came and spoke, and that was the beginning of several years when we attracted high profile speakers that even colleges around were not having. Our athletes got to hear from the very best!

It was a great honor to be named "Coach of the Year" by the *Lincoln Journal Star* in 1965. I felt grateful for the outstanding young men that I had the privilege to coach.

Claire Stramel

Scotus High School 1967 - 1971

- Head coach for the 1967 Class C state football champions

I did not realize at the time the tradition at Scotus, but was excited to coach the Shamrocks. After we signed a contract, my wife Sharon taught Home Economics for two years and I was coaching football and was doing some teaching and counseling which was rare in those days. The fans, players and I were not happy when there was a loss. The players worked very hard to rectify this situation and I thank my assistant coaches Jim Puetz and Vern Younger for their suggestions and help. The coaches were all new that year so it was interesting to coach and many decisions were made at the last minute. We were later selected by the *Omaha World-Herald* as state champions my first year at Scotus. This was extremely important to Scotus and our athletes. I think the overall respect by the community was a big influence on our decision to teach and coach for several years. It took a couple of years for me to realize how much it meant to be a coach at Columbus Scotus.

In terms of influences I have had on coaching, my college coach said if you have speed, spread them out and run the ball. Well, we had great speed with Joe Blahak and Bill Kosch and our line was very quick.

We taught the line technique instead of being physical and we were successful.

At our first practice I asked all the lineman to go with Coach Puetz. Six kids walked over to the side. We knew we had to make some lineman out of some good athletes who wanted to be backs but they soon bought into playing their new position.

I received many suggestions on how to run the program and I always tried to listen and then evaluate. I realized that results would ultimately be my responsibility. I had an instinct on what to do and that is how I made my decisions at game time.

I had many fond memories and it usually happened on the bus ride home, mentally reviewing how the kids responded to different situations.

Funniest: These are my memories about football. I know there were other moments that the other coaches would possibly share with the programs they coached.

At our very first home game that I coached we (coaches) found out that the Shamrock players sat on the east side of the field. I thought, "OK, no problem", but we must have had a hundred alumni over there along the sidelines and there were no restraints (there was mass confusion). We had a hard time finding players. At one point I was asking the other coaches what happened to our cornerback? Where is he? They told me he was out. I looked around and he was over visiting with a man in a suit. I walked over and asked what was going on? The back held up his hand and I could see that he had a broken finger. I grabbed his hand and pulled on the finger and popped it back into position. I quickly wrapped it with tape and said "get your butt back in there". The man in the suit then stuck out his hand and said "Coach, I am Dr. Sojka, your team physician, you did the right thing and have him come in and see me in a couple of days". The next home game we decided to be on the west side (grandstand) and so we ended a home game tradition of having Scotus players on the east side of the field.

Another interesting and I thought funny story was: We were playing our arch-rivals David City Aquinas at David City. One of our lineman came out of the game holding his stomach and we thought he had taken a low hit. We told him to lie down on his back and try to relax. One the Aquinas fans hollered at me telling me we had a man down. I was trying to ignore him when he shouted out "He is only interested in the money and not his players". I obviously was not making a lot of money and we coaches laughed at that comment for a long time.

Lyle Nannen was the coach at West Point Central Catholic and we always played them the first game of the season. We always had a soap scrimmage the weekend before our first game under the lights. Lyle would always come and scout us. One year as we went out on the field we noticed a sign at the top of the grandstands on the east side. The sign said "THIS SEAT IS SAVED FOR LYLE NANNEN". Below the sign was a white toilet seat. Lyle later admitted, "That was a good one".

Another experience which shows the good attitude and strength of our players was on the first home game one of the captains came to me and said we have a tradition here to make a visit at church before we get on the bus to go to the field. I had not researched the traditions enough to know this but the kids were able to come forward and let us coaches know.

The game I still remember the most is the night we were playing Cathedral for the conference title. Both teams had won their division and played for the league championship. We were leading by a few points with only a few seconds to go in the game. On a 4th and long their quarterback threw up a "dying quail" and our defensive back was waiting for it to come down and suddenly slipped and fell allowing the offensive end to catch the ball and go to the end zone and Cathedral won the game.

I have to mention two players who had great talent and were very coachable: Joe Blahak and Bill Kosch. We also had a lot of hard working kids who had the desire and positive attitude to get the job done.

Two athletes that I thought were very good was Gene Harmon from Schuyler and John Howell from Cathedral. The best coach I coached against was Roger Higgins from Omaha Cathedral.

One memorable experience I had was we had just moved into a new apartment in Columbus and I looked out the window and there were two or three carloads of boys out in front of our house. I went out to see what was going on and they were all football players and introduced themselves and wanted to welcome us to Columbus Scotus. We were very impressed and they let me know that several would-be starters and players had transferred out of Scotus and that they were anxious to prove they could do the job for Scotus. We won the Class C state championship the first year.

We had high expectations of the athletes and their conduct during the game. The athletes were very good at maintaining those standards and rarely gave excuses or blamed others for their inability to get the job done. I was also proud of our winning record over the four years I coached there. I think winning the Class C state championship our first year was a very proud moment for me.

In the fall of 2015, I had a call from Joe Blahak who was a great athlete for Scotus and I was fortunate to coach him in football his junior and senior year. Joe went on to play at the University of Nebraska and was All-Big Eight for three years and was a starter on the two national championship teams in 1970 and 1971. He played for the Minnesota Vikings in Super Bowl IX. The NFL celebrated the 50th anniversary of the Super Bowl this past year and presented a gold football to any players who played in a Super Bowl. The award was presented to the high school that the player attended. Joe called me and asked if I could be there when the football was presented to Scotus Central Catholic High School. My wife and I did attend that game with Joe and his family. I was proud of Joe for his accomplishments and that Scotus High School has an opportunity to apply for a $5,000 grant from the NFL.

Thanks for the opportunity to share some of my memories about four very good years of my coaching, teaching and counseling years.

Frank Spenceri

Scotus High School 1970 - 1988

- Head boys basketball coach, 1970-1988
- Head cross country coach, 1970-1988
- Head golf coach, 1973-88
- Assistant football coach, 1970-72
- Athletic director, 1978-1988
- Head coach, Nebraska Coaches Association All-Star basketball game, 1980
- Shamrock Athletic Hall of Fame inductee, 1999

In May 1970, Pat, I, and our children Scott and Lisa pulled into Columbus, Nebraska. And for the next 18 years Columbus Scotus became a very impactful influence on our family – a very positive, fun, and emotional impact.

The years I spent as head coach in basketball, cross country, and golf and as an assistant coach in football, were years filled with a whole bunch of great memories.

What made the "Shamrock Impact" so positive was a host of reasons: Great school with a fantastic tradition, very involved alumni, very caring and involved parents, a super school staff and most important a very talented and hard-working group of student-athletes to work with.

My fondest memories are the relationships with all the great parents, alumni, athletes, and staff. Scotus is very lucky to have an outstanding mix of all of those people. It's something that not every school has, and I cherished the chance to work with so many great people.

Over the years, I've had many mentors in the coaching profession, most especially Don Leahy and Tom Brosnihan, my football, basketball, and baseball coaches at Creighton Prep. Another mentor was Dud Allen, who hired me as an assistant basketball coach at Omaha Holy Name while I was still attending college.

I've always viewed the role of the coach as the maestro of an orchestra, whose job it is to get each musician to do their job to the best of their individual abilities. In high school the athletes change each year, so it's up to the coach to make changes that will allow that year's mix of athletes to reach their full potential.

Coaching for so many years, there are countless great memories. Some of the ones that really stand out were the win over Aquinas in the district tournament in 1975 (our first win over them in three years); the last-second loss to Aurora in the 1975 districts; our games at the state tournament in 1981 and 1982; the final game at Memorial Hall in 1980 when we rallied to beat Aquinas 60-56; and the first game in the Dowd Activity Center a couple weeks later when we beat undefeated Council Bluffs St. Albert; the 82-81 triple overtime win over Lakeview in districts in 1974; the 102-96 win over Wahoo Neumann in 1974 when Conrad Slusarski had 40 points and Gregg Grubaugh had 34. And of course, winning the 1981 state championship in golf at the Elks Country Club was something I'll never forget.

One humorous incident I remember was when Gregg Grubaugh was a freshman. He had outstanding talent and I moved him up to the varsity. We didn't have enough varsity uniforms for him to get one, so I dug around and found an old one that sort of matched our varsity jerseys. Unfortunately, it was too big for Gregg. He told me that he wasn't ready to play varsity and that he didn't want to go out on the court in that uniform. I told him to "get in the game and shoot the ball". He did – and that was the beginning of an incredible career.

Over the years, I was blessed to coach many great athletes. Obviously, Gregg Grubaugh and Bret Kumpf would right at the top of that list. Others would have to include Chris Hoffman, Steve Heimann, Pat Engelbert, Mark Brezinski, Jim Feehan, and Tim Engelbert. And I had the chance to coach my son Scott and we were able to make it to the State tournament twice together. That's a memory I will always cherish. A coach is like a jockey on a horse. The jockey doesn't win the race; the horse does. At Scotus, I was lucky to have a lot of good horses to ride.

Coaching as long as I did, I saw many outstanding athletes on opposing teams. Tom Kropp of Aurora, Chuck Jura and Gene Harmon of Schuyler, and Russ Uhing of Hartington Cedar Catholic were among the best.

And opposing coaches – there were many great ones. Dale Kerkman was an assistant coach for me at Omaha Holy Name and went on to be the head coach at Aquinas for many years. Our games against Aquinas in those days were always close and hard-fought and Dale was a great competitor. Jim Kane at Elkhorn Mount Michael, Fred Northrup at Grand Island Central Catholic, and Lyle Nannen at West Point Central Catholic were some of the other outstanding coaches.

The one thing I'm most proud of during my years at Scotus was that we always fielded teams that were exciting to watch and accomplished everything they could. We always left it all on the court and played as hard as we could. That could happen only because the kids were all very coachable.

I was also blessed to be around many other great coaches at Scotus. Jim and Gary Puetz, Vern Younger, John Petersen, Randy Berlin – they were all outstanding coaches and good friends.

Thanks to everyone for everything. God bless you all.

Jim Puetz

Scotus High School 1967 – 2005

- Coached 31 years at Scotus
- Football 1967-2001 (assistant coach 1967-70, head coach 1971-2001)
- Track & field head coach 1967-1993
- Golf head coach 1996-2005
- Career record as a football head coach: 236-96-6
- Football state champions, 1984, 1993
- Track state champions, 1978, 1979
- Track State runner-up, 1969 and 1985, 18 district championships, 19 conference championships
- Nebraska High School Hall of Fame inductee, 2007
- Shamrock Athletic Hall of Fame inductee, 2004
- Nebraska Coaches Association Skip Palrang Award for outstanding contributions to high school football, 2016

Serving as a Shamrock coach meant many things to me – pride, tradition, winning, good athletes, parents, assistant coaches, and community support.

I arrived in 1967, along with Claire Stramel and Vern Younger. We only had five or six boys from both the junior and senior class out for football that first year. About 25 boys from that year's senior class had transferred to Columbus High the previous summer after a disagreement with the superintendent. Despite such low numbers, we had very talented players like Bill Kosch and Joe Blahak and were able to win the Class C state championship that year.

Gene Pillen, my high school coach at David City St. Mary, had a tremendous influence on me, as did Gary Puetz and Vern Younger, who served as assistant coaches with me at Scotus.

There are a couple of funny memories over the years, including kicking a water cooler at halftime in the locker room at Pawnee Park and throwing a helmet into the milo field at Lakeview. The helmet incident was part of a halftime "pep talk" I was giving to the team after what I thought was a poor first half effort. The problem came when it was time to start the second half and we couldn't find the helmet – it belonged to a two-way starter. Luckily, some frantic searching by the managers located the helmet.

Another helmet-tossing incident came at Pawnee Park in 1994. We had played a poor first half after the team attended the funeral for the father of a player earlier that day. Both incidents were followed by good second halves for us and we won both games.

Game-day experiences that stand out were pre-game dinners, team Masses with Fr. Wayne, and the pre-game spirit shown by the players and students.

One game-day experience I'll never forget happened in 1973 in our opening game at Ord. We were leading late in the game with the ball around midfield. Dan Steiner, our outstanding two-way lineman, came out of the game and said he had to use the restroom. I told him to get back in the game, but eventually his position coach, Dale Heth, convinced me to let him use the restroom. A couple plays later, we had to punt – and Steiner was our punter and was still in the restroom. The backup punter (Joe "The Toe" McMeekin) came in but fumbled the snap (it was raining) and Ord recovered and went down to score and win the game at the very end. It was our only loss in a 9-1 season.

I had the opportunity to coach many great athletes at Scotus – Joe Blahak, Bill Kosch, Dan Brock, Dan Steiner, Dave Steiner, Mike Cielocha, Jeff Podraza, Karl Hroza, Jeff Herdzina, Scott Sobota, Brandon Drum, and Chad Mustard. The best athletes I coached against were both from Schuyler – Tim Johnk and Marty Kobza.

Over the years, I faced many great coaches, including Roger Higgins (Omaha Cathedral), Gene Hunting (Schuyler), Ron Mimick (Aquinas), Jeff Beller (Norfolk Catholic), Carl Tesmer (Grand Island CC and

Hastings St. Cecilia), Bob Schnitzler (Battle Creek) and Fr. Bob Roh (Aquinas track).

Lots of memories over the years at Scotus, but the ones that stand out are winning state championships in track (1978 and 1979), football (1984 and 1993) and beating Lincoln Pius X in football in 1997 (they were Class B state champions that year with an outstanding team and we were the only blemish on their record).

I was blessed to have many outstanding athletes over the years, plus a fine coaching staff, including Gary Puetz, Vern Younger, Randy Berlin, and Rick Grubaugh. We also had great support from the community and staff.

Something I'll never forget was the time I was kicked out of the game at Wahoo Neumann. In the first half, Coach Gary Puetz was called for a 15-yard penalty for yelling at the officials. In the second half of the game, I was letting the officials know that I didn't like another one of their calls and I received a penalty. Then the official told me I had to leave the game for a second penalty. Gary told him, "But that penalty in the first half was on ME!" The official told us that a new rule that year meant two penalties on *anybody* on the sideline meant the head coach would automatically be ejected. I guess we missed the rules meeting that year. We had no idea that rule was in effect. I spent the remainder of the game eating a hot dog and visiting with the fans. The person taking films of the game for us noticed me at the concession stand and made sure that he had plenty of footage of me eating that hot dog. By the way, we won that game big.

I also will always remember scouting trips, coaching clinics, and the famous bus race at the 1969 district track meet at Schuyler. In those days, there was a two or three hour break between the afternoon preliminaries and the evening finals. All the coaches from the meet went to Johnnie's Steakhouse to eat. When we got back to the stadium, we found out what our team had been up to while we were gone.

Both the Scotus and Aquinas bus drivers had left the keys in their buses. Kids from both schools decided to race the buses around the parking lot.

Scotus won – our driver was Bob Kosch, who was an amazing athlete. Bob was the kind of athlete who could will people to compete at his level, whether it was football or bus races.

We had a lot of success, so every loss was heart-breaker. At the top of that list is losing on a last-second field goal against Aquinas in the playoffs 1997. We had a great team that year and could have won a state championship. Aquinas ended up winning the state title that year. What was really tough about that loss was the fact that Aquinas didn't kick extra points all year – they always went for two after touchdowns - so they really didn't have a kicking game. But they managed to hit a field goal from more than 40 yards out to beat us.

A couple of other events stand out. In 1992, we were flagged for 60 yards in penalties in a loss at Battle Creek (the rule about the head coach getting ejected after two penalties wasn't in effect yet). And in 1984, we were hosting Omaha Roncalli in the state football semifinals. The Roncalli cheerleaders brought a big banner that they hung on the east stands that read "Beat the Discoverers". The Shamrocks – not the Discoverers – won that night in a great game and we went on to beat Gothenburg for the championship.

In my second year at Scotus (1968), we read somewhere that by lengthening a person's stride, you could make them run faster. So with the help of Bill Kosch's dad, we fashioned a bar that hooked to the back end of a pickup truck. We had three players at a time grab hold of the bar and then we would gradually speed up the pickup as we drove down the street with the players running as fast as they could to keep up. I'm not sure if that helped us get any faster, and luckily nobody got hurt. We only did that for one season.

We also had the best group of student managers over the years that a school could ever have – Gary Witt, Charlie Wilhelm, Tracy Grubaugh, Mike Bernt, and "*The Great One*": John Kopetzky.

Editor's Note: Coach Puetz forgot to mention quite possibly the two greatest athletes he ever had the privilege to coach: Rudy Kolache and Francis the Shotputter. Rudy Kolache led the state in the pole vault, once clearing a then-unheard of height of 14'-2". Francis was also a state leader in the shotput, and had a uniquely "stylistic" shot putting method. Unfortunately, both of these fine athletes was plagued by injuries throughout their career and were not able to compete at many track meets.

Also, unfortunately, they existed only in Coach Puetz's mind (and in Shamrock legend).

Vern Younger

Scotus High School 1967 - 2011

- Forty-four year career of teaching and coaching at Scotus
- Head basketball coach, 1967-70
- Athletic Director, 1970-78
- Freshman football coach, 1967-2007
- Assistant basketball coach, 1970-73
- Assistant track coach, 1967-2011
- Nebraska Coaches Association Assistant Coach of the Year, 1985-86
- Archdiocese of Omaha Teacher of the Year, 2008
- Shamrock Athletic Hall of Fame inductee, 2007

During the spring of 1967 I was hired to be the 1967-1968 Scotus head varsity basketball coach, assistant football coach and assistant track coach as well as be a full-time teacher. Little did I know at the time, I would be coaching against many well-seasoned and excellent coaches such as Jay Muma (Schuyler), Fred Northrup (Grand Island Central Catholic), Jim Kane (Elkhorn Mount Michael), Lyle Nannen (West Point Central Catholic), Roger Higgins (Omaha Cathedral) and Ed Spethman (Fremont Bergan).

Victories were tough to come by during my three years as head basketball coach at Scotus, but during the 1968-1969 season, led by Joe Blahak and Ken Bator, we were able to fashion an eight-game win streak with upset wins over Omaha Cathedral at home and West Point Central Catholic on the road. Many of the players on the 1969-1970 team will probably remember the return trip to Omaha Cathedral. Not only did they humble us on the court with their state championship-to-be team, some of their less than ideal student fans beat up our cars on the way out of town. Tweet Placzek or Tracy Grubaugh could probably expand on this story.

Coach Frank Spenceri took over the Scotus basketball program during 1970-1971 season and I remained in the basketball program as the freshmen coach/bus driver. I'm sure some of Coach's first team members will remember missing the bus for the return trip home after a loss at Elkhorn Mount Michael. Although Coach Spenceri had some rather colorful language at times, he was a great coach and was responsible for resurrecting the Scotus basketball program.

From the 1970-1971 school year through the 1977-1978 school year I was hired to be the Athletic Director at Scotus. Although I ushered in the girls' athletic program at Scotus following the Title IX mandate, I take little credit for the success of the girls' program. Coach Gary Puetz, who I helped hire, was instrumental in the hiring of Coach John Petersen. Boy, were those two great hires and the rest is history.

Coach Jim Puetz was my mentor in football and track. It was totally fun being on his staff for so many years. He let his assistant coaches coach and I was able to be very successful in his program as his freshman coach from 1967-2007. Watching young freshman players become great Scotus athletes was a great joy to me.

In addition to being on the coaching staff of the 1967, 1984 and 1993 State Champions, watching Bill Kosch (one of the very best gamers ever at Scotus) and Joe Blahak (probably the most explosive athlete I have ever seen at Scotus) during my first few years at Scotus and later watching them star in football at Nebraska were defining moments for me in football. It was not difficult to become a Big Red fan coming from Kansas after attending my first Nebraska game and being able to watch Bill and Joe play.

In track, my coaching duties for the most part consisted of coaching the sprinters, hurdlers and the sprint relay. Every modern day Scotus outdoor boys sprint, hurdle and relay record was set by athletes I coached. I take little to no credit for the records set by all-time Scotus great Mike Cielocha, although he was a member of an all-class gold medal 880 relay team that ran 1:29.9 in 1978 that I did coach. Other members of that team were Mike Savage, Vern Kobus and John Heimann. The 400-meter relay record of 42.97 was set in 1985 and was anchored by state 100-meter sprint champion Keith Neal. Other members of that team were versatile hurdler/jumper Jeff Podraza, Robert Miller and my son Dave Younger.

The high hurdle record is still owned by Tom Sobotka. Tom was the Class B state champion in 1976 while running a school record 14.3. The intermediate hurdle record is owned by Ron Starzec who ran a 39.9 in 1981. Eventually the boys and girls programs were combined and I was able to coach Andrea Drum to a 100-meter high hurdle record and Audrey Pfeifer to a 300-meter intermediate record.

Great track memories would include watching Joe Blahak run, jump and do just about everything there was to do in track, being on the staff of the 1978 and 1979 Mike Cielocha-led state championships, watching the smooth-as-silk Tom Sobotka run the hurdles, and not-so-smooth but competitive Ron Mimick, watching the tracksters compete during the Good Friday Relays (always won by the sprinter/hurdlers), watching Karl Hroza jump and Pat Engelbert throw, and watching Ron Starzec crash over the last intermediate hurdle (with a big lead) at conference in 1980 and get up to finish 6th. Ron's 6th place finish enabled the Scotus boys to continue a win or tie streak that would reach 18 consecutive conference championships.

Anyone that has been around Scotus long enough will have witnessed or heard about some of the following funny or not-so-funny events.

Coach Jim Puetz being dismissed from a Wahoo Neumann football game because of a Coach Gary Puetz penalty. The word is Coach Jim was later observed eating a hotdog during the game by the concession stand. Yes, we won big that game.

Scotus going from winning a football game at West Point Central Catholic on a Dave Ebner TD pass reception to losing the game because Dave was called for offensive pass interference. When the dust cleared, the penalties on the Scotus bench were half the distance to our own goal (this was before the two penalties and the head coach is gone rule; not pretty, but comical).

The bus wreck in 1970 on the way home from a basketball loss at Fremont Bergan near the meat packing plant west of Schuyler. No serious injuries, but very scary. We were able to avenge that loss the following week at home.

Losing our opening 1973 football game to Ord on a cool misty night due to Scotus standout Dan Steiner(punter) needing to use the restroom during crunch time. Yes, we needed to punt when he was gone. The snap was dropped and the punt was blocked which led to very late TD by Ord. That was the only loss for that team and I remember it as one of Scotus' best, led by defensive standout Dave Steiner and a host of other good players.

The helmet toss into a milo field at Lakeview, the cooler break at halftime, the floor stomp during a homecoming halftime, the lights going out at Neumann in 1977, etc.

As I said before, it was fun and sometimes very entertaining being on Coach Jim Puetz's' staff. Let's just say Jim is "One of a Kind".

Excluding the Scotus athletes, these are some of the memorable individuals that our teams competed against or I was able to see participate in high school. Seven-footer Chuck Jura led Schuyler to a Class B state championship and beat Scotus during the season. Tom Kropp from Aurora could dominate in any sport. Marty Kobza could throw the shot and discus like nobody I have ever seen. I was one of the officials that measured his state record shot put throw. John Howell, Omaha Cathedral running back. We played against him three times and he rung us up for 750 yards rushing. Ryan Went from Lakeview was another back that was very difficult to stop. Scott Poehling from Fremont Bergan could run like Mike Cielocha. Aaron Brandt from Wahoo Neumann stood alone when it came to the hurdles.

Although I was not real successful during my tenure as Scotus basketball coach, I'm very satisfied that I remained at Scotus for 44 years and coached during most of that time. The bulk of the male athletes and a few of the female athletes mentioned in this book are student/athletes that I have coached at some level and as you can see there are some really great ones.

Being named the Nebraska High School Assistant Coach of the Year in 1985-86, being presented the Service to Scotus Award twice (in 1996 and 2011), being named the Gerhold (2005) and Archdiocese of Omaha (2008) Teacher of the Year and being inducted into the Shamrock Athletic Hall of Fame in 2007 as a coach are highlights of my career at Scotus and are reasons why I will always bleed "GREEN".

Gary Puetz

Scotus High School 1975 – 2016

- Football assistant coach, 1975-2001
- Track assistant coach, 1975-1995
- Athletic Director for 21 years from 1995-2016; Scotus won 34 state championships in that time
- Freshman boys and junior high girls basketball coach
- *Omaha World-Herald* Class C All-Sports Champion, 2014-15 and 2015-16
- NSAA Cup All-School Champion (Class C) 2008-09, 2013-14, 2014-15, 2015-16
- Shamrock Athletic Hall of Fame inductee, 2012

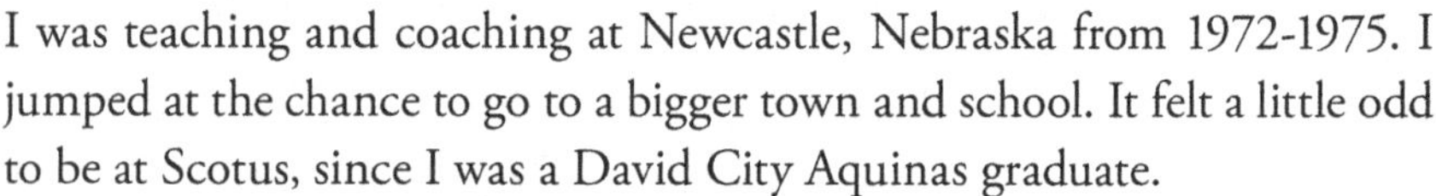

I was teaching and coaching at Newcastle, Nebraska from 1972-1975. I jumped at the chance to go to a bigger town and school. It felt a little odd to be at Scotus, since I was a David City Aquinas graduate.

Any game or meet against Aquinas was a fond memory. It seemed like half of the parents and athletes for Aquinas were my cousins. The state championships we won in football and track were great moments I'll never forget. One memory I'd like to forget is Jim and I getting 60 yards in penalties at Battle Creek in 1992. It didn't affect the outcome of the game; Battle Creek had a great team that year and won the State Championship. I think we played them closer than anyone else all year.

Then there was the time I got Jim Puetz kicked out of a game at Wahoo Neumann (or at least helped him get kicked out). Check out his page for the details on that one.

I don't have a single most memorable game-day experience. There was just an excitement of every competition. Our coaches and kids always worked hard and expectations were always high.

There were many great athletes I coached at Scotus: Jim Feehan, Steve Bonk, Mark Kurtenbach, Bob Klopnieski, Pat Engelbert, Travis Brock, Brandon Drum, and Chad Mustard to name a few. The best athlete I coached against was Tim Johnk of Schuyler.

I competed against many other great coaches. In football, they were Bob Schnitzler of Battle Creek, Gene Hunting of Schuyler, Tim Turman of Neumann, and Ron Mimick of Aquinas, to name a few. The best opposing track coach was Bill Kohl of Elkhorn.

Looking back, my most memorable experiences as a coach included our state football championships in 1984 and 1993 and beating Lincoln Pius X in 1997. Also, coaching my sons Nick and Joe – they were good players and it was an honor to coach them.

The thing I'm most proud of during my years at Scotus is getting to work with so many great people, and the high quality of the kids we coached.

In addition to coaching football and track, I also served as a freshman boys basketball coach in my early years, and helped get junior girls basketball started in the early 1980s. One incident from those years stands out. The other team shot the ball and missed. The Scotus girl got the rebound and looked over at me on the bench and yelled, "COACH! ARE WE ON OFFENSE OR DEFENSE?" The two officials had to stop the game because they were laughing so hard. We've come a long way since then.

The coaching clinics were always a good time over the years. I think all Scotus coaches could tell a lot of stories … but most are best left untold!

It is hard to believe 41 years have gone by. It has been an honor to work with, teach, and coach at Scotus. The quality of the Scotus administrators, faculty, parents, students and staff (especially Annette Hash) have all been great!

Merlin Lahm

Scotus High School 1986-2016

- Head boys basketball coach, 1989-2005
- Assistant boys basketball coach, 1986-88
- Head cross country coach, 2006-16
- Head boys track & field coach, 2009-16; coached six individual state champion jumpers
- Boys cross country state champion coach, 2011
- Girls cross country state champion coach, 2012, 2013, 2016

I arrived at Scotus Central Catholic in 1986, working amidst Hall-of-Fame coaches Jim Puetz, Gary Puetz, Vern Younger, Frank Spenceri, John Petersen, and Dan Mahoney. They were a fine group of mentors from which to learn. Each year our football and boys basketball programs were among the best in the state. Volleyball and girl' basketball were on their way to the same...or greater...level of prominence. The boys track team had earned a state runner-up finish the previous year, and the girls track team was top quality. It was a great time to be a Shamrock.

Those first years I was a high school assistant in basketball and track, and a junior high football coach. When Frank Spenceri retired two years later, I took over the head boys basketball position and gave up coaching football. I was the jump coach in track and, thirty years later, I serve the same duty. Around 1994 we restructured our track staff, and members coached both boys and girls in their events. The 2004-2005 season was my last as head basketball coach. When Dan Mahoney moved out of state the following year, I took over the boys and girls cross country programs. I became the head boys track coach in 2009.

In twenty-nine years of coaching the jumps, athletes in jumping events have won twenty-nine state meet medals and five individual state championships, along with a number of individual runner-up finishes.

The girls track program won one state championship during that time period under head girls coach Janet Tooley. Our boys track team won two of the last three conference championships, and three of the last four district titles. Kris Almquist, Chris Gannon, Tyler Roewert, Jamie Tooley, and Derek Lahm were the jumpers that earned individual state jump titles. Also notable among jumpers is Julie Trouba, who medaled at state in the high jump four times. In addition, since I've been head boys coach, Taylor Suess won the all-class gold medal in the discus, Cody Mroczek won the 400m dash (twice) and also the all-class gold medal in the long jump.

Scotus competed in the boys state basketball tournaments in 1993 and 1996. We had only one losing season from 1988-89 to 1999-2000. That was the 1991-92 season, which we followed with a state tournament appearance in 1993. The most heartbreaking memory I have coaching at Scotus came in the first round of the state tournament in 1996. We lost to Wahoo by one point on a tip at the buzzer in overtime. Wahoo went on to easily win the next two rounds and the state title. We feel like we had a chance to do the same had we kept that tip from occurring. The team in 1996 included future NFL player Chad Mustard, and a number of other fine players.

Another basketball team I remember with pride is the 1999-2000 squad. Though I'm not sure we were the most athletic team on the court in any game we played, this team overachieved to finish the season 12-8. Our goal was to have no more than 12 offensive possessions in each of the first three quarters. We generally were able to do that and broke the school defensive scoring average per game record, which has since been broken. Pat Brockhaus and Father Steve Emanuel were varsity assistants that year. Fr. Emanuel was fond of saying, "You don't have to be a thoroughbred. It's OK to be a mule if you know you're a mule."

Through the years, I have especially enjoyed competition with Aquinas, Neumann, and Lakeview. They seem to be our biggest current rivals. I have fond memories of battles with famous Nebraska high school basketball coaches Jim Kane of Mount Michael, Bob Uhing of Wayne, Wes Sheppard of Lincoln Christian, Kevin Scheef of Aquinas and Wahoo, and Bill Gavers of Grand Island CC. I apologize to the many other notable coaches I've left off this list.

The girls cross country team I coached beginning in 2005 was not far removed from the highest levels of success they'd achieved under Coach Mahoney, but the boys program had not experienced much success at the state level. In 2011, we won the first boys cross country state championship in school history. In 2014 the boys were state runner-up. The girls won state championships in 2012, 2013, and 2016 following a state runner-up performance in 2010. Our program has a current streak unequaled by any other Class C program in the state - qualifying both our girls and boys cross country teams for the state meet each of the past six years.

The finest girl cross country runner I coached was Morgan Benesch. Though she never won an individual state championship (she finished runner-up at state three times and third-place once), Morgan eclipsed the time of all Scotus runners before her, including past Scotus individual state champions. Nebraska has since changed the distance girls run in cross country, so those records will never be broken. The most accomplished male runner I have coached in cross country is Nathan Ostdiek. He finished as the individual runner-up as a junior and as a senior. Nathan has the fastest Scotus time in history on four of six courses we run on, and the second fastest time on the other two courses.

Of course, nothing is possible in coaching without talented and committed athletes. We are fortunate at Scotus to have students who want to be involved. In the 2014-2015 school year, over 91% of the student body was involved in at least one NSAA-sponsored activity, and 95% were in at least one NSAA or school activity. I also attribute our success to the parents, who encourage and support their sons and daughters. We could not survive without the volunteer work of groups like the Shamrock Club, Mother's Club and the individual work of a multitude of individuals.

Some of my most cherished memories involve coaching my own children. I coached each one of our three children in youth basketball, helped coach the boys in baseball, Jessica in cross country, and all three children in track.

In 2012, all three children won a state track meet medal: Derek won the Class B triple jump, Grant placed in the same event, and Jessica earned a medal in the 400m dash.

I greatly appreciate the opportunity to share these reflections. I am humbled to be included with the many wonderful Scotus coaches, athletes, and supporters noted within the covers of this book. Thank you.

John Petersen

Scotus High School 1977-2016

- Coached 36 years at Scotus
- Volleyball head coach, 1977-2013
- Girls basketball head coach, 1977-1999
- 863-136 record in volleyball
- Volleyball state champions 15 times, state runner-up 7 times
- 28 state volleyball tournament appearances
- 14 consecutive state finals appearances, 1993-2006
- 9 undefeated volleyball seasons
- State record (all sports) 115-match winning streak
- 353-148 record in basketball
- State basketball champions three times, state runner-up one time
- Nebraska Coaches Association Volleyball Award for significant contributions to high school volleyball, 2003
- National High School Athletic Coaches Association (NHSACA) National Coach of the Year, 2012
- NHSACA Hall of Fame inductee, 2008
- *Lincoln Journal Star* Coach of the Year, 1994, 2007
- *Omaha World-Herald* Coach of the Year, 1991
- Shamrock Athletic Hall of Fame inductee, 2014

Nearly forty years ago I received a call from a close friend of mine, Gary Puetz. We had taught together in Newcastle, Nebraska for three years. He had left two years earlier to join his brother Jim at Scotus Central Catholic. I was currently teaching at Little Rock, Iowa. It seems like yesterday when he called to inform me that there was a math teaching job along with head volleyball and girls basketball coaching positions. My wife Marilyn and our two young daughters Amy and Jessie made the move south and I guess the rest is history. I cannot imagine that there could have been a better place for my family and me. What a great ride it has been!

It was 1977 and the Scotus girls athletic programs were in still in their infancies as volleyball and track had been in existence for less than 10 years. Girls basketball had just completed their first year of fielding a team. The girl athletes were eager to compete, eager to learn, and of course, eager to win. The boys programs had been extremely successful for years so there was hope the female athletes could accomplish some of the same level of success. I was fortunate enough to step into an ideal situation. There were multiple coaches already on the staff who served as excellent mentors for my development as a coach. Coach Frank Spenceri taught me many of the fundamentals of coaching basketball that I used throughout my career. Also, the football and track coaches - Jim Puetz, Gary Puetz, and Vern Younger - gave me multiple insights on how to be a coach.

People often say that our girls have always been able to win consistently, but it did take time to reach the level of being able to compete for state championships. My first year, 1977-78, we went 8-7 in volleyball and 3-13 in basketball. The first year there were approximately 60 girls grades 9 thru 12 out for volleyball, and I had no assistant for the year. I had to coach the 9th, junior varsity, and varsity teams each night as well having to schedule two practices a day to accommodate that many athletes.

Our athletic director hired Joe Barbaglia (Columbus Hospital Administrator) as my assistant in basketball so that helped. I was proud of those girls as they made great strides and were willing to work extremely hard to improve. The first breakthrough on the state level was in 1982 as the volleyball team went 20-2 and qualified for the state tournament, ultimately losing in a tight match in the first round. We finally qualified for the state basketball tournament in 1988 but also losing in the first round. Unfortunately, there was not a "wild card" method to get into the state tournament as we would have had multiple other teams qualify. An example was the 1985-86 and 1986-87 basketball teams that did not qualify even though they compiled a 41-3 record over those two seasons.

Coaching at Scotus for 37 years as the head volleyball coach and 23 years as the head girls basketball coach (also another 13 years in the program) has provided so many memories.

There are several memories that I wish the outcome could have been different:

The 1993 state volleyball final versus Grand Island Central Catholic was a matchup of two great teams. In those days matches were played two out of three sets to 15. We split the first two sets and led in the third set 11-2 but just could not get over the hump, ultimately losing 15-13. I was so disappointed for that group of girls as they were extremely talented but lost to a GICC team that was made up of four girls who played D-1 collegiate volleyball.

In the 1995 state basketball final versus Hastings Adams Central our senior point guard, Shauna Greiner, broke her nose on the second play of the game and missed the first half. We lost by six, but I think we may have won if not for that injury.

The 2000 state volleyball team was going for our sixth consecutive state title versus a talented Central City squad. We won the first set 15-0 and had six match points in the second set only to lose the set. We never recovered from losing that second set and lost the match in the third set.

The 2004 state volleyball team won their first 28 matches of the season and carried the burden of extending our state leading record of 115 straight volleyball victories. It all came to an end on the night of the state championship match as a talented Lincoln Lutheran team beat us by winning the fifth set to claim the title. My regret was that we did not use a different blocking scheme that night, hindsight.

There have been so many fond memories that it is impossible to convey all of them, but here are just a few.

The first state championship in the history of Scotus girls athletics was accomplished by the 1986 volleyball team. The team had to beat an incredibly tough Hartington Cedar Catholic team in the district final. They prevailed in the state Class B championship final by defeating Grand Island Northwest. The victory set the stage for future Scotus teams showing that it was possible for our girls teams to compete and win at the state level.

In the 1998 state girls basketball championship game we were playing North Bend on a night in which a howling snowstorm took place. With roads that were treacherous to travel, we may have had 50 fans in the stands. North Bend had a large contingent of followers that were at the game that night and who continually chanted, "Where's your fans?" We outscored them 14-1 in the second quarter and won by 17 points for our third consecutive basketball title.

The 2009 state volleyball championship match was one of my favorite all-time memories. We were playing GICC for the 8th time in a state final (we did win six of them). Earlier in the season they had beaten us three times, they were 35-0, and of course were number one in C-1. Somehow, someway, our team found a way to win 3-2 in an incredible atmosphere at the Nebraska Coliseum. It was a great victory when very few people expected us to win. By the way, GICC's coach Sharon Zavala is certainly one of the very best coaches that I have had the pleasure of coaching against.

The 1996 and 1998 volleyball teams were undefeated but also were ranked #1 all-class. This was quite an accomplishment for a team playing in Class C-1.

I am so thankful for many things during my tenure as a coach at Scotus. The consistency that our teams have had over the years has been incredible. I have been so blessed to have coached talented, dedicated, and hard-working girls. They not only excelled as athletes, but also as students, and now are excelling as doctors, lawyers, accountants, pharmacists, chiropractors, teachers, and many other professions. Just great kids! I can't express how much I love each and every one of them.

The consistency also came from the many dedicated coaches that worked in the volleyball and basketball program. It is impossible to name them all, but I would be remiss if I did not honor the following: in volleyball junior high coaches Gary Luchsinger, Tracy Kucera, Jane Dusel-Misfeldt, and Joan Lahm, freshman coach Julie Blaser, volunteer assistant coach Joe Held, and varsity assistants Marla Mueller and Janet Tooley. Special thanks goes out to Coach Tooley for being an incredible assistant for nearly 25 years. In basketball my longest tenured assistants were Julie Blaser in junior high and Scott Miller, who was my assistant coach for 10 years when we won three state titles, also an incredible coach. Our team's success is a direct tribute to all of these coaches' abilities.

I am blessed to be called a Columbus Scotus Central Catholic Coach. What a great privilege it has been to be a part of this school! Thank you to all who have been a part of our volleyball and girls basketball programs.

Jeff Ohnoutka

Scotus High School 2006 - 2016

- Head coach of state runner-up in boys basketball, 2015
- 134-84 record as head coach

Having the opportunity to be a coach at Scotus was a real privilege and something I took great pride in. When you walk into Scotus and see the banners, trophies, plaques it is clearly obvious that success is part of the culture here. When you coach at Scotus, you also understand that you are have been entrusted with a responsibility to continue that winning culture. That is something I never took lightly.

When I came to Scotus eleven years ago, I had the opportunity to learn from some of the finest coaches in the state in their particular sport. From each of these coaches I learned the following things.

Gary Puetz: Trust your players. Give them the tools to be successful and then show confidence in them on game days.

Janet Tooley: Never get outworked. Coach Tooley is without a doubt one of the most competitive people I have ever met.

John Petersen: Be driven every day. Coach Petersen used every opportunity that he was around his players to try and make them better. He covered every scenario.

Merlin Lahm: Master Motivator. Coach Lahm gets his track athletes to believe they can do anything. Anybody who convinces teenagers that bad weather is to their advantage is really motivating people!

Jon Brezenski: No excuses! I love his approach with our athletes. He convinces them that the team is the most important thing and give up their individual desires. He is very honest with players and they respect that.

There were numerous things that happened that I will always remember but if I narrowed it down to one it would be the victory in 2015 over Neumann in the state semifinals. Just to see the enjoyment on the faces of our players and assistant coaches and fans was priceless. The thought that we were going to play for a state championship was really overwhelming. There had been so many times where it seemed that was not possible. I was just so happy for our school.

In 2007 I took over the program at Scotus. I inherited a team that had no seniors. We had a talented group of juniors but we had to learn how to win. That first year we played five games before Christmas and I think every game was against a ranked team. We lost every game. I remember sitting in the locker room in Wayne after the last game before Christmas and everybody was crying. It was one of the toughest moments of my career. We had been close in every game but we could not find a way to get it done. We were crying because we were putting so much into this and seeing no rewards. The reason I remember this is that team went on to win nine games and the next year went through a stretch where they beat five rated teams. I know this is about a memory I would like to forget but in a way that moment in Wayne was forever burned in my memory.

Before every game we put our arms around each other and pray. That tradition was created out of desperation one night at Lincoln Christian around six years ago. Our team was not playing well and I made the decision that night that we were going to put ourselves on the line for each other. We decided to put our arms around each other and understand that we were all in this together. It quickly became a part of our game day ritual.

For me though there is no better feeling in the world then after a win when we "clap it up" in the locker room. The adrenaline rush I get from that feeling makes me feel like I am 18 years old. To see our kids excited with each other and for each other is a really neat thing.

My most memorable experience is all the relationships I have developed because I coached basketball. I am so grateful to the players who were part of our program. They bought in and decided that we were going to be successful.

My assistant coaches have been dedicated men who always wanted what was best for our program. Take Mike Vuncannon, our current assistant, for example. He is a father of five who not only coaches our junior high and varsity but also coaches club basketball. His commitment to the program is unmatched. Scotus is very lucky to have someone like him.

The thing you enjoy as a coach is the competition. The practices and the game strategies all designed to give your team an edge on game night. Winning is really fun and I found pretty early in my career that I hated losing way more than I liked winning. So you have to be a competitive person to be good at this job.

I am extremely proud of the program we have built at Scotus. We have had the opportunity to play in the state semifinals the last three years in a row. We have created a program that is one of the best in Class C-1. Kids now grow up wanting to play basketball for Scotus. It took an unbelievable amount of work by a lot of people to make that happen…but it was all worth it. That's the Shamrock Way!

Jon Brezenski

Scotus High School 2005-2016

- Head soccer coach 2006 – Present
- Four-Time state champion as head boys soccer coach (2009, 2014, 2015, 2016)
- Assistant football coach 2005 – Present
- Assistant coach, 2015 state championship football team

As a Scotus alum, I take great pride in now being a coach at Scotus. I feel a sense of obligation to "give back" to Scotus for teaching me so many things as a student-athlete. I want to teach our current student-athletes the values and beliefs my coaches instilled in me when I was student-athlete.

My wife (Kristie Korth-Brezenski) and I made the decision to move back to Columbus in October 2004 during my last year of PT school at UNMC. When Gary Puetz called me in January 2005 and we talked about the possibility of coaching at Scotus, I was excited. I was offered the head boys soccer position and also a position on the football staff. It has been great to coach at Scotus since 2005. The soccer program has been able to win four state championships (2009, 2014, 2015, 2016) and our football team won a championship in 2015. To be a part of the successes and contributed to Scotus' athletic tradition as a coach has been a real blessing.

I have tried to instill the principles I learned from my coaches and teachers. I don't want to leave anyone out on this one. Jim Puetz taught me the importance of organization and motivation and you also have to make practices fun so the kids enjoy playing for you. Gary Puetz taught me organization and the importance of the small things to develop players. Vern Younger taught me the importance of building a program from the ground up, utilizing coaches in your program to develop athletes over time and for the long term. Rick Grubaugh (our offensive coordinator in the 1990s) taught me the importance of film study and the importance of knowing your opponents Merlin Lahm is in my mind, the best coach ever in terms of knowing your opponent by studying them and looking for the small things to use to your advantage. I've used his teachings in my ability to scout opponents for soccer and for football. Finally, John Petersen taught me so many things and I never played for him. He taught me what it takes to build a program, the importance of drilling fundamentals first, and making sure your athletes can be good at the skills required for success. I've been able to take something from all of these former coaches to help mold me into the coach I am today.

I have been blessed so far during my time as the soccer coach to win four state championships (2009, 2014, 2015, 2016). Each of those championships has been special. The memories the players share with me after the fact are the greatest things. To see the joy on their faces after we have won four championships is what I always remember. One of the best things I enjoy is getting together with former players during our Scotus Alumni Soccer Tournament during the first weekend in August. Sitting with them and hearing their stories and memories…sometimes things I don't even remember, are some of the most enjoyable times.

The 2015 Scotus football championship season was awesome. The journey we had with the team was incredible. We had to overcome a lot of adversity to achieve our goal. The final game against a talented Norfolk Catholic team was incredible and to see all the joy on our players and fellow coaches' faces was something I will cherish for a long time.

The 2009 Class B state soccer championship against Columbus High was amazing. We played in front of a large crowd at Morrison Stadium on Creighton's campus. The stands were split into Maroon and Green, right down the middle. It was an intense match, going back and forth. We were able to score in the 97th minute to win the match 1-0. I have always found this goal to be ironic because it occurred in the 97th minute and 1997 was also the year of our first soccer championship. It was my first state championship as a head coach.

The 2014 and 2015 state championship matches were also fantastic. The 2014 final against Gretna went into overtime and we scored a couple of minutes into the period on an own-goal and then controlled the second overtime to secure the win.

In 2015, we defeated our rival, Omaha Skutt, 3-0. After a scoreless first half, we had a "spirited" talk at halftime and challenged the team to come out and dominate the second half like we knew we were capable. The team responded and scored three minutes into the half and then added two more goals with about 15 minutes to play to earn our fifth championship.

During the 2016 season, our soccer program was able to accomplish what no other boys program in the state of Nebraska has ever done...win a third consecutive championship. There were very high expectations for our program in 2016. We returned almost everyone from our 2014 and 2015 state championship teams and we started the season ranked #1 All-Class. We ran into a rough start, going on 0-2 in the St. Ignatius Cup at Omaha Creighton Prep during the second week of the season. The losses on that Saturday were a blessing for our team as it really took off any type of early pressure and letting us know what our team needed to work on in order to be successful. We were able to get back on track and ran off a pretty impressive string of wins, including the Metro Cup at Millard South, defeating Omaha Central and then #1 Omaha Westside in the finals. We suffered a loss to Columbus High in the district final in a shootout, but the loss did not have a negative impact. We felt like we left the field as the better team and as Jackson Kumpf said so confidently, "We get down to Morrison Stadium, no one will beat us."

We were able to win both of our opening games against Lexington (2-0) and Columbus High (2-1) to set up the final against #1 Elkhorn South, who entered the game 18-0. It was a classic soccer match and the boys played extremely well in front of a very large crowd. We were able to dodge a couple of bullets early in the second half to keep the game 0-0. As the second half wore on, we were able to take control of the match, but missed a couple of great chances to take the lead. We continued to work hard and press Elkhorn South to maintain control of the game to set up a most memorable finish.

With under a minute to play, Caleb Ostdiek was able to get on the loose end of a crossing pass from Cole Harrington and send a high, lofting ball into the box. Cole jumped up and flicked the ball with his head to Nathan Ostdiek, who hit a one-time shot off the near post inside of the goalkeeper and scored! Nathan proceeded to rip off his shirt and was then tackled by his teammates in front of our fans in an epic moment in Nebraska high school sport history! The goal and celebration will live on forever as one of the greatest moments in my playing and coaching career.

The goal really epitomized what these past three years were for our program. We had a hard-working and determined group of players who pushed each other each day in practice. The group was able to find the collective balance of having a fun at practice, but then also to get serious and push themselves and one another to that next level. Our program motto is BELIEVE and this 2016 team never wavered in their journey to make history.

I have coached some great athletes during my time as a coach at Scotus, so it is tough to really single out any one player. I think the collection of players during my time as the soccer coach has been very good, which obviously makes winning a little easier. Our teams have been true "teams" and team members have been able to contribute in their own way to our successes.

Tom Hoover and Jim Swanson, the co-head coaches at Omaha Creighton Prep, are very successful and also very good friends. I really enjoy playing against their teams each year, as those matches help to improve our team. I also learned many great things from speaking with them, not only about coaching, but also about being a good husband and father.

In football, I have had the opportunity to coach against Ron Mimick (David City Aquinas) and Jeff Bellar (Norfolk Catholic). Both of these coaches are arguably two of the best, so preparing to play them makes you a better coach. I have enjoyed the opportunity to talk with Coach Mimick in the off-season to learn things from him on how to run a program and have been able to carry those things over in my coaching career as both a soccer coach and football coach.

During the 2015 state soccer semifinal against Lexington, one of our top players was improperly dismissed during the match. To see our team rally and win 3-1 and come together in their preparations for our state championship match against Omaha Skutt and defeat them soundly 3-0 in the final was a testament to the resolve of our kids. The bus rides home following our state soccer championships have always been one of the most enjoyable things for me. The time we spend as a group off the field, whether it be going out to eat, singing on the bus ride home, or taking pictures at Morrison Stadium following our state championship wins are always some of the fondest memories.

Winning the state championships in soccer and in 2015 in football have been great experiences, but my proudest moments occur when former players come back and reminisce about their experiences. To hear what they enjoyed playing for me and what they remember the most as players is always interesting. To see former players go on to college and then eventually get married and become fathers, is enjoyable and when you hear from them that you had a positive impact on their lives going forward is probably the greatest thing.

I am proud I have been able to help continue the successes of our athletic programs. We are the fifth-smallest school in Nebraska to have soccer and now have the most Class B State Championships with six is something very special to me as a coach and to our former players.

Some of the greatest coaching stories cannot be told. But honestly, coaching at Scotus is a true blessing and I feel very fortunate to be a part of the coaching staff. Being able to reconnect with my former coaches and teachers on a professional level is something I do not take for granted. Scotus is a very special place, with very special people, who are dedicated in providing a positive, faith-based life experience for our students. To be able to in some way contribute to Scotus athletics and to have some type of positive impact on young people is something I cherish every season.

Janet Tooley

Scotus High School 1987 – 2016

- Head girls track coach, 1995-2016
- Head boys track coach, 1995-1996
- Class B girls state track champion, 2009
- Class B girls state track runner-up, 1998, 2002
- National High School Athletic Coaches Association Girls Track & Field National Coach of the Year Finalist, 2014
- Assistant volleyball coach, 1987-2013
- Nebraska Coaches Association Assistant Coach of the Year, 1995

I was hired in 1987 and my first coaching duties included junior high track and 8th grade volleyball. Jim Puetz and Dan Mahoney (my unofficial mentor) were the head track coaches and ran very organized and competitive programs. It was exciting to be a part of something that was already so successful as well as eventually (in 1990) serving as a varsity assistant with John Petersen, who was in the early stages of creating our volleyball dynasty!

One distinct memory from those junior high track coaching days was our 6:00 a.m. practices. Despite the early hour, it always looked as if it was a Friday night home football game as the cars would stream into Pawnee Park to drop off 120+ athletes for practice! On those pre-dawn, cold spring mornings, we would have the entire team out doing their warm up laps with yes, some trying to hide out behind the high jump mats! For away meets we traveled in an SCC "convoy" consisting of the bus, which I drove, and at least six mini vans driven by parents. Even though we won the majority of our meets, with the large numbers we had on the team, a successful day also included making sure no one was left behind!

Now, fast forward to 1995 when I stepped into the Shamrock varsity head track & field coaching position. I was definitely following some "greats":

Jim Puetz and Dan Mahoney. I had big shoes to fill, but also a successful legacy to build upon. Julie Blaser and I took on the role of co-head coaches of both the boys and the girls programs. This was a first at Scotus, females coaching male athletes at the varsity level, and it took a bit of getting used to for the guys, but actually ended up being the beginning of a great run of success for the coed track program. I have had the privilege to coach many talented and dedicated athletes as well as to work with some very knowledgeable and dedicated coaches who put in more than just a few years helping to make our program such a success. Track athletes will remember not only the head coaches but also the assistants that worked with them daily. The likes of Jim and Dan as well as Barb Malicky, Gary Puetz, Vern Younger, Merlin Lahm, Rick Grubaugh, Kevin Dodson, Nathan Arneal, Jeff Ohnoutka, Roger Krienke, Kim Grubaugh, Ron Starzec and Danielle (Bender) Wessel are some notables. I apologize to anyone I have inadvertently neglected to mention due to lack of space! They are all great Shamrocks!

What a whirlwind of memories there have been during these past 20 years at the varsity level, many stored somewhere in one of our infamous "State Meet Itineraries"! As anyone who has ever competed in sports knows, despite hard work and putting forth your best effort, things don't always work out the way we would like. It's hard to forget those district meets when due to illness, injury or just bad luck, quality individuals or relays failed to qualify for Burke. We have had some state meet heartbreaks, including a bad starter's gun in the 200-meter prelims and a few miscues on our relays.

We've had seasons when weather didn't cooperate and we still went out and practiced in rain, sleet and snow early in the spring and then encountered 100+ degree heat at the state meet. Certainly some tough memories but fortunately many more great ones! Most SCC track athletes will remember the long-standing traditional Good Friday Relays and the more recently added, raw egg toss competitions. Those tough USC workouts are hard to forget, as well as the lower-intensity pre-meet workouts and "park runs". We can't forget the "Queen of Victory" prayer with every departure and the thank you prayer on our way home. Fun times include taking victory laps after a team championship and singing the school fight song on the way home. Other great memories evolve around food—especially DQ days and our Easter Break team breakfasts!

In 2004 our facilities at Pawnee Park were refurbished, giving us one of the best venues in the state. Since the upgrade, SCC has become the annual host of our Centennial Conference meet, with former coach Nathan Arneal on the PA. This is like a "mini state meet" with the level of competition that is there. Going up against quality programs like Bishop Neumann, Hastings St. Cecilia, Boys Town and GICC to name a few, is always a fun challenge. Area rivals Pierce, Lakeview, Wayne and Boone Central keep us training hard to stay at the head of the pack. The number of major meets, conference and district championships that our program has won over the years is amazing. I am so grateful to be a small part of all of this!

With space limited, I will close mentioning the SCC history that was made on May 23, 2009: our first Class B girls state track & field team championship. It was a much different experience than what I had been fortunate to be a part of many times in our volleyball program. There was no final whistle at match point and no Rowdy Dowdy's going crazy in the stands as Amber Ewers and Sami Spenner were getting into the blocks of the 200-meter finals. All they had to do was successfully get out of those blocks, finish the race, and we would bring home Scotus' first girls track & field team championship trophy.

I will never forget standing on the hill, overlooking the Burke track and those 20-some seconds watching as they crossed that finish line placing 1-2! As I made my way through the crowd to congratulate the girls, most in the stands had no idea that we had just won the meet, top it off our first team state championship - but we did! Certainly a moment in my career that I will never forget as well as all of the special athletes I've had the privilege to coach!

What an awesome feeling it is to be a part of Scotus. Thanks for giving me this opportunity to share some wonderful memories and, don't ever forget, it's always *a great day to be a Shamrock!*

Dan Mahoney

Scotus High School 1977 – 2004

- Head girls track coach, 1980-94
- Assistant girls track coach, 1978-79
- Head girls cross country coach, 1978-2004
- Head boys cross country coach, 1997-2004
- Three-time girls cross country state champion head coach, 2000, 2001, 2002
- Four-time girls cross country state runner-up head coach, 1991, 1999, 2003, 2004
- Shamrock Athletic Hall of Fame inductee, 2007

When I arrived at Scotus as a first year teacher and coach in the fall of 1977 it quickly became clear that I was very fortunate to begin my coaching career at a school with such a collection of great coaches. Jim and Gary Puetz, Frank Spenceri, Vern Younger, and John Petersen were or would become some of the best in the state. Observing and learning from these coaches provided me with the basic foundations and inspirations needed for a rookie coach.

My coaching career began as Barb Malicky's assistant track coach in 1978. Then from 1980 to 1994 I was head girls track coach with assistance at various times from Barb, Greg Bauer, and Rick Grubaugh. It was a time when Scotus was blessed with many talented female athletes and many school records were broken.

We had some great rivalries, especially against David City Aquinas. During this time there were many conference and district championships won as well as numerous Class B individual state champions in various events.

In the fall of 1978, three of the girl distance runners from the previous track season expressed an interest in running cross country. The problem was that there was no official girls cross country at that time. If the girls wanted to compete they would have to run against the boys. The girls (Anne Syslo, Julie Jarecke, and Sheryl Liebig) accepted the challenge and thus the first unofficial Scotus girls cross country team was born. Two years later the state would have the first official girls state cross country meet. During those early years we struggled to just get enough girls out to form a team. But as time went on we increased our numbers and became more successful. By the 1990's we usually had one of the largest teams in our class. At those first state meets there was no admission charge to get in because hardly anyone attended. We were lucky if a few parents showed up. How times have changed! Now there are huge crowds with a large number of Scotus parents and fans cheering on the Shamrocks.

I would coach cross country for twenty-seven years, with the last eight years including the boys team. The girls teams would go on to win three state championships (2000-2001-2002) and have four state runner-up performances (1991-1999-2003-2004), as well as three individual state champion runners (Molly Engel, 2000; Angela Fisher, 2001; and Kayla Engel, 2002). Like track, there would be some great cross country rivalries. At the state meet we battled Coach Steve Reeves' Gothenburg girls teams for the state title four consecutive years.

I have many fond memories, but perhaps the best was our first girls cross country state championship in 2000. The best coach I coached against was George O'Boyle from Lincoln Pius X; George is one of the best coaches in the country.

The girls cross country teams winning three state championships in a row were the most memorable, while having three different individual state champion runners during those same years.

I was extremely fortunate to be a coach at a school with such a strong sports tradition. Scotus students, parents, faculty and administrators were very supportive of all activities and sports. I would like to thank all those athletes that I have coached for all their hard work and dedication. It has been a privilege to have been associated with so many outstanding athletes and coaches.

SHAMROCK ATHLETIC HALL OF FAME

Ken Cielocha '54

Shamrock Hall of Fame – Athlete

Inducted 1999

- Four-year letterman in football and three-year letterman in track
- Member of 9-0 1953 State Championship football team
- Qualified for State track in 440 yard relay 1952, 1953, 1954
- All-State football running back 1953
- *Omaha World-Herald* Weekly Honor Roll three times 1953
- National Honor Society 1953
- All American football team 1953

Clinton Gates '55

Shamrock Hall of Fame – Athlete

Inducted 1999

- Four-year letter winner in football, playing guard of offense and linebacker on defense
- First team Class B All-State in football 1954
- First team All-Class All-State in football 1954
- Member of St. Bonaventure/Scotus football chain gang for more than 30 years and an active member of the Shamrock Club and 250 Club

Bill Backes '61

Shamrock Hall of Fame – Athlete

Inducted 1999

- Lettered in football, basketball, and track
- Honorable Mention All-State in football 1960
- Average 17 points per game in basketball 1960-61
- Third place at State track low hurdles 1961

Dave Kudron '64

Shamrock Hall of Fame – Athlete

Inducted 1999

- Two-year letter winner in football 1962, 1963
- Two-year letter winner in basketball 1963, 1964
- Three-year letter winner in track 1962, 1963, 1964
- First State track All-Class gold medal winner in school history 120 yard high hurdles (14.7) 1964
- Honorable Mention All-State in football 1963 and basketball 1964
- First team All-State track 1964
- Competed on 1964 State Championship track team

Bill Kosch '68

Shamrock Hall of Fame – Athlete

Inducted 1999

- All State football 1967
- Played in Shrine Bowl 1968
- Captain of 1967 Class C State Championship football team
- All-Centennial Conference in football and basketball (averaged 16 points per game)
- Finished 2nd in the 180-yard low hurdles and 3rd in the 120-yard high hurdles at State track meet 1968
- Scotus Athlete of the Year 1968

Joe Blahak '69

Shamrock Hall of Fame – Athlete

Inducted 1999

- First team Class B All-State in football 1968
- Played on 1967 State Championship football team
- Played in Shrine Bowl 1969
- Class B State Champion long jump 1968
- Class B State Champion long jump and 180 yard low hurdles 1969
- State track All-Class gold medal long jump and 180 yard low hurdles 1969
- Scotus Athlete of the Year 1969

Brenda Grubaugh '74

Shamrock Hall of Fame – Athlete

Inducted 1999

- Winner of four State track meet gold medals - 50, 100, and 200 yard dash 1973 and 100 yard dash 1974
- Set state record in 50 yard dash 1973
- Scotus Athlete of the Year 1974
- Helped usher Shamrock girls athletics into statewide prominence
- Both daughters of Brenda and her husband Paul are Scotus graduates

Mike Cielocha '79

Shamrock Hall of Fame – Athlete

Inducted 1999

- Lettered in track, football, and basketball
- First team Class B All-State in football 1978
- Played in Shrine Bowl 1979
- Class B State Champion 220 and 440 yard dashes 1977
- Class B State Champion 220 and 440 yard dashes and 880 yard relay 1978
- Class B State Champion 100, 220 and 440 yard dashes and 880 yard relay 1979
- State track All-Class gold medal 440 yard dash 1977
- State track All-Class gold medal 220 and 440 yard dashes and 880 yard relay 1978
- State track All-Class gold medal 100 and 440 yard dashes 1979

Glen Kucera '81

Shamrock Hall of Fame – Athlete

Inducted 1999

- All-State football 1979, 1980
- Played in the Shrine Bowl 1981
- Current school record holder for number of receptions and receiving yardage in a single game, season, and career
- All-State basketball 1981
- Qualified for State track 1980, 1981
- Scotus Athlete of the Year 1981

Karl Hroza '86

Shamrock Hall of Fame – Athlete

Inducted 1999

- First team Class B All-State in football 1984, 1985
- First team Super State in football 1985
- Played in Shrine Bowl 1986
- Class B state triple jump champion 1985, 1986
- Holds Scotus triple jump record of 47'
- Played basketball
- Scotus Athlete of the Year 1986

Pat Engelbert '87

Shamrock Hall Of Fame – Athlete

Inducted 1999

- All-State In Football 1985, 1986
- All-Class All-State 1986
- Played In Shrine Bowl 1987
- All-Conference In Basketball 1985, 1986
- All-Conference Basketball Tournament Team 1986, 1987
- State Track Meet Shot Put Runner-Up 1987
- Current School Record Holder In Shot Put (57'-9")
- Scotus Athlete of the Year 1987

Kelly Nicolas '87

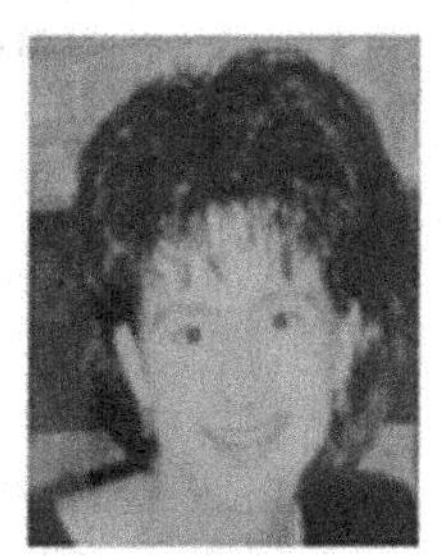

Shamrock Hall of Fame – Athlete

Inducted 1999

- Competed in basketball, volleyball, and track
- All-State basketball 1986, 1987
- All-State volleyball 1986
- Played on the 1986 State Championship volleyball team
- Played in the Nebraska All-Star volleyball and basketball games 1986
- State track meet qualifier 1984, 1985, 1986, 1987
- Holder of numerous school basketball records
- Scotus Athlete of the Year 1987

Kelli Martin '87

Shamrock Hall of Fame – Athlete

Inducted 1999

- First team Class B All-State in volleyball 1985, 1986 and all-conference 1984, 1985, 1986
- First team Class B All-State in basketball 1986, 1987 and all-conference 1983, 1984, 1985, 1986
- Played on the State Championship volleyball team 1986
- Played in the Nebraska Coaches Association All-Star basketball game 1987
- Scored over 1,000 career points in basketball
- Silver medal at State track meet in discus 1987 and holds current school record of 125'7"
- Holds many school and state volleyball records
- Scotus Athlete of the Year 1987

Dean Soulliere '54

Shamrock Hall of Fame – Coach

Inducted 1999

- Head football and track coach and Athletic Director 1959-65
- Head coach of the State Championship Track team 1964
- Quarterback for the undefeated 1953 football team (final Class B ranking #2) and head coach of the undefeated 1964 football team (Final Class B ranking #3)
- Head coaching record in football of 29-11
- Shrine Bowl coach 1963
- *Lincoln Journal Star* High School Coach of the Year 1964

Frank Spenceri

Shamrock Hall of Fame – Coach

Inducted 1999

- Head basketball, cross country and golf coach and assistant football coach 1970-1988
- Athletic/Activities Director, Assistant Development Director and Alumni Coordinator
- Head coach of the State Championship boys golf team 1981
- Several State tournament teams in basketball, several district championships in cross country
- Initiated the Columbus Catholic school intramural basketball program

Paul "Dutch" Ernst

Shamrock Hall of Fame – Coach

Inducted 1999

- First coach for St. Bonaventure High School (1936-50)
- Coined "Shamrocks" for St. Bonaventure/Scotus Central Catholic teams
- First basketball team qualified for State tournament (1936-37)
- He added the first six-man football team in Columbus and the first parochial team outside of Omaha and Lincoln (1941)
- Head coach of 8-0 football team, the first undefeated team in school history (1943)
- He added track (1941) and 11-man football (1946)
- "Dutch" coached entirely as a volunteer

Al Grubaugh

Shamrock Hall of Fame – Booster

Inducted 1999

- A tremendous supporter of Scotus athletics and an important resource for coaches for many years
- The enthusiasm and sportsmanship that he brought to booster club meetings as well as athletic events were inspirational
- His unselfish support and dedication to Scotus athletics set a standard for all to emulate
- All four children of Al and his wife Bess graduated from Catholic high schools

Bon & Helen Shadle

Shamrock Hall of Fame – Boosters

Inducted 1999

- One of Bon's favorite pastimes was Scotus athletics
- Helen also shares a passion for athletics and is known as one of the school's most loyal spectators
- Helen also enjoys attending the school's band and theater performances
- Bon spent many hours running chairs at football games, selling tickets for basketball games and helping at track meets
- Bon was a past President of the Shamrock Club, one of the early organizers of the Shamrock Night fundraiser and the KC Track meet
- All six of their children graduated from Scotus

Editor's Note: Helen Shadle passed away in November 2015 at the age of 92. She attended her final Scotus football game in 2015, less than two months before her passing.

Lee & Shirley Hroza

Shamrock Hall of Fame - Boosters

Inducted 1999, 2000

- Lee is a 25-year member and past President of the Shamrock Club
- He helped the Shamrock Club develop into a significant financial and volunteer resource for Scotus athletics
- He headed the 250 Club
- He was treasurer of the Junior Olympic track meet for 18 years
- Shirley provided refreshments for the Junior Olympic meets, assisted with fundraising events and is a devoted fan of all Shamrock activities
- All six of their children are Scotus graduates

Leonard & Cece Feehan

Shamrock Hall of Fame – Boosters

Inducted 1999, 2000

- Greatest fans of Scotus athletics
- Leonard was an original member of the Shamrock Club
- Leonard and Cece have missed no more than 20 games since the early 1950s
- Devoted supporters of all Scotus athletics, Leonard has been a leader in the Knights of Columbus for more than 45 years and was a significant supporter of the KC Track meet
- Cece was the first President of the Scotus Mothers Club
- All seven of their children attended Scotus

Glenn Shonka

Shamrock Hall of Fame – Booster

Inducted 1999

- A charter member and one of the first officers of the Shamrock Club, Glenn and his wife Lucille seldom missed a Shamrock athletic event whether home or away
- From 1956-1974, all eight of their children attended, participated in athletics and/or cheerleading and graduated from St. Bon's/Scotus
- An important booster event, The Glenn Shonka Open was organized in 1980 in Glenn's memory

Bill Mimick '66

Shamrock Hall of Fame – Athlete

Inducted 2000

- Four-year letter winner in football
- First team Class B All-State 1965
- Played in Shrine Bowl 1966
- Football team MVP and All-Conference selection 1965
- Honorable Mention Class B All-State in basketball 1965
- Second team Class B All-State 1966
- Basketball team MVP in 1965, 1966
- 20.1 points per game average 1965 and 17.2 points per game average for career
- Held school record in shot put, discus, and high jump
- Scotus Athlete of the Year 1966

Dan Brock '72

Shamrock Hall of Fame – Athlete

Inducted 2000

- Three-year letter winner in football and track
- Two-year letter winner in basketball
- State track meet qualifier in shot put 1971, 1972
- Third place finish at State in shot put 1972
- All-Class All-State (*Omaha World-Herald*) and All-State Class B (Lincoln *Journal Star*) in football 1971
- All-conference in football 1970, 1971
- Second team all-conference in basketball 1972
- Captain of football and basketball teams 1971-72
- Scotus Athlete of the Year 1972

Lana Torczon '81

Shamrock Hall of Fame – Athlete

Inducted 2000

- Three-year letter winner in volleyball 1978, 1979, 1980 and basketball 1979, 1980, 1981
- Four-year track letter winner 1978, 1979, 1980, 1981
- First team All-State in basketball 1981
- Honorable Mention All-State in volleyball 1980 and basketball 1980
- All-conference in volleyball 1979, 1980 and basketball 1980, 1981
- Played in Coaches All-Star basketball game 1981
- Set several school records in basketball, including rebounds in a season (248) 1981
- Member of school record two mile relay 1981
- Scotus Athlete of the Year 1981

Jeff Podraza '85

Shamrock Hall of Fame – Athlete

Inducted 2000

- Three-year letter winner in football 1982, 1983, 1984
- Honorable Mention All-State and All-Conference 1983, 1984
- Recorded longest punt in Shrine Bowl history (76 yards) 1985
- Played on 1984 State Championship football team with a 13-0 record and a school record 8 shutouts
- Three-year letter winner in basketball 1983, 1984, 1985
- Led the team in blocked shots, rebounds, and steals 1985
- Four-year letter winner in track 1982, 1983, 1984, 1985
- Held several school records in track and was a 1985 State track medalist in 110 meter high hurdles (2nd), All-Class 110 meter high hurdles (5th), long jump (6th), and a member of the 2nd place 4x100 meter relay team (with current school record time)
- Scotus Athlete of the Year 1985

Albert Tucek '45

Shamrock Hall of Fame – Booster

Inducted 2000

- Four-year letter winner in track
- Qualified for State track meet 1943, 1944, 1945
- In 1945, was undefeated in the mile and finished 4th in Class C at State
- Three-year letter winner in basketball
- Co-captain of 1945 team (13-5) that was the first team to win the Platte County Tourney
- After graduation, ran clock for basketball games from 1946-1984
- Active booster and past President of the Shamrock Club (1961)

Tony '42 & Phyl (Foltz) Zabawa '42

Shamrock Hall of Fame – Boosters

Inducted 2000

- Tony played basketball for four years and was team captain senior year
- Tony was the school's first male cheerleader
- Phyl was a member of the girls basketball team and Pep Club
- Tony drove the bus for teams and Pep Club, ran the clock for football games, and is a charter member of the Shamrock Club, serving a term as President
- Phyl chaperoned the Pep Club bus, leading the Rosary on the way to games and both Tony and Phyl chaperoned the youth center and many dances
- Phyl often assisted with concessions for athletic contests
- Both Tony and Phyl are active and very loyal fans of Shamrock athletics, have been active in fundraising for the school, and all eight of their children graduated from St. Bonaventure/Scotus

Kristi Sobota '91

Shamrock Hall of Fame – Athlete

Inducted 2001

- Three-year letter winner in volleyball
- Played on the 1990 State Championship volleyball team (26-0)
- First team All-Class All-State 1990
- First team Class B All-State 1989, 1990
- Four-year letter winner in basketball
- School record holder for most rebounds in a career (583)
- Four-year letter winner in track
- Three-time State meet qualifier in shot put
- Al Grubaugh Award 1990
- Scotus Athlete of the Year and Sertoma Athlete of the Year 1991

Dan Steiner '75

Shamrock Hall of Fame – Athlete

Inducted 2001

- First team Class B All-State in football 1974
- Second team Super State 1974
- First team All-Catholic All-American 1974
- All conference 1974
- Played in 1975 Shrine Bowl
- Two-time State track qualifier 1974, 1975
- District Champion in shot put 1975
- Fourth place at State track in shot put (52'9") 1975
- Scotus Athlete of the Year 1975

Dick '52 & Joan (Gregorius) '54 Tooley

Shamrock Hall of Fame – Boosters

Inducted 2001

- Dick and Joan's devotion to their alma mater is extraordinary
- As a student, Dick was involved in football, basketball and track and received the school's Babe Ruth Award in 1952
- He is a past President of the Shamrock Club and has been an active member since the booster club's inception
- In high school, Joan played in both the band and pep band and she continues to support the performing arts and athletic programs through her loyal attendance at performances and sports events
- All six of their children are Scotus graduates

Larry Liss '64

Shamrock Hall of Fame – Athlete

Inducted 2002

- Four-year letter winner in track and one-year letter winner in football
- Set school records in the 100 yard dash (9.7) 1964, 220 yard dash (22.5) 1963, broad jump (21'3.5") 1963, 880 yard relay with John Iossi, Harry Blahak, and Dave Kudron (1:34.2) 1963
- State champion 100 yard dash and State runner-up 220 yard dash 1963
- Competed on 1964 Class B State Championship track team
- State track All-Class gold medal 100 yard dash and All-Class Silver Medal 220 yard dash 1964

Mary Fehringer '88

Shamrock Hall of Fame – Athlete

Inducted 2002

- First team Class B All-State in volleyball 1987
- Played on the State Championship volleyball team 1986 (26-0)
- Played on the State tournament basketball team 1988
- Set school record in the high jump (5'6") and placed 2nd at State track meet in high jump 1987
- Scotus Athlete of the Year and KLIR Athlete of the Year 1988

Cletus Fischer

Shamrock Hall of Fame – Coach

Inducted 2003

- First full-time head football coach (1950-55) compiling a record of 35-8 and Class B top ten rankings in three of his five years
- 1953 team went undefeated (8-0) and earned final ranking of #2 in both the *Lincoln Journal Star* and *Omaha World-Herald*
- He coached five All-State athletes
- Head basketball coach for three years (32-17)
- Head track coach for five years
- He "jump-started" the Shamrocks into today's modern era of success in football and track

JoDe Cieloha '94

Shamrock Hall of Fame – Athlete

Inducted 2004

- Four-year letter winner in basketball, three-year letter winner in volleyball and soccer and one year letter winner in track
- Played on State runner-up volleyball team 1991, 1993 and #3 team 1992
- First team Class B All-State in volleyball 1992, 1993
- First team Super-State 1993
- Set school record for blocks in a season and career
- Played on basketball team ranked #2 in Class B 1994
- First team All-State in basketball 1994
- Scotus Athlete of the Year 1994

Jeff Herdzina '94

Shamrock Hall of Fame – Athlete

Inducted 2004

- Three-year letter winner in football
- Played on State Championship football team (13-0) 1993
- Set single season rushing record (2,181 yards) 1993
- First team All-Class All-State and Class B All-State 1993
- School record for scoring in a game (30), season (225), career (309)
- Class B Player of the Year 1993, Shrine Bowl participant 1994
- Huskerland magazine Class B All-Decade team 1990-1999
- In soccer, led Class A in goals scored 1993, 1994
- First team All-State 1993, 1994
- Participated in 1994 Shrine soccer game
- Four-year letter winner in basketball
- Honorable Mention All-State 1993, 1994
- One-year letter winner in track
- Member of 1600 meter relay team that finished 6th at State meet 1991
- Scotus Athlete of the Year and KLIR Athlete of the Year 1994

Jim Puetz

Shamrock Hall of Fame – Coach

Inducted 2004

- Head football coach 1971-2001, head track coach 1967-1993 and head boys golf coach 1996-2004
- Compiled a career football record of 236-96-6 including two State Championships (1984, 1993)
- Nebraska High School football Coach of the Year 1985, 1997
- Nebraska High School Coach of the Year 1994
- In track, directed two State Championship teams (1978, 1979), two State runner-up teams (1969, 1973) and 18 District Championship teams
- Nebraska Coaches Association Career Milestone Level IV both football, track
- Taught social studies and physical education during his Scotus career
- "A player's coach and a true Shamrock"

Shauna Greiner '96

Shamrock Hall of Fame – Athlete

Inducted 2006

- Three-year letter winner in volleyball
- Starter on two teams with combined 55-1 record 1994, 1995
- First team Class C-1 All-State and Second team Super-State 1995
- Played on State Championship team 1995 and State runner-up team 1994
- Three-year letter winner in basketball
- Started on two teams with combined 44-6 record 1995, 1996
- Second team Class C-1 All-State 1995
- Played on State Championship team 1996 and State runner-up team 1995
- Four-year letter winner in soccer
- First team Class B All-State 1996
- Finalist, *Omaha World-Herald* Female Athlete of the Year 1996
- Scotus Athlete of the Year 1996

Chad Mustard '96

Shamrock Hall of Fame – Athlete

Inducted 2006

- Four-year letter winner in track, three-year letter winner in football and basketball
- Played on the State Championship football team 1993
- Honorable Mention All-State in football 1994
- First team All-State 1995
- Second team All-Class All-State 1995
- First team All-State in basketball 1996 with 20 points per game average
- Set school record for blocked shots in game, season, and career
- Played on State tournament team 1996 that finished 20-4 and ranked #4
- State track qualifier 1995, 1996
- Finished 5th in triple jump at State track 1996
- Scotus Athlete of the Year 1996

Carmen Burbach '97

Shamrock Hall of Fame – Athlete

Inducted 2007

- Four-year starter in volleyball (102-3 record), on two state championship teams (1995, 1996) and two state runners-up (1993, 1994)
- First team All-State 1994, 1995, 1996
- Honorary captain on the 1995 and 1996 All-State teams
- Second team Super State 1995
- First team Super State and honorary captain 1996
- Huskerland Prep Magazine volleyball Player of the Year 1996
- In basketball, three-year starter on state runner-up teams (1995) and state championship teams (1996, 1997)
- Second team All-State 1997
- Also lettered in track
- 1997 Scotus Athlete of the Year

Jesse Kosch '93

Shamrock Hall of Fame – Athlete

Inducted 2007

- Four-year player in football and broke the Class B single game rushing record with 376 yards against North Platte St. Patrick
- Current school career record holder for rushing yards (3,454)
- First team All-State punter 1991, 1992
- Played basketball two years, lettering in 1991
- Participated in track 9th-11th grade and was the first freshman to lead the team in scoring
- Qualified for state track meet 1990, 1991, 1992
- Second team All-State in soccer 1993, and was third-leading scorer in the state
- Most Valuable Player, and the only player from both rosters not from a Class A school in the 1993 Shrine All-Star soccer game
- 1993 Scotus Athlete of the Year

Dan Mahoney

Shamrock Hall of Fame – Coach

Inducted 2007

- Head girls cross country coach 1978-2005
- Head boys cross country coach 1997-2005
- Head coach of State Championship girls team 2000, 2001, 2002 and four State runner-up teams 1991, 1999, 2003, 2004
- Three individual State Champion runners 2000, 2001, 2002
- Nine District Championship teams, nine District Runner-up teams, and eight Conference Championship teams
- Head girls track coach 1978-2004
- Three individual State Champion athletes, two State Champion relays
- Three District Championship teams and three District Runner-up teams
- Nine Conference Championship teams and three Conference Runner-up teams
- Nebraska Coaches Association Cross Country Coach of the Year 2002
- Nebraska Coaches Association 25-Year Award 2002 and Milestone Award for Girls Cross Country 2005
- Taught social studies and science at Scotus for 28 years, Scotus Outstanding Service Award 2005

Vern Younger

Shamrock Hall of Fame – Coach
Inducted 2007

- Assistant varsity football coach 1967-2005 (38 years) and helped coach three state championship teams (1967, 1984, 1993)
- Head freshman football coach 1967-2003, finishing with a 140-42 record
- In basketball, coached as head/junior varsity/freshman (1967-74)
- In track, was varsity assistant from 1969-1996, working with state championship teams (1978, 1979)
- Athletic director 1970-77, helped usher in girls athletics at Scotus
- Nebraska Coaches Association Assistant Coach of the Year 1986-87
- Recipient of the 25-year coaching award 1992
- Taught biology, physiology, and PE for 40+ years and was sophomore class sponsor 40+ years

Marc Wolfe '78

Shamrock Hall of Fame – Booster
Inducted 2008

- A thirty-year member of the Shamrock Club and has served as Secretary for more than 20 years rarely missing the Club's monthly meetings in performance of his duties.
- Has been the keeper of the clock at all home varsity football and basketball games for more than twenty years and for volleyball games for many years, and has been a loyal volunteer at the finish line for Scotus track teams.
- His knowledge of Shamrock athletics and loyalty to his alma mater is unquestioned and an inspiration for all.

Kristie Korth '98

Shamrock Hall of Fame – Athlete

Inducted 2008

- Started on State Championship volleyball teams 1995, 1996, 1997
- First team Class C-1 All-State and All-Class volleyball tournament team 1997
- Started on State Championship basketball teams 1996, 1997, 1998 and State runner-up 1995
- First team Class C-1 All-State basketball 1998
- Honorable mention Class C-1 All-State basketball 1996, 1997
- Played on the 1998 State Championship soccer team and set a state record of 28 season assists
- First team All-Nebraska soccer 1997, 1998
- First team Class B All-State soccer and honorary captain 1998
- First team Class B All-State soccer 1997
- Second team All Nebraska 1996 and Honorable Mention All State soccer 1995
- *Omaha World-Herald* Nebraska Female Athlete of the Year 1998
- Scotus Athlete of the Year 1998

John Kopetzky '80

Shamrock Hall of Fame – Booster

Inducted 2010

- Lettered 11 times as a student manager for boys sports football 1976-79 (4 letters), track 1978-79 (2 letters) and a very rare 5-year letter winner in basketball (1976-80)
- As a student manager he recorded and maintained game statistics, repaired equipment and provided general support for athletic training and sports medicine activities
- Nominated for the Shamrock Hall of Fame by a significant number of alumni, one comment clearly stood out: "He provided service-oriented leadership and changed the paradigm that participation in sports did not have to be on the playing field"

Jim Dolezal '81

Shamrock Hall of Fame – Booster

Inducted 2010

- Lettered five times as a student manager for the boys basketball and track teams
- Member of the State Championship track team 1978 and the 1981 boys State basketball tournament semi-final squad - the only team in Scotus basketball history to win a game at the state tournament
- For more than 30 years after graduation, he has supported Scotus athletics by providing outstanding coverage as a sportswriter for the Columbus Telegram (since 1983) and as broadcaster for Three Eagles Communications (since 1997).
- He has also served as Master of Ceremonies on numerous occasions for the Scotus Athletic Banquet

Kim Rickert '98

Shamrock Hall of Fame – Athlete

Inducted 2011

- Three-year letter winner in volleyball
- Played on State Championship volleyball team 1995, 1996, 1997
- Second team All State 1997
- Member of the North team in the 1998 All-Star volleyball match in Lincoln
- Started four years in basketball
- Played on the 1995 State runner-up team and State Championship teams 1996, 1997, 1998
- First team All-State in basketball 1998
- Lettered in track four years and State meet qualifier sophomore year

Rhea Wemhoff '97

Shamrock Hall of Fame – Athlete

Inducted 2011

- Three-year starter in volleyball, on two undefeated State Champion teams 1995, 1996 and State runner-up team 1994
- First team All-State 1996, Honorable Mention 1994, 1995
- Three-year starter in basketball, on two State Championship teams 1996, 1997 and one State runner-up team 1995
- First team All-State 1996, 1997 and Honorable Mention 1995
- Lettered in track three years

Jewelia Grennan '99

Shamrock Hall of Fame – Athlete

Inducted 2012

- Three-year letter winner in volleyball, on State Championship teams 1996, 1997, 1998
- First team Class C-1 All-State 1997, 1998
- First team Super State 1998
- Huskerland Prep magazine Class C-1 Player of the Year 1999
- Four-year letter winner in basketball, on State Championship teams 1997, 1998
- First team Class C-1 All-State 1999, second team All-State 1998
- Three-year letter winner in soccer, on State Championship team 1998, State runner-up team 1999, State tournament qualifier 1997
- Honorable Mention Class B All-State 1998
- Scotus Female Lifter of the Year and Female Athlete of the Year 1999

Stephanie Kruse '99

Shamrock Hall of Fame – Athlete

Inducted 2012

- Three-year letter winner in volleyball, on State Championship teams 1996, 1997, 1998
- First team Class C-1 All-State 1998
- Three-year letter winner in basketball, on State Championship teams 1997, 1998
- Honorable Mention Class C-1 All-State 1998
- Four-year letter winner in soccer, on State Championship team 1998, State runner-up team 1999, State tourney qualifiers 1996, 1997
- First team Class B All-State and honorary captain 1999
- All Nebraska second team 1999
- *Lincoln Journal Star* Super-State first team 1999
- Second team All-State 1998
- Honorable Mention All-State 1996, 1997
- Played in Shrine soccer game, 1999

Gary Puetz

Shamrock Hall of Fame – Coach
Inducted 2012

- Assistant football and track coach 1975-2001 (27 years). During that time, Scotus won two state football titles. As line coach, he coached 27 All-State athletes
- In track, Scotus won two state titles and was runner-up twice. As throws coach, he coached many state qualifiers and medalists
- Athletic/Activities Director at Scotus 1995-present. During that time, Scotus won 28 state championships in seven sports
- Scotus received nine *Omaha World-Herald* All-Sports awards and four NSAA CupAll-School awards
- Nebraska Coaches Association Assistant Coach of the Year Award 1991 and NSAA Distinguished Service Award 2012

Tom Rogers '99

Shamrock Hall of Fame – Athlete
Inducted 2013

- Three-year letter winner in football
- First team All-State in football 1997, 1998
- Invited to, and played in, Down Under Bowl in Australia 1997
- Four-year letter winner in soccer and played on State Championship team sophomore year
- First team All-State in soccer 1998, 1999
- Super State All-State 1999
- KLIR Athlete of the Year 1999

Heather VanAckeren '00

Shamrock Hall of Fame – Athlete

Inducted 2013

- Four-year letter winner volleyball, basketball, and soccer
- Played on seven State Championship teams
- In volleyball, started for State Championship teams 1998, 1999
- First team All-State 1998, 1999
- Honorable Mention All-State 1997, Third Team Super State 1999
- Four-year team record 110-5 with four State Championships
- In basketball, played on State Championship teams 1997, 1998
- Started for three years with a record of 83-15
- Four-year letter winner in soccer
- Played on 1998 State Championship team
- Honorable Mention All-State 1999
- Scotus Athlete of the Year, Lifter of the Year, KLIR Athlete of the Year 2000

Molly Engel '01

Shamrock Hall of Fame – Athlete

Inducted 2013

- Four-year letter winner in cross country and track and competed at State meets in both sports all four years
- First team All-State in cross country 1998, 1999, 2000
- First team Super State 2000
- At State cross country meet, finished 20th in 1997, 8th in 1998, 7th in 1999, and 1st in 2000
- At State track meet in 1998, finished 2nd in the 4x800 with a school record time of 9:43.3; 5th in the two mile, 4th in the one mile, and the team finished as State runner-up
- At State track meet in 1999, finished 3rd in the 4x800, 6th in the two mile and one mile
- At State track meet in 2000, finished 1st in the 4x800, 3rd in the one mile
- At State track meet in 2001, finished 3rd in the 4x800
- Scotus Athlete of the Year 2001

Meghan Pile '02

Shamrock Hall of Fame – Athlete

Inducted 2014

- Four-year starter in volleyball; on State Championship teams in 1998, 1999, and 2001 and on the State runner-up team in 2000, combined record of 113-3
- First team Class C-1 All-State 2001, Second team Class C-1 All-State '99, '00
- Third team Super State 2001
- Current school career record holder for most digs (695)
- Four-year letter winner in basketball and played on two State tournament teams including the 2002 State runner-up team (21-5)
- Second team All-State 2002
- Four-year starter in soccer; on State Championship team 2002 (16-4) and State runner-up teams 1999, 2000
- First team All-State 2001, 2002
- First team Super State 2002, second team 2001
- Scotus Athlete of the Year and KLIR Athlete of the Year 2002

John Petersen

Shamrock Hall of Fame – Coach

Inducted 2014

- Head volleyball coach 1977-2013
- Head girls basketball coach 1977-1999
- Freshman/JV girls basketball coach 2000-2013
- Volleyball record 828-136 with 15 State Championships and 7 State Runners-up in 27 State tournament appearances
- Basketball record 353-115 with 3 State Championships and 1 State runner-up in 5 State tournament appearances
- *Omaha World-Herald* Nebraska Girls Coach of the Year, 1991
- *Lincoln Journal Star* Nebraska Girls Coach of the Year 1994, 2007
- Nebraska Coaches Association volleyball Coach of the Year 1993, 2001, 2006
- Nebraska Coaches Association volleyball Award 2003
- National High School Athletic Hall of Fame inductee 2008
- National High School volleyball Coach of the Year 2012

Heidi Sobota '05

Shamrock Hall of Fame – Athlete

Inducted 2015

- In volleyball, played on the 2002 and 2003 State Championship teams and the 2004 State runner-up team
- First team All-State 2004, third team Super State 2004
- In basketball, played on the 2004 State Championship team
- In soccer, four-year starter and played on the 2002 State Championship team
- First team All-State 2003, 2004, 2005
- Second team Super State 2004, 2005
- Scotus Gatorade Player of the Year and the KLIR Athlete of the Year 2005
- Played soccer for Briar Cliff University
- Second team all-conference 2005
- Played on the Charger team that finished third in regionals
- Team captain at Northwest Missouri State; First team all-conference

Laura Dolezal '04

Shamrock Hall of Fame – Athlete

Inducted 2015

- In volleyball from 7th grade though her senior year, Laura's teams never lost a match. Played on three State Championship teams 2001, 2002, 2003
- First team All-State 2003
- Played in the Nebraska Coaches Association All-Star volleyball game 2004
- In basketball, played on the 2004 undefeated State Championship team (24-0) and the State runner-up team 2002
- In soccer, played on the State Championship teams 2001, 2002
- First team All-State 2003, 2004
- Finalist, *Omaha World-Herald* Nebraska High School Female Athlete of the Year 2004
- Scotus Athlete of the Year and KLIR Athlete of the Year 2004
- Played college volleyball at Wayne State College and selected first team All-Nebraska Division II 2004, 2005, 2006, 2007, Northern Sun Intercollegiate Conference Libero of the Year 2005, 2006, first team All NSIC 2005, 2006, 2007 and first team All NSIC region 2006, 2007

Don & Karen (Gdowski) '73 Mroczek

Shamrock Hall of Fame – Boosters

Inducted 2014

- Don has coordinated football gate volunteers for 30 years, is a 32-year Shamrock Club member, is a past President (two terms)
- He has been the track finish line clerk for more than 20 years, and coached Scotus youth basketball teams for 25 years and was assistant basketball coach for 2 years
- He has co-chaired the Columbus Area Chamber's Holiday basketball Tournament for 31 years and plays Santa Claus at Scotus events
- Don and Karen co-chaired the Scotus Gala in 1994 and have decorated for the Gala for the past 15 years
- Karen chaired the Scotus Mothers Craft Boutique for 13 years and created and directs the Scotus Bid-A-Bag fund-raiser, now in its 6th year

Annette Hash

Shamrock Hall of Fame – Booster

Inducted 2015

- Arrived at Scotus in 1984 and has served the school as both the administrative assistant to the activities director and as the assistant director of development
- Has supported numerous Scotus coaches, athletes, and activity events, nearly all 34 Scotus Gala dinner auctions, ten Scotus Education Fund Drives and countless other development activities
- Received the Scotus Outstanding Service Award 2003
- For her distinguished service to Shamrock athletics and development, Scotus welcomes Annette as a booster in the Shamrock Hall of Fame!

Al Niedbalski '71

Shamrock Hall of Fame – Booster

Inducted 2016

- Three-year letter winner in football and one year letter winner in basketball
- Co-founder of the Alumni basketball Tournament, 1984
- Long time Shamrock Club member and officer
- Scotus School Board member 1995-2000, including one year as Board President
- Helped lead construction of the McLaughlin Activity Field
- Public address announcer for football, volleyball, and basketball, 2001-present
- Co-chair of Columbus Golf Committee, which helped bring the NSAA Girls Golf State Championship to Columbus the past seven years

Jamie Tooley '06

Shamrock Hall of Fame – Athlete

Inducted 2016

- Three-year letter winner in volleyball
- Played on State Championship team 2005, 2006 and State runner-up team 2004 and was a part of the Nebraska all-sport all-time win streak of 115
- Honorable Mention All-State 2005, First team Class C-1 All-State 2006
- Second team All-Class All-State 2006
- Three-year letter winner in basketball
- Played on State Championship team 2004
- Honorable Mention All-State 2006
- Four-year letter winner and State qualifier in track
- Finished 3rd at State in 3200 relay 2004, Finished 6th at State in triple jump 2005
- Finished 1st at State in triple jump with a school record (37'6"), 4th in the long jump, and 5th in 400 relay 2006
- Scotus Athlete of the Year, Lifter of the Year, KLIR Athlete of the Year 2006

SHAMROCK TEAM AND INDIVIDUAL RECORDS

FOOTBALL SINGLE GAME RECORDS			
	PLAYER	RECORD	YEAR
MOST POINTS SCORED	Tony Korth	36	2004
MOST RUSHING YARDS	Tony Korth	391	2004
MOST PASSING YARDS	Doug Duren	338	1980
MOST RECEIVING YARDS	Glen Kucera	223	1980
MOST PASSES COMPLETED	Doug Duren	23	1980
MOST PASSES CAUGHT	Glen Kucera	11	1980
MOST PASSING TD'S	Doug Duren	5	1980
MOST TOTAL TACKLES	Dave Steiner	26	1973

FOOTBALL SEASON RECORDS			
	PLAYER	RECORD	YEAR
MOST POINTS SCORED	Jeff Herdzina	225	1993
MOST RUSHING YARDS	Jeff Herdzina	2,181	1993
MOST PASSING YARDS	Doug Duren	1,557	1980
MOST RECEIVING YARDS	Glen Kucera	1,001	1980
MOST PASSES COMPLETED	Doug Duren	90	1980
MOST PASSES CAUGHT	Glen Kucera	49	1980
MOST PASSING TD'S	Doug Duren	18	1980
MOST TOTAL TACKLES	Rick Schumacher	153	1978

FOOTBALL CAREER RECORDS			
	PLAYER	RECORD	YEAR
MOST POINTS SCORED	Jeff Herdzina	309	1991-93
MOST RUSHING YARDS	Jesse Kosch	3,454	1990-92
MOST PASSING YARDS	Dan Briggs	2,604	1969-71
MOST RECEIVING YARDS	Glen Kucera	1,291	1979-80
MOST PASSES COMPLETED	Dan Briggs	147	1969-71
MOST PASSES CAUGHT	Glen Kucera	64	1979-80
MOST PASSING TD'S	Dan Briggs	26	1969-71
MOST TOTAL TACKLES	Dave Steiner	246	1971-73

FOOTBALL TEAM RECORDS		
CATEGORY	RECORD	YEAR
MOST WINS IN A SEASON	13-0	1984 1993
MOST DEFENSIVE SHUTOUTS	7	1984
AVG. POINTS ALLOWED PER GAME	4.2	1978

VOLLEYBALL MATCH RECORDS			
	PLAYER	RECORD	YEAR
KILLS	Monica Boeding	26	2009
BLOCKS	Katie Beiermann	9	2008
ASSISTS	Liz Hadland	55	2005
DIGS	Kara Moore	31	2011
ACES	Kelli Martin	12	1985
SERVING POINTS	Kelli Martin	24	1985

VOLLEYBALL SEASON RECORDS			
	PLAYER	RECORD	YEAR
KILLS	Lauren Hellbusch	278	2011
BLOCKS	JoDe Cielocha	74	1992
ASSISTS	Morgan Thorsen	883	2014
DIGS	Kim Stutzman	359	2014
ACES	Kelli Martin	112	1985
SERVING POINTS	Alyssa Kuta	253	2014

VOLLEYBALL CAREER RECORDS			
	PLAYER	RECORD	YEAR
KILLS	Monica Boeding	835	2007-09
BLOCKS	JoDe Cielocha	174	1991-93
ASSISTS	Jordan Chohon	2,322	2009-11
DIGS	Meghan Pile	695	1998-2001
ACES	Kelli Martin	262	1983-86
SERVING POINTS	Jordan Chohon	681	2009-11

VOLLEYBALL TEAM RECORDS		
CATEGORY	RECORD	YEAR
KILLS, SEASON	1,076	2014
BLOCKS, SEASON	179	2014
ASSISTS, SEASON	968	2014
DIGS, SEASON	1,550	2014
ACES, SEASON	290	1985
CONSECUTIVE WINS	115	2001-04

BOYS BASKETBALL GAME RECORDS			
	PLAYER	RECORD	YEAR
POINTS	Mark Brezenski	48	1982-83
REBOUNDS	Conrad Slusarski	22	1974-75
ASSISTS	Rich Pensick Eric Pinger	13	1981 1990
STEALS	Mark Brezinski	12	1982-83
3-POINTERS	Grant Lahm	8	2014-15
BLOCKS	Dalton Taylor	7	2014-15

BOYS BASKETBALL SEASON RECORDS			
	PLAYER	RECORD	YEAR
POINTS	Grant Lahm	587	2014-15
REBOUNDS	Conrad Slusarski	305	1974-75
ASSISTS	Joe Quattrocchi	139	1989-90
STEALS	Mark Brezinski	82	1982-83
3-POINTERS	Grant Lahm	105	2014-15
BLOCKS	Dalton Taylor	56	2014-15
FIELD GOAL %	Travis Brock	65.2%	1989-90
FREE THROW %	Chad Gonka	91.3%	1995-96
3-POINT %	Grant Lahm	49.0%	2014-15

BOYS BASKETBALL CAREER RECORDS			
	PLAYER	RECORD	YEAR
POINTS	Grant Lahm	1,970	2011-15
REBOUNDS	Gregg Grubaugh	576	1972-75
ASSISTS	Joe Quattrocchi	279	1989-91
STEALS	Mark Brezinski	164	1980-83
3-POINTERS	Grant Lahm	300	2011-15
BLOCKS	Dalton Taylor	91	2013-15
3-POINT %	Grant Lahm	46.0%	2011-15

BOYS BASKETBALL TEAM RECORDS		
CATEGORY	RECORD	YEAR
TEAM DEFENSIVE AVERAGE	45.1	2014-15
TEAM OFFENSIVE AVERAGE	73.9	1980-81
SEASON RECORD	23-5	2014-15

GIRLS BASKETBALL GAME RECORDS			
	PLAYER	RECORD	YEAR
POINTS	Chris Orr	33	1987-88
REBOUNDS	Linda Warth Lana Torczon	21	1978-79 1980-81
ASSISTS	Megan Tooley	10	1990-91
STEALS	Kristie Korth Alyssa Foltz	11	1995-96 2010-11
3-POINTERS	Shauna Greiner Sami Spenner Monica Boeding	5	1995-96 2008-09 2008-09

GIRLS BASKETBALL SEASON RECORDS			
	PLAYER	RECORD	YEAR
POINTS	Chris Orr	376	1987-88
REBOUNDS	Lana Torczon	248	1980-81
ASSISTS	Megan Tooley	97	1989-90
STEALS	Kelly Nicolas	105	1985-86
3-POINTERS	Shauna Greiner	37	1995-96
FIELD GOAL %	Angie Naughtin	60.0%	1993-94
FREE THROW %	Darlene Rinkol	89.0%	1990-91

GIRLS BASKETBALL CAREER RECORDS			
	PLAYER	RECORD	YEAR
POINTS	Kelly Nicolas	1,075	1984-87
REBOUNDS	Kristi Sobota	583	1988-91
ASSISTS	Megan Tooley	313	1988-91
STEALS	Kelly Nicolas	310	1984-87
3-POINTERS	Monica Boeding	51	2008-10

GIRLS BASKETBALL TEAM RECORDS		
CATEGORY	RECORD	YEAR
TEAM DEFENSIVE AVERAGE	26.6	2001
TEAM OFFENSIVE AVERAGE	62.2	1986
SEASON RECORD	25-0	1996 2004

BOYS CROSS COUNTRY RECORDS			
	RUNNER	TIME	YEAR
HOME COURSE 5K	Nick Preister	16:31	2011
	Dave Rhode	16:56	1985
	Joel Ostdiek	16:58	2011
	Nathan Ostdiek	17:05	2014
	Erik Hash	17:07	1993
STATE COURSE 5K	Tim Zuerlein	16:57	1981
	Nick Preister	17:14	2011
	Joel Ostdiek	17:21	2011
	Nathan Ostdiek	17:23	2014
	Zeph Swope	17:27	2008

BOYS CROSS COUNTRY TEAM RECORD		
CATEGORY	RECORD	YEAR
BEST TEAM RECORD	108-3	2014

GIRLS CROSS COUNTRY RECORDS			
	RUNNER	TIME	YEAR
HOME COURSE 5K	Kaylee Tonniges	20:19	2013
	Jessica Schaecher	20:45	2013
	Brooke Olmer	20:49	2013
	Jessica Lahm	21:20	2013
	Carly Fehringer	21:20	2013
STATE COURSE 5K	Jessica Schaecher	20:22	2013
	Kaylee Tonniges	21:20	2014
	Carly Fehringer	21:29	2013
	Jaimee Beauvais	21:30	2014
	Brooke Olmer	21:31	2013
HOME COURSE 4K	Morgan Benesch	15:13	2012
STATE COURSE 4K	Morgan Benesch	14:57	2012

GIRLS CROSS COUNTRY TEAM RECORD		
CATEGORY	RECORD	YEAR
BEST TEAM RECORD	118-1	2013

BOYS INDIVIDUAL GOLF RECORDS			
	PLAYER	SCORE	YEAR
9 HOLES	Derrick Diermann	34	2010
18 HOLES	Brady Vancura	70	2011
MOST TOURNEYS WON, SEASON	Brady Vancura	4	2011
MOST TOURNEYS WON, CAREER	Brady Vancura	7	2008-11
STATE CHAMPION	Brady Vancura		2011

BOYS TEAM GOLF RECORDS		
	SCORE	YEAR
9 HOLES	157	2014
18 HOLES	308	2014
MOST TOURNEYS WON, SEASON	3	2014
STATE CHAMPIONS		1981

GIRLS INDIVIDUAL GOLF RECORDS			
	PLAYER	SCORE	YEAR
9 HOLES	Jacy Gasper	36	2010
18 HOLES	Jacy Gasper	74	2010
36 HOLES	Jacy Gasper	154	2010
MOST STATE MEDALS	Jacy Gasper	4	2007-10
STATE RUNNER-UP	Danielle Bernt Jacy Gasper		2002 2010

GIRLS TEAM GOLF RECORDS		
	SCORE	YEAR
9 HOLES	175	2002
18 HOLES	351	2002
36 HOLES	706	2002
STATE RUNNER-UP		1998 2013 2014

BOYS SOCCER GAME RECORDS			
	PLAYER	RECORD	YEAR
GOALS	Jeff Herdzina	5	1993
ASSISTS	Cody Zimmerman	4	2012 2014
SAVES	Jake Huss	30	2012

BOYS SOCCER SEASON RECORDS			
	PLAYER	RECORD	YEAR
GOALS	Jeff Herdzina	33	1993
ASSISTS	Cody Zimmerman	18	2014
SAVES	Josh Jepsen	170	2006
SHUTOUTS	J. Eickmeier G. Buelt S. Schumacher E. Chohon	10	1998 2001 2009 2015
GOALS AGAINST AVERAGE	Chase Beiermann	0.650	2008

BOYS SOCCER CAREER RECORDS			
	PLAYER	RECORD	YEAR
GOALS	Jeff Herdzina	91	1992-94
ASSISTS	Cody Zimmerman	35	2011-14
SHUTOUTS	Jeff Eickmeier	25	1996-98
GOALS AGAINST AVERAGE	Chase Beiermann	0.863	2006-08

GIRLS SOCCER GAME RECORDS			
	PLAYER	RECORD	YEAR
GOALS	Sara Kunneman	5	1998

GIRLS SOCCER SEASON RECORDS			
	PLAYER	RECORD	YEAR
GOALS	Sara Kunneman	43	1998
ASSISTS	Kristie Korth	28	1998
SHUTOUTS	Melanie Bonk	13	1996

GIRLS SOCCER CAREER RECORDS			
	PLAYER	RECORD	YEAR
GOALS	Kristie Korth	73	1995-98
ASSISTS	Kristie Korth	58	1995-98
SAVES	Mollie Jones	642	2005-08
SHUTOUTS	Melanie Bonk	43	1995-98

GIRLS SOCCER TEAM RECORDS		
CATEGORY	RECORD	YEAR
BEST RECORD	18-1	1999
GOALS SCORED	115	1998
GOALS ALLOWED	8	1999
SEASON SHUTOUTS	13	1996 1998

BOYS TRACK & FIELD RECORDS			
EVENT	PLAYER	RECORD	YEAR
100 M DASH	Mike Cielocha	10.50	1978
200M DASH	Mike Cielocha	21.40	1977
400M DASH	Mike Cielocha	47.90	1977
800M DASH	Tim Zuerlein	1:57.70	1982
1600M RUN	Fred Maguire	4:29.95	1991
3200M RUN	Tim Zuerlein	9:55.60	1982
110/100 MH HURDLES	Tom Sobotka	14.30	1976
300M INT/ LOW HURDLES	Ron Starzec	39.90	1981
400M RELAY	J. Podraza R. Miller D.Younger K. Neal	42.97	1985
1600M RELAY	M. Strecker B. Przymus G. Lahm C. Mroczek	3:25.67	2015
3200M RELAY	T. Zuerlein T. Cielocha J. Sutko D. Stopak	8:07.30	1981
LONG JUMP	Joe Blahak	23'0"	1969
TRIPLE JUMP	Karl Hroza	47'0"	1985
HIGH JUMP	Mike Ernst Matt Beller	6'5"	1985 1995
POLE VAULT	Josh Spenner	14'0"	2011
SHOT PUT	Pat Engelbert	57'9"	1987
DISCUS	Ryan Mustard	167'5"	2014

GIRLS TRACK & FIELD RECORDS			
EVENT	PLAYER	RECORD	YEAR
100 M DASH	Brenda Grubaugh	12.10	1974
200M DASH	Amber Ewers	24.50	2008
400M DASH	Amber Ewers	57.17	2010
800M DASH	Renee Bowman	2:20.00	1998
1600M RUN	Renee Bowman	5:15.70	1998
3200M RUN	Angela Fisher	11:16.00	2002
110/100 MH HURDLES	Amanda Cielocha	15.00	2002
300M INT/ LOW HURDLES	Kellie Korth	45.90	2007
400M RELAY	A. Paprocki S. Spenner M. Boeding A. Ewers	49.76	2009
1600M RELAY	J. Kosch R. Bowman M. Boeding A. Ewers	4:04.00	1995
3200M RELAY	L. Hegemann M. Engel M. Schmidt R. Bowman	9:43.30	2009
LONG JUMP	Sami Spenner	17'73/4"	2009
TRIPLE JUMP	Jamie Tooley	37'6"	2006
HIGH JUMP	Mary Fehringer	5'6"	1987
POLE VAULT	Tara Starzec	11'8"	2013
SHOT PUT	Becky Puetz	42'3"	1989
DISCUS	Kristina Flint	134'10"	2006

SHAMROCK ATHLETES OF THE YEAR

St. Bonaventure / Scotus Athletes of the Year					
YEAR	MALE	FEMALE	YEAR	MALE	FEMALE
1959	Dennis Novotny		1988	Steve Soulliere	Mary Fehringer
1960	Larry Staroscik		1989	Travis Bock	Camille Sobota
1961	Bill Backes		1990	Travis Brock	Karey Keeshan
1962	Ted Starostka		1991	Eric Pinger	Kristi Sobota
1963	Bill Shonka		1992	Matt Naughton	Brenda Sliva
1964	Dave Kudron		1993	Jesse Kosch	Jessica Peterson
1965	John Iossi		1994	Jeff Herdzina	JoDe Cieloha
1966	Bill Mimick		1995	Brandon Drum	Angie Naughton
1967	Jim Legenza, Steve Shadle		1996	Chad Mustard	Shauna Greiner
1968	Bill Kosch		1997	Nick Mroczek	Carmen Burbach
1969	Joe Blahak		1998	Aaron Legenza	Kristie Korth
1970	Bob Kosch		1999	Matt Mroczek Thadd Recek	Jewelia Grennan
1971	Stan Liss		2000	Jeremiah Grell	Heather Van Ackeren
1972	Dan Brock		2001	Jeff Kosch	Molly Engel
1973	Tom Zabawa		2002	Craig Pekny	Meghan Pile
1974	Tim Thomas	Brenda Grubaugh	2003	Josh Melliger	Jennifer Sackett
1975	Gregg Grubaugh Dan Steiner	Cheryl Wieser	2004	Brian Malicky	Laura Dolezal
1976	Tom Sobotka	Kathy Korger	2005	Pat Schaecher	Kayla Engel Ann Beiermann
1977	Chris Hoffman	Jackie Melliger	2006	Eric Puckett	Jamie Tooley
1978	Tim Hroza	Connie Hajek	2007	Kyle Mroczek	Liz Hadland
1978	Rick Schumacher	Linda Warth	2008	Michael Novicki	Kellie Korth

1980	Tim Engelbert	Jackie Paprocki	2009	Chase Beiermann	Katie Beiermann Sami Spenner
1981	Glen Kucera	Lana Torczon	2010	Shawn Schumacher	Monica Boeding
1982	Tim Zuerlein	Laurie Hajek	2011	Brady Vancura	Amber Ewers
1983	Mark Brezinski	Jo Rhode Trish Hroza	2012	Ryan Miksch	Jordan Chohon
1984	Jim Paprocki Todd Kudron	Sheri Svoboda	2013	Derek Lahm	Kara Moore
1985	Jeff Podraza	Karen Tooley	2014	Cody Zimmerman	Laura Miksch
1986	Karl Hroza	Wendy Nicolas	2015	Grant Lahm	Kelsey Kessler
1987	Pat Engelbert	Kelli Martin Kelly Nicolas	2016	Jake Bos	Sarah Schumacher

SHAMROCK ATHLETIC TIMELINE

1930s

1931: First St. Bonaventure basketball team.

1936: Paul "Dutch" Ernst begins his 14-year career as Shamrock coach.

1937: Basketball team qualifies for the state tournament; the only Shamrock team to make it to the state tourney until 1981.

1940s

1941: First St. Bonaventure track team (spring) and six-man football team (fall).

1943: Football finished 8-0. Frank Tagwerker named All-State as a junior. He gave up his senior year and joined the Navy in 1944.

1946: 11-man football is introduced.

1950s

1950: Coach Ernst retires after 14 years of coaching football, basketball, and track. During his entire tenure, he was a volunteer.

1950: Cletus Fischer is hired as the first full-time Shamrock football, basketball, and track coach. In five years, his football teams went 35-8 and were ranked in the top 10 four times. He compiled a 32-17 record in basketball.

1953: Football finishes 8-0 and is ranked #1 during the regular season in the *Lincoln Journal Star* poll; final ranking of #2 in both the *Journal Star* and *Omaha World-Herald.*

1958: Memorial Hall opens, providing the Shamrocks with their first home court. Previously, they practiced in an old barn on the corner of 16th Street and 19th Avenue and played home games at Columbus High School.

1960s

1964: St. Bonaventure captures the Class B State Track Championship.

1964: Final St. Bonaventure football team finishes undefeated with a final ranking of #3.

1965: On July 1, St. Bonaventure High School becomes Scotus Central Catholic, supported by nine parishes (St. Bonaventure, St. Anthony and St. Isidore in Columbus; St. Mary and St. Augustine in Schuyler; St. Joseph in Platte Center; St. Rose in Genoa; St. Lawrence in Silver Creek; and St. Stanislaus in Duncan).

1967: Scotus named Class C football champions by the *Omaha World-Herald.*

1970s

1973: Girls athletics begin with volleyball and track.

1978: Scotus wins Class B Boys Track & Field State Championship.

1979: Scotus wins Class B Boys Track & Field State Championship.

1980s

1980: Shamrock Activity Center (later Dowd Activity Center) opens with a boys basketball win over Council Bluffs St. Albert.

1981: Scotus wins Class B Boys Golf State Championship.

1984: Scotus wins Class B Football State Championship.

1986: Scotus wins Class B Volleyball State Championship.

1990s

1990: Scotus wins Class B Volleyball State Championship.

1993: Scotus wins Class B Football State Championship.

1995: Scotus win Class C-1 Volleyball State Championship, the first of five titles in a row.

1996: Scotus wins Class C-1 Girls Basketball State Championship, the first of three in a row.

1996: Scotus win Class C-1 Volleyball State Championship.

1997: Scotus wins Class C-1 Girls Basketball State Championship.
1997: Scotus wins Class B Boys Soccer State Championship.
1997: Scotus wins Class C-1 Volleyball State Championship.
1998: Scotus wins Class C-1 Girls Basketball State Championship.
1998: Scotus wins Class B Girls State Soccer Championship.
1998: Scotus wins Class C-1 Volleyball State Championship.
1999: Scotus wins Class C-1 Volleyball State Championship.

2000s

2000: Scotus wins Class C Girls Cross Country State Championship.
2001: Scotus wins Girls and Boys Class B Soccer State Championship.
2001: Scotus wins Class C-1 volleyball State Championship.
2001: Scotus wins Class C Girls Cross Country State Championship.
2002: Scotus wins Girls Class B Soccer State Championship.
2002: Scotus wins Girls Class C Cross Country State Championship.
2002: Scotus wins Class C-1 Volleyball State Championship.
2003: Scotus wins Class C-1 Volleyball State Championship.
2004: Scotus wins Class C-1 Girls Basketball State Championship.
2004: Scotus sets a Nebraska all-time all-sport record with its 115th consecutive volleyball win.
2005: Scotus wins Class C-1 Volleyball State Championship.
2006: Scotus wins Class C-1 Volleyball State Championship.
2008: Scotus wins Class C-1 Volleyball State Championship.
2009: Scotus win Class B Boys Soccer State Championship.
2009: Scotus wins Class B Girls Track & Field State Championship.
2009: Scotus wins Class C Boys Cross Country State Championship.
2009: Scotus wins the Class C Girls NSAA Cup for 2008-2009 school year, the first of five Girls NSAA Cups in a row.
2009: Scotus wins the Class C All-School NSAA Cup for 2008-2009 school year.
2009: Scotus wins Class C-1 Volleyball State Championship.

2010s

2010: Scotus wins the Class C Girls NSAA Cup for 2009-2010 school year.

2011: Scotus wins Class C-1 Volleyball State Championship.

2011: Scotus wins the Class C Girls NSAA Cup for 2010-2011 school year.

2012: Scotus wins the Class C Girls NSAA Cup for 2011-2012 school year.

2012: Scotus wins Class C Girls Cross Country State Championship.

2013: Scotus wins the Class C Girls NSAA Cup for 2012-2013 school year.

2013: Scotus wins Class C Girls Cross Country State Championship.

2014: Scotus wins Class B Boys Soccer State Championship.

2014: Scotus wins the Class C Girls NSAA Cup for 2013-2014 school year.

2014: Scotus wins the Class C All-School NSAA Cup for 2013-2014 school year.

2015: Scotus wins Class B Boys Soccer State Championship.

2015: Scotus wins the Class C Boys NSAA Cup for 2014-2015 school year.

2015: Scotus wins the Class C All-School NSAA Cup for 2014-2015 school year.

2015: Scotus wins the Class C NSAA Cup for the 2014-2015 school year.

2015: Scotus wins Class C-1 State Football Championship.

2016: Scotus wins Class B Boys Soccer State Championship.

2016: Scotus wins the Class C Boys NSAA Cup for the 2015-2016 school year.

2016: Scotus wins the Class C All-School NSAA Cup for 2015-2016 school year.

2016: Scotus wins Class C Girls Cross Country State Championship.

In the 2015-2016 school year, Scotus had an outstanding record in all sports, including two state championships and eight top five finishes. By sport, here are the final rankings by the Nebraska School Activities Association:

Football	STATE CHAMPION
Boys Cross Country	#4 at State meet
Girls Cross Country	#12 at State meet
Girls Golf	#10 at State meet
Volleyball	#4 at State tournament
Boys Basketball	#3 at State tournament
Wrestling	#5 at State tournament (Class B)
Boys Golf	#3 at State meet (Class B)
Boys Track & Field	#3 at State meet (Class B)
Girls Track & Field	#9 at State meet (Class B)
Girls Soccer	State tournament qualifier, #5 in final *Lincoln Journal Star* poll
Boys Soccer	STATE CHAMPION

STATE CHAMPIONSHIP TEAMS AND ALL-TIME ALL-STATE ATHLETES

ST. BONAVENTURE / SCOTUS STATE CHAMPIONSHIP TEAMS		
SPORT	CHAMPS	YEARS
Football	4	1967, 1984, 1993, 2015
Volleyball	15	1986, 1990, 1995, 1996, 1997, 1998, 1999, 2001, 2002, 2003, 2005, 2006, 2008, 2009, 2011
Girls Basketball	4	1996, 1997, 1998, 2004
Boys Track & Field	3	1964, 1978, 1979
Girls Track & Field	1	2009
Boys Cross Country	1	2009
Girls Cross Country	5	2000, 2001, 2002, 2012, 2013, 2016
Boys Golf	1	1981
Boys Soccer	6	1997, 2001, 2009, 2014, 2015, 2016
Girls Soccer	3	1998, 2001, 2002
Total Team State Championships	**44**	

VOLLEYBALL ALL-STATE SELECTIONS					
1982	Julie Paprocki	1996	Staci Rosche	2004	Haley Buelt
1985	Courtney Tooley	1996	Julie Trouba	2005	Jen Haney
1985	Kelli Martin	1996	Rhea Wemhoff	2005	Jamie Tooley
1986	Kelli Martin	1997	Kristie Korth	2005	Liz Hadland
1986	Kelly Nicholas	1997	Kim Rickert	2006	Liz Hadland
1986	Courtney Tooley	1997	Jewelia Grennan	2006	Laura Blair
1987	Mary Fehringer	1998	Heather VanAckeren	2008	Katie Beiermann
1988	Camille Sobota	1998	Stephanie Kruse	2008	Monica Boeding
1989	Kristi Sobota	1998	Jewelia Grennan	2008	Sami Spenner
1990	Kristi Sobota	1999	Heather VanAckeren	2009	Andrea Odbert
1990	Megan Tooley	1999	Amanda Sackett	2009	Monica Boeding
1991	Jenni Styskal	1999	Meghan Pile	2010	McKenzie Leu
1991	Tracy Wessel	2000	Kristen Blair	2010	Jordan Chohon
1992	JoDe Cieloha	2000	Meghan Pile	2011	Jordan Chohon

1993	Renee Fuhr	2000	Natasha Bender	2011	Lauren Hellbusch
1993	Tiffany Bonk	2001	Meghan Pile	2011	Kara Moore
1993	JoDe Cieloha	2001	Natasha Bender	2012	Lauren Hellbusch
1993	Renee Fuhr	2002	Jen Sackett	2012	Kara Moore
1994	Amy Johnson	2002	Renee Beiermann	2012	Payton Chohon
1994	Carmen Burbach	2002	Taylor Harsh	2012	Alyssa Foltz
1995	Shauna Greiner	2003	Taylor Harsh	2013	Payton Chohon
1995	Carmen Burbach	2003	Laura Dolezal	2014	Meghan Peiper
1995	Audrey Pfeifer	2003	Ann Beiermann	2015	Meghan Pieper
1996	Carmen Burbach	2004	Heidi Sobota	2015	Courtney Labenz
1996	Audrey Pfeifer	2004	Ann Beiermann		

GIRLS BASKETBALL ALL-STATE SELECTIONS					
1986	Kelli Martin	1994	JoDe Cieloha	1998	Kristie Korth
1986	Kelly Nicholas	1995	Angie Naughton	1999	Jewelia Grennan
1987	Kelli Martin	1996	Rhea Wemhoff	2002	Meghan Pile
1987	Kelly Nicholas	1996	Shauna Greiner	2003	Mandi Schumacher
1988	Chris Orr	1997	Rhea Wemhoff	2004	Mandi Schumacher
1991	Kristie Sobota	1998	Kim Rickert		

GIRLS SOCCER ALL-STATE SELECTIONS					
1996	Shauna Greiner	2000	Meghan Pile	2007	Natasha Scholz
1997	Jodi Eikmeier	2001	Katie Korth	2009	Katie Beiermann
1997	Kristie Korth	2001	Meghan Pile	2010	Jordan Chohon
1997	Sara Kunneman	2001	Natasha Bender	2011	Jordan Chohon
1998	Holly VanAckeren	2002	Meghan Pile	2012	Jordan Chohon
1998	Kristie Korth	2003	Nicole Mielak	2012	Stephanie Jarecke
1998	Melanie Bonk	2004	Brittany Williams	2013	Emily Kosch
1998	Sara Kunneman	2004	Heidi Sobota	2013	Kara Moore
1998	Stephanie Kruse	2004	Laura Dolezal	2013	Payton Chohon
1999	Amanda Sackett	2005	Heidi Sobota	2014	Emily Kosch
1999	Stephanie Kruse	2006	Jen Haney	2014	Payton Chohon
2000	Heather VanAckeren	2007	Katie Beiermann		

GIRLS TRACK & FIELD GOLD MEDAL WINNERS		
1973	Brenda Grubaugh	50, 100, 220 Yard Dash
1974	Brenda Grubaugh	100 Yard Dash
1982	C Witt, L Hajek, P Stopak, S Svoboda	3200M Relay
1985	Annette Sueper	3200M Run
1989	Becky Puetz	Shot Put
1992	J Jazwick, K Stopak, L Liss, T Gablenz	400M Relay
1993	Keri Stopak	100M Dash
1995	J Trouba, J Kosch, L Hegeman, R Boman	3200M Relay
1998	Renee Boman	1600M Run
2000	C Bierman, K Ames, L Beller, M Engel	
2002	Katie Swanson	100M Dash
2006	Jamie Tooley	Triple Jump
2009	A Paprocki, A Ewers, M Boeding, S Spenner	400M Relay
2009	Amber Ewers	200M Dash, *400M Dash
2010	Amber Ewers	*400M Dash
2011	Amber Ewers	400M Dash
2013	Tara Starzec	*Pole Vault

GIRLS CROSS COUNTRY STATE CHAMPIONS					
2000	Molly Engel	2001	Kayla Fisher	2002	Kayla Engel

FOOTBALL ALL-STATE SELECTIONS *(Denotes All-Class Selection)					
1953	Ken Cielocha	1983	Jim Paprocki	1996	Chris Cielocha
1954	*Clinton Gates	1984	Karl Hroza	1996	Nick Puetz
1962	John Torczon	1984	Keith Neal	1997	Jonah Bargman
1964	Keith Johnson	1984	Steve Bonk	1997	Thadd Recek
1965	Bill Mimick	1984	Todd Jarecke	1997	Tom Rogers
1967	Mark McLaughlin	1985	Bob Klopnieski	1998	Jeff Eickmeier
1967	*Bill Kosch	1985	Karl Hroza	1998	Jesse Fischer
1968	Joe Blahak	1985	Pat Engelbert	1998	Thadd Recek
1968	Steve Wieser	1986	*Pat Engelbert	1998	Tom Rogers
1969	Bob Kosch	1987	Eric Heigi	1999	Drew Brock
1971	*Dan Brock	1989	Travis Brock	2000	Jeff Kosch
1974	*Dan Steiner	1991	Jesse Kosch	2000	Jesse Benda
1974	Ron Mimick	1992	Jesse Kosch	2011	Cody Placzek
1975	*John Fischer	1993	Brandon Drum	2013	Cody Zimmerman
1976	Jim Feehan	1993	Chris Kinnison	2014	Jake Bos
1978	Tim Tinius	1993	Jeff Herdzina	2015	Jake Bos
1978	Mike Cielocha	1993	Scott Sobota	2015	Marcus Dodson
1979	Glen Kucera	1994	*Brandon Drum	2015	Baeley Pelster
1980	Glen Kucera	1995	Chad Mustard	2015	Carson Fuscher
1982	Kevin Molczyk	1995	Sam Graus	2015	Cole Harrington

BOYS BASKETBALL ALL-STATE SELECTIONS					
1975	Gregg Grubaugh	1993	Mick Collins	2014	Grant Lahm
1981	Bret Kumpf	1996	Chad Mustard	2015	Grant Lahm
1981	Glen Kucera	2013	Grant Lahm	2016	Dalton Taylor
1983	Mark Brezinski				

WRESTLING GOLD MEDALISTS					
2015	Alec Foltz	2016	Marcus Dodson		

BOYS SOCCER ALL-STATE SELECTIONS					
1993	Jeff Herdzina	2005	Ben Milnar	2014	Jake Bos
1994	Jeff Herdzina	2006	Chris Herdzina	2014	Ryan Fuchs
1997	Aaron Legenza	2006	Clint Torczon	2015	Caleb Ostdiek
1997	Jon Brezinski	2006	Josh Jepsen	2015	*Alec Foltz
1997	Lenny Sliva	2007	Danny Zach	2015	Jake Bos
1998	Jon Brezinski	2008	Chase Beiermann	2015	Baeley Pelster
1998	Justin Fry	2009	Chase Beiermann	2015	Evan Chohon
1998	Tom Rogers	2009	David Gokie	2015	Jackson Kumpf
1999	EJ Brezinski	2009	Jared Ostdiek	2016	*Jake Bos
1999	Tom Rogers	2009	Shawn Shumacher	2016	Alec Foltz
2000	Tyson Becher	2010	Aaron Bos	2016	Jackson Kumpf
2001	Greg Buelt	2010	Shawn Shumacher	2016	Evan Chohon
2001	Aaron Mielak	2012	Cody Zimmerman	2016	Caleb Ostdiek
2001	Brock Pillen	2013	Cody Zimmerman	2016	Baeley Pelster
2001	Tyson Becher	2014	Cody Zimmerman	2016	Nathan Ostdiek

BOYS TRACK & FIELD GOLD MEDAL WINNERS *(Denotes Grand Champion)		
1964	Larry Liss	*100 Yard Dash
1964	Dave Kudron	180 Yard Low Hurdles
1967	Steve Shadle	*440 yard Dash
1968	Joe Blahak	100 Yd Dash, Long Jump, 180 Yd LH
1969	Joe Blahak	Long Jump, 180 Yd LH
1976	Tom Sobotka	120 Yard High Hurdles
1977	Mike Cielocha	220 yard Dash, *440 yard Dash
1978	Mike Cielocha	*220 yard Dash, 440 yard Dash
1978	J Heimann, L Kobus, M Cielocha, M Savage	*880 Yard Relay
1979	Mike Cielocha	*100, 220, *440 Yard Dash
1979	B Bosak, M Cielocha, M Jahn, M Savage	880 Yard Relay
1979	Rick Schumacher	Triple Jump
1985	Karl Hroza	Triple Jump
1985	Keith Neal	100M Dash
1986	Karl Hroza	Triple Jump
1990	Kris Almquist	Long Jump
1999	Chris Gannon	Triple Jump
2002	Tyler Roesvert	Triple Jump
2009	Taylor Suess	*Discus
2013	Derek Lahm	*Triple Jump
2015	Cody Mroczek	400M Dash
2016	Cody Mroczek	*Long Jump, 400M Dash

FROM THE EDITORS

John Kopetzky

Scotus Class of 1980

In my six years of junior high and high school at Scotus, I was an "athlete" (and I use the term loosely) for exactly one season – football in 8th grade under legendary coach Bob Young. That one season was a brutal reminder that some people are cut out to be athletes, and some are cut out to be student managers. Without question, I was among the latter group. Thankfully, the athletes and coaches at Scotus let me fulfill my dream of being a Shamrock and I was the manager for varsity basketball for five years, football for four, and track for two.

I was able to be part of two state, district, and conference championship teams in track, a conference championship and four top ten teams in football (27-10-1 record) and a conference championship, two district runner-up, and three top ten teams in basketball (64-38 record). And along the way, I was able to see outstanding performers and coaches, both Shamrocks and opponents, and log countless memories of great moments. Above all, I was given the chance to be part of something greater than myself – to be part of a team, to be part of the tradition of Scotus Central Catholic.

I grew up in a home that was 100% Scotus, with three older sisters (Jeanne '70, Kathy '73 and Julie '74) and a younger brother (Kent '89) who lived and died with the Shamrocks. My dad sold tickets for many years on the visitors' side of Pawnee Park and so I got to go to every home game and played football in the grass near the south end zone with my friends from St. Anthony's. During basketball season, my friends and I ran around Memorial Hall, folded our programs into paper airplanes and tried to get them stuck in the ceiling insulation. Although I wasn't exactly sure what a safety or cornerback was, I puffed my chest out with pride at the exploits of Shamrocks Joe Blahak and Bill Kosch when they played for Nebraska.

I dreamt about someday being part of the Scotus tradition. And, for six glorious years, I was able live that dream.

There are so many memories of my years as a Shamrock, it's impossible to list one as the best. But there are many that stand out: Mike Cielocha flying around a track in the 440; Tim Hroza's speed and moves on the football field; Steve Heimann's patented baseline jumper that almost never missed; the magical 1978-79 girls basketball season, where Scotus came out of nowhere and went 14-5, losing in double overtime in the district finals (and I came home from the game with a black eye, courtesy of Bill Wieser jabbing me in the eye with the pole on the Irish flag he was waving); earning a varsity letter as a student manager when I was in the 8th grade and being the first guy in my class to be able to wear a letter jacket; the legendary "S" Club initiation in 1976; the standing-room-only crowds at the district basketball games at Platte College in 1975 when I was in 7th grade, where we beat Aquinas 55-53 before losing a heart-breaker to Aurora in the finals, 66-64; calling in the scores after the games and having to convince the *Omaha World-Herald* that yes, our quarterbacks really *were* named Brezinski and Prososki; all the hype leading up to the 1978 State track meet, when it looked like a two-team race between Scotus and Schuyler; leading the team out onto the court through the Pep Club "spirit line" for the final varsity basketball game ever at Memorial Hall in 1980 (a come-from-behind 60-56 win over Aquinas); the double-overtime, 76-75 win at Holy Name in 1977 that clinched our first-ever Centennial Conference championship; watching Bret Kumpf work his magic on the basketball court without ever, *ever* getting rattled; starting the 1976 football season 0-2 with a controversial loss (there was *no* way Dave Ebner committed offensive pass interference on the winning touchdown pass) at West Point Central Catholic and riding home on top of the players' pads in the back of Coach Younger's pickup truck (luckily there was a topper on the truck so I didn't have to worry about falling out); getting asked to speak at a pep rally as a freshman and promptly announcing that we were "...going to beat the s**t out of Lakeview!"; not being asked to speak at a pep rally again until I was a senior for some reason; the Thursday football practices at Victory Mall (where the Dowd Activity Center stands now); hearing Coach Younger tell his hurdlers to "STRIDE OUT";

playing endless games of sports trivia with Jim Dolezal during practices; destroyed water coolers and tipped-over basketball racks as Coaches Puetz and Spenceri sought to (ahem) motivate us; hearing the immortal chant of "F ... O ... O ... T ... B ... A ... L ... L ... FOOTBALL TRACK!"; getting to announce to the crowd at the basketball game on February 22, 1980 (our final home game that year) that the U.S. had beaten the Russians in Olympic hockey; having the support of an incredible Pep Club and student body; road trips to volleyball and girls basketball games; singing polkas (led by Pat Novicki) in the bus after football games; and the list could go on and on. But the statute of limitations has not expired on many other incidents so they'll have to remain unpublished.

The excellence and standard of success that was set decades before I arrived at Scotus was palpable. We expected to win - *every game.* Even when we were struggling in a game or a season (which wasn't that often), there was an expectation that we would find a way to win – *because we were Scotus.* For me personally, that carried over into non-athletic competitions like speech and one act play. We were *Scotus.* We were going to win. Period. It wasn't arrogance, but simply the knowledge that we had worked hard, prepared well, had good coaching and a track record of success.

When we lost to Hartington Cedar Catholic in the district basketball final in my senior year, my career as a Shamrock came to a close. In the locker room after the game, faced with the cold hard reality that it was all over, I cried uncontrollably for one of the few times in my life. At the time, I viewed it as sadness that one of my dreams – qualifying for the state basketball tournament – was going to be unfulfilled. Looking back on it, I now know that the tears were a subconscious realization on my part that a truly special phase of my life was over. It is a phase that I will always cherish.

This book has been a labor of love. I am grateful to Mark Kurtenbach for pushing this idea for so many years and for keeping me on task during the process. This book has helped me to consider in a new way everything that Scotus means to me. I hope that your memories of St. Bonaventure and Scotus bring you as much joy as mine do for me.

I am proud to dedicate my work for this book to my parents, Walt and Lucille Kopetzky. They made many sacrifices so that all of their children had the opportunity to receive a Catholic education, supported us in our many activities, and set a wonderful example of service for us to follow.

It's been more than 35 years since I graduated from Scotus, but one thing remains the same today as it did back in 1980: I cannot imagine having had a better high school experience than I had at Scotus. I really can't. The experiences I had in my years there had a lifelong impact on who I am as a person, and I will always be eternally grateful for the opportunity I was given to be a part of something truly special. Even though the years since my graduation have taken me away from Columbus, and as a parent I've been a part of another outstanding Catholic school community at Lincoln Pius X, I am proud to say I am, and will always be, profoundly grateful to be a member of the Green Nation. (And we're talking ***Shamrock*** green here, folks.)

As has been stated by many others in the pages of this book, **IT'S ALWAYS A GREAT DAY TO BE A SHAMROCK.**

Mark Kurtenbach

Scotus Class of 1980

Like John, I grew up in a Scotus family. Mom graduated from St. Bonaventure; Dad worked at Scotus and was on the chain gang for home football games. I grew up watching great football players at Memorial Stadium from the grandstands or sideline like Tom Blahak, Dan Steiner, Dan Martin, and Pat Novicki (with his high-top black leather cleats from the 50's). I watched Gregg Grubaugh, Conrad Slusarski, and Steve Heimann dominate the court in the old Memorial Hall gym, and was amazed watching Tom Sobotka clear the hurdles on the cinder track at Pawnee Park.

It was a tradition in the 1970's after every football win for the players on the bus to do a victory chant as a 'shout-out' to the coaches. It went like this:

"He's a Man, He's a Man, He's a ***Scotus Man*** ... Puetz! Puetz! Puetz!" ... and so it went for the Head Coach and all the Assistant Coaches. Jim Puetz was a master of motivation and a great coach – and he knew how to have fun with the players.

I'm not sure when that tradition started or if it still continues, but I always thought it was a good one. In a way, it was the acknowledgement of the players back to the coaches; a show of team unity and a way to celebrate the team's success. And, it was fun to yell something on the bus after a win (and there were a lot of them).

Behind most traditions is a backstory; some purpose or meaning that is hidden behind what is seen or heard. After all, traditions are only meaningful if you pass them on. I believe this traditional victory chant by a bunch of high school football players had a deeper meaning.

The tradition of the ***Scotus Man*** and the ***Scotus Woman***.

Rewind to October, 1978: Scotus versus Boystown. After a hard-fought three and a half quarter slugfest against undefeated and ranked Boystown, Scotus was on top 7-0. A busted play and long scramble by speedy quarterback Al Connerly left the Cowboys with first and goal on the 8-yard line with a minute and change to play.

As a junior, I had the great privilege to play shoulder-to-shoulder with my older brother Gary on the defensive line in our 6-2 scheme. The 1978 Scotus defensive unit posted six shutouts that season and still holds the record for fewest average points per game by an opponent (4.2). It was all coming down to four plays.

First down: A two-yard gain. Second down: We stuffed 'em - no gain. Third down: Another couple of yards. Fourth down ... clock is running, no timeouts left, ball placed on the four-yard line. It all comes down to this.

I remember the defensive huddle prior to the final play; it was *pandemonium*. I remember linebacker Tom Hoffman literally frothing at the mouth. I remember Gary Puetz's coaching when taking on a bigger player ("You keep hittin' him 'til he *quits!*"). I remember catching a glimpse of my Dad near the sideline. I remember every player in that huddle yelling 'there is *no way* they're gonna score'. The huddle breaks; both teams line up. Everything is in slow motion.

Before the snap, I remember thinking, "There's ***no way*** they're gonna score."

Connerly rolls out (not sure if he was going to pitch, run, or throw). There's a huge surge by Tim Tinius up the middle. Connerly is corralled by defensive end Paul Johnson who forces a fumble. Tim Engelbert scoops up the ball and begins a rumble toward the opposite goal, and is "assisted" along the way by my brother, Gary. Tim and Gary go down, the clock runs out, game over, another shutout, Scotus wins.

Now *that* is what being a ***Scotus Man*** is all about.

The pages of this book are filled with the stories of Scotus Men and Scotus Women. These are the athletes and coaches who embody the personality of the blue-collar town of Columbus and the qualities of Scotus and its athletic programs; determined, hard-working, loyal, tough-minded ... and maybe even a little rough around the edges. As you will find in the stories of the athletes and coaches, these common themes rise to the surface.

It is a true honor and has been a lot of fun to bring these stories together. The story of Scotus athletics is a story worth telling, not only because of the success and honors the athletes, coaches, and teams have achieved, but because of the support by students, fans, and alumni over the *generations.* For John and I as editors of this book, contributing in a small way to the rich tradition and legacy of Scotus Athletics has been a very meaningful part of our lives.

For my part, any effort that I have put into this book is dedicated to my parents, Alvin and Elaine Kurtenbach; they too are determined, hard-working, loyal, and tough-minded. Their daily selfless sacrifices to send me to Scotus and the love and support that they showed me over the years cannot be measured.

I hope you enjoy reading this book as much as I have had in helping to put it together.

PHOTOS

Columbus Daily Telegram Photo from the 1967 Track Season – Even through the school had been renamed to Scotus Central Catholic, the track tank tops still had the St. Bonaventure emblem on them (!). From left: Bill Kosch, Joe Blahak, Steve Shadle. All three are members of the Shamrock Athletic Hall of Fame, Blahak holds the school long jump record (23'), Shadle won the gold medal in the 440 Yard Dash, and Kosch blistered a 15.0 second in the high hurdles.

Stephanie Kruse catches air during a soccer match in 1999

School record holder Morgan Benesch running cross country in 2012

1999 state volleyball champs celebrate

Father and son state football champions Steve Bonk (1984) and son Ross (2015)

Meghan Pile executing one of her 695 career digs

Kim Rickert pulls down a rebound against Lakeview

2009 Class B state track & field champions

Tom Rodgers hammers
Aquinas defenders

Sami Spenner squares
up for a jumper
at the state basketball tournament

Scotus' first state volleyball champions - 1986

Monica Boeding in 2010 action

Grant Lahm drives to
the hoop en route
to his 1,970 career points

1993 Shamrock linemen before a big game

Scotus fires off the line against Schuyler
in 1979 opening game action at Pawnee Park

Joe Blahak presenting Gary Puetz with the NFL's Golden Anniversary football

Marcus Dodson pictured in his 2016 state wrestling title match

Shamrock Pride!

Platte Conference
basketball champions

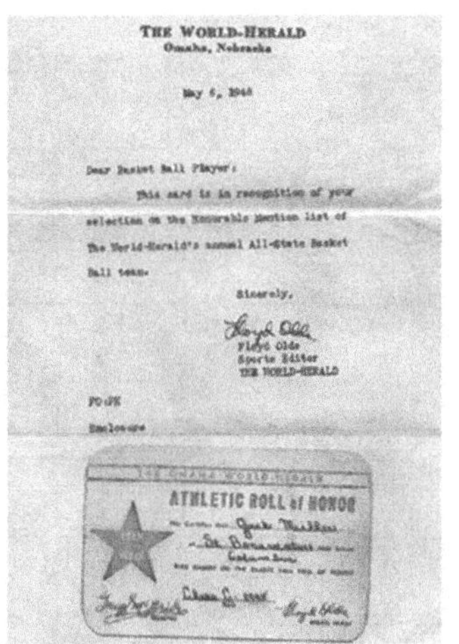

THE WORLD-HERALD
Omaha, Nebraska

May 6, 1948

Dear Basket Ball Player:

This card is in recognition of your selection on the Honorable Mention list of The World-Herald's annual All-State Basket Ball team.

Sincerely,

Floyd Olds
Sports Editor
THE WORLD-HERALD

FO:JK

Enclosure

ATHLETIC ROLL of HONOR

Letter to Jack Miller
in 1948 notifying
him of his Honorable
Mention Selection
to the *Omaha World Herald*
All-State basketball team

Jordan Chohon battles at the
net in state championship
volleyball action

Scotus girls celebrate another
state volleyball
championship in 2011

Liz Hadland chalks
up another assist

Bill Kosch intercepts a
pass for the Huskers
while Joe Blahak blocks a defender

Johnny Unitas poses with
Bill Backes at the 1960 St.
Bonaventure Athletic Banquet

Amber Ewers and Sami
Spenner finish
1-2 at the state track meet

When St. Bonaventure High School was centralized and renamed Scotus High School, Paul "Dutch" Ernst was the first coach at St. Bon's, and Dean Souillere was the last coach

Mike Cielocha breaks the tape in the 1978 state track meet

Bret Kumpf goes baseline in 1981 basketball action

The 1978 Class B state track & field champions

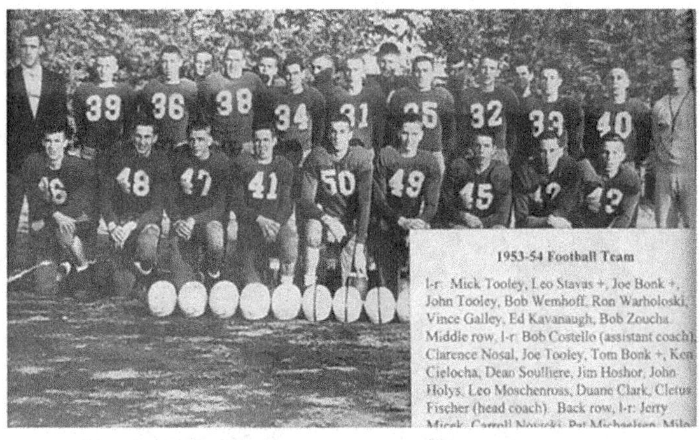

1953–54 St. Bonaventure football team

Printed in the United States
By Bookmasters